K060

estab

She was living on Kyushu,
her home town Kumamoto
is the island below Shikoku

The old man was her
companion, helped her
carry ___ and provided
a different view point

THE 1918 SHIKOKU PILGRIMAGE

OF TAKAMURE ITSUE

an English translation of *Musume Junreiki*

translated by Susan Tennant

The 1918 Shikoku Pilgrimage of Takamure Itsue: an English translation of *Musume Junreiki*

translated by Susan Tennant

First edition Copyright © 2010 Susan Tennant

All rights reserved. No part of this book may be reproduced or transmitted in any form or by any electronic or mechanical means including photocopying, recording or by any information storage and retrieval system without written permission from the publisher, except for the inclusion of brief quotations in a review.

Temple and vajra drawn by
Bev Greene

ISBN 1450540759

Published by

Bowen Publishing
D-101
Bowen Island, BC
Canada V0N 1G0

TABLE OF CONTENTS

Section I: Departure	7
Section II: Heading to Shikoku at Long Last	77
Section III: Along the Inland Sea	179
Map of the Pilgrimage Route	230
What is the Shikoku Pilgrimage?	231
Who was Takamure Itsue?	235
Why did Takamure make the Pilgrimage?	236
Takamure's Life Before the Pilgrimage	237
Takamure's Romance with Hashimoto	241
Takamure becomes a Celebrity	245
Takamure's Pilgrimage Journey	246
Takamure's Life after the Pilgrimage	250
The Importance of Takamure's Account	254
Tanka poems and *Goeika* hymn	258
Glossary	260
Selected Bibliography	267

PREFACE

In the summer of 1918 Takamure Itsue left her home in Kumamoto on the southern island of Kyūshū, walked most of the way across the island before boarding a train to Ōita, and then took a ferry to the island of Shikoku. She then walked approximately 1400 kilometres following an ancient 88 temple pilgrimage path. En route, she wrote 105 newspaper articles about her experiences which were published in a Kyūshū newspaper. Later, in 1979, these articles were published in book form as *Musume Junreiki (The pilgrimage journal of a young woman)*, a book which has since been republished several times.

The book which you have in your hands is an English translation of *Musume Junreiki*. If reading this translation whets your appetite to learn more about Takamure Itsue and the Shikoku pilgrimage, you will find information about both in the appendices at the end of this volume. Takamure's reasons for making the pilgrimage were complicated and her life equally complex.

There is also a glossary of Japanese terms. The first time that a Japanese term is used in the book, its meaning is explained in a footnote but a glossary of terms is provided as well. Readers will also find information about the Shikoku pilgrimage as well as a map of the pilgrimage route.

Japanese custom has been followed throughout in giving the family name first followed by the given name.

May those who read these book be as charmed by Takamure and her experiences as I have been.

ACKNOWLEDGEMENTS

First, I must thank Takamure's sister in law, Hashimoto Shizuko, for giving me permission to translate *Musume Junreiki*. In addition, thanks are due to Horiba Kiyoko, the editor of *Musume Junreiki,* a Japanese feminist historian well known for her research on Takamure Itsue, who put me in touch with Hashimoto Shizuko.

Musume Junreiki (*The pilgrimage journal of a young woman*) was difficult to translate. The 105 newspaper articles which comprise the book were written in 1918 using the old Japanese writing system and there are many kanji and expressions in the articles which are no longer used. In addition, Takamure Itsue's writing style has many peculiarities.

I could not have translated this book without help from many people, all of whom I wish to thank. The four woman with whom I co-wrote *Awa 88: a bilingual guide to the pilgrimage temples in Tokushima Prefecture*, Shinohara Nobuko, Kametaka Yoko, Negishi Keiko and Yamada Takako, helped me understand the Shikoku pilgrimage, its history and traditions and its place in the hearts of the Japanese.

Nakamura Masami, of Iwakura, Aichi Prefecture, helped me to read the Japanese text, as did Kakuse Kumiko of Nagoya University. Professors Hamaguchi Keiko and Tsuno Kosuke of the former Tosa Women's Junior College, Prof. Okumura Eiko of Kobe Women's University helped me with the *goeika* as did some of the priests of the pilgrimage temples and Taniguchi Myōshō of Muryōkōin temple on Mount Koya. Prof. David Moreton of Tokushima Bunri University was encouraging and helpful and Prof. Ian Reader of the University of Manchester kindly gave me permission to use his map of the pilgrimage route. Bev Greene provided the drawing of the temple and the vajra.

Professor Eiichi Kageyama (Retired) of Takushoku University generously gave me many hours of his time and assisted me by researching and supplying useful information and by reading and correcting my preliminary translations of *Musume Junreiki*. This book would not exist without his help.

If there are others whom I have failed to mention, please accept both my thanks and my apologies.

Susan Tennant
Bowen Island, Canada
February 2010

takamureitsu@yahoo.ca

- ended up in textile factory
- goes home to work as TA at father's school at age 20, meets future husband Hashimoto Kenzō
- she pledges eternal love but he's not ready so she leaves
- anarchist: pro-working poor, but opposed to Marxists who attacked marriage as a bourgeois institution.

Section 1: Departure

- Poet: wrote "tanka", 31-syllable poem with pattern 5-7-5-7-7
- Anarchist feminist journal: March 1930 - June 1931
- Slogans: 1) Negate Authoritarianism!
  2) Down with men!
  3) rebirth for the female!

Article 1: BEFORE THE PILGRIMAGE

Even I myself don't know why I resolved to make the pilgrimage, but the following is part of a letter I wrote to Miyazaki Daitarō.[1] I will be very pleased if you can understand, even just a bit, the kind of person I am by reading this section of the letter.

"Today is the fourteenth of May. These days I am madly addicted to reading— morning, noon, and night, even when drawing water, even when cooking rice. I just have to read. If I don't read, it's utterly unbearable.

Please don't ask what the reason is; even I myself don't know. At times I wonder if I've gone crazy. However, there doesn't seem to be anything particularly the matter. Only, it's strange that I easily become extremely emotional and distressed, and that I can cry noisily and copiously.

Also, it is absolutely horrifying how my imagination, limitlessly, endlessly, and boundlessly, extends really grotesque, dark wings. There are times that I have a sharp pain in my heart because I vividly picture the scene of my death.

In the evening, while strolling among the rows and rows of tombstones in the precincts of the old temple where I am temporarily allowed to stay, I often sense something coming suddenly and looming right in front of my eyes. I wonder if this is an image projected by my vague dread of magnificent, mysterious things. When I watch calmly as though I were a spectator and observe myself, I really do see a black shape coming sternly and gravely towards me, about which I can do nothing.

This is actuality. Actuality threatens me because it is actual; the ideal threatens me because it is ideal. In the first place, where does life end and where does death lead?

Going on a pilgrimage—that's particularly easy for

---

[1] Names are written Japanese style with the surname first. Miyazaki was then City Editor of the Kyūshū Nichi Nichi Newspaper and had the pen name of Kōtei.

me. There is nothing in the world more painful than stagnating. I even think that venturing recklessly into an unknown world has perhaps more significance than that."

(I have omitted the rest. This is the letter that I never sent to Mr. Miyazaki.)

May twenty-fourth. After eating supper I visited the Kannon Dō[2] on Kannon-zaka[3] and had the pleasure of meeting the resident nun for the first time. She is an extremely gentle and serene person and while talking with her I felt a yearning such as one feels in the midst of a spring breeze. I felt strongly that what was most important was practice rather than theory, and virtue rather than knowledge.

"Go on a pilgrimage? That is commendable, but I don't know much about pilgrimages. How about visiting Mr. Yamamoto Sōgan in Shinsaiku-machi?"[4]

I thanked her, excused myself, and returned home. Then, the next day, the twenty-fifth, I went without delay to Mr. Yamamoto, listened to him talk about various things, and at the same time received careful, kind instruction about pilgrimages, including clothing and what not.

To be honest, at first I was thinking of the Saigoku pilgrimage[5] to the thirty-three temples of western Japan which are related to former Emperor Kazan,[6] but I gave that up and decided on a pilgrimage to Kōbō Daishi's eighty-eight temples on Shikoku Island.[7] My heart danced when I was shown such things

---

2 A dō is a temple building and can be large or small. This is the same temple that she tried to run away to at the age of 12 when she wanted to be a nun. (see Article 104)
3 Horiba, the editor of *Musume Junreiki,* notes that there is now a Jizō Dō where the Kannon Dō once stood. *Saka (Zaka)* means slope.
4 This is New Saikumachi. The original Saikumachi was a business area of Kumamoto City.
5 This is a pilgrimage to thirty-three temples in western Japan which enshrine Kannon Bosatsu. There are eleven temples in Kyōto, six in Shiga, five in Ōsaka, four in Nara, three each in Wakayama and Hyōgo, and one in Gifu. Because of her link with Kannon Bosatsu, this pilgrimage would have appealed to her.
6 Reigned AD 984-986.
7 Kōbō Daishi (774-835), the founder of Shingon Buddhism in Japan, poet,

as the *wasan* (hymns of praise)[8] and the *goeika* (pilgrimage hymns).[9]

The first of the eighteen *wasan* praising Kōbō Daishi says, "First, the next life is the only important thing, so never neglect your faith." It ends with "Namu Daishi, Namu Daishi, Namu Daishi, Henjōson"[10] and is signed by Nagaoka Shūken, retired chief priest,[11] resident in Ryūjōin on Mount Kōya in Kii Province.[12]

Here is one section of the "Temple Establishment" *wasan*:[13]

> When you look into the origin
> Of the eighty-eight holy sites,
> In Enryaku 23 (805),
> Kōbō Daishi entered China
> And received Shingon Esoteric Buddhism teachings
> From Keika[14] Ajari.
> He then entered cloud-shrouded Vulture Mountain[15] in

---

artist, educator, engineer, scholar, calligrapher, and political statesman, is considered by many Japanese to be a saint, a semi-divine entity who did not die in 835, but entered into an eternal meditative state on Mount Kōya in Wakayama Prefecture.

8 A Buddhist hymn in praise of such things as a Buddha, *bodhisattva*, founder of the sect, a doctrine, or a sutra.

9 Each pilgrimage temple has its own *goeika* which praises such things as the benefits of the principal deity and the scenery around the temple. In the old days pilgrims sang the appropriate *goeika* as they approached the temple.

10 *Namu* means to respect, to revere. This phrase can be translated as "I put my faith in Kōbō Daishi" or "Glory to Kōbō Daishi" or 'I sincerely believe in Kōbō Daishi" or even "Homage to Kōbō Daishi".

11 The word used, 施印（せいん, means a retired chief priest who has gone to live in a monastery other than the one in which he held the leading rank.

12 Now Wakayama Prefecture.

13 Takamure calls this the *Yamabiraki wasan* but it is called the *Shikoku hachi jū hakka sho michibiraki wasan* in 仏教和賛五百題（Five hundred Buddhist *wasan*）by Fujii Sahei, published by Yamashiro ya in Taishō 5. (Horiba's note)

14 Keika (Hui-kuo) was the seventh patriarch of esoteric Buddhism. Ajari means teacher or master and it is a rank given to an eminent priest of Esoteric Buddhism.

15 Vulture Peak is a small mountain near the ancient Indian city of Ragir where the Buddha preached sixteen years after his enlightenment. In fact,

India
And made a pilgrimage through the sacred areas
Of the eight pagodas related to Shakamuni.[16]
In order to make all Japanese
Accept Buddhism throughout the land,
He brought back soil from the eight pagodas.
He multiplied the number eight by ten,
Added the eight original pagodas,
Divided the sand into eighty-eight portions,
And on these divided parts of sand,
Built the temples which became
The eighty-eight sacred sites of Shikoku.

I became a little worried when I read,

Robed in hemp,
Wearing a wicker hat
A straw bag on the back,
A bag with three robes[17]
Short straw sandals[18] called *zōri,*
A box eighteen centimeters in length and six centimeters in width
Hanging around the neck for *fuda* slips,[19]
Carrying a pilgrim's staff in the right hand,
And a Buddhist rosary in the left.[20]

Kōbō Daishi never visited India.
16 After the historical Buddha (Shakyamunii) died, his remains were divided into eight parts and eight pagodas were erected.
17 Pilgrims do not carry a bag with three robes as priests used to do. The *wagesa*, the narrow strip of cloth worn around the pilgrim's neck (7.5 cm wide and 60 cm long) represents these three robes.
18 Traditional rough straw sandal with a thong between the big toe and second toe and tied on to the foot with straw straps. They were worn when taking a long journey on foot. The *zōri* mentioned in the *wasan* do not cover the full length of the foot and thus are uncomfortable for walking.
19 These are small pieces of paper that pilgrims put into a special box at each temple. On them are the pilgrim's name, address, prayers for happiness, peace and prosperity, and a drawing of Kōbō Daishi.
20 This is also a *wasan*.

I was told that my clothes also had to be like these. Mr. Yamamoto told me that *waraji*[21] sandals are better than *zōri*. I was a little uneasy, but the hat, staff, and so on seemed intriguing.

While I was lost in a trance, Mr. Yamamoto kindly dug out a pilgrim's staff upstairs and gave it to me saying, "This is for you."

It was made in the shape of the Buddhas of the five wisdoms.[22] The five wisdoms are space, wind, fire, water, and earth—symbolized by the head, shoulders, ribs, abdomen, and hips. Talking this way, I may sound like a scholar, but really, it is nothing other than what Mr. Yamamoto told me. I don't know why but my face flushes when I think of going on the pilgrimage holding this staff.

Article 2: BEFORE THE PILGRIMAGE (Continued)

On the afternoon of the twenty-ninth, I went to the home of Mr. Miyazaki, to consult with him. Unfortunately, he was not at home, so for quite a long time his wife and I fretted together about various things.

"You know, when a person is dressed in pilgrim clothes,

---

21 These are straw sandals that are tied on the foot rather than kept on by thongs.

22 The five wisdoms are (a) the mirror-like wisdom which arises when one attains enlightenment and that which reflects all sense perceptions is purified; (b) the wisdom of equality which arises after all feelings of pleasantness, unpleasantness and indifference have been purified; (c) the wisdom of individual analysis which arises when the factor of discrimination, which distinguishes one object from another is purified; (d) the wisdom of accomplishing activity which arises when the basic ability to perform acts according to particular circumstances is purified; and (e) the wisdom of the sphere of reality which arises when consciousness is purified and becomes the mind that is the seed of the wisdom truth body of a Buddha. The corresponding five Buddhas are Ashuku, Hōshō, Amida, Fukūjōju and Dainichi. The five Buddhas correspond to the five elements of esoteric Buddhism and the top of the pilgrim staff is shaped to represent these five elements. The spherical top represents air and sits upon a semi-lunar shape representing wind. Below that is a triangular shape representing the fire element followed by a round shape representing the water element. At the bottom is the square earth element.

they are given rice or all manner of other things.[23] So, to begin with, learn how to make a bag."

"Oh dear, that's embarrassing. Whatever will I say when I receive things?"

"And then how does one wear *waraji* straw sandals?" The two of us racked our brains again but in the end couldn't figure it out at all. She gave me a tonic called Kitan and a traveling case called a *kōri*[24] and I returned home.

The next day, the thirtieth, a messenger came from the newspaper by bicycle just as I was about to go out. "I'm so glad," I said, speaking loudly without meaning to.

Late that evening I visited Mr. Miyazaki and he told me about various things. Now, finally, it has become a reality. Dreamily, I returned to my lodgings and at once began my preparations. The clothing will be roughly as follows:

- a sedge hat with a turned down brim (*sugegasa*)
- a traveling case on a wooden frame for the back (*kōri*)
- a vest split on the sides and with a stripe on the back[25] (*oizuru*)
- cloth bands around the legs[26] (*kyahan*), white socks with split toes (*tabi*), straw sandals (*waraji*) and hand covers[27] (*tenuki*)
- a *fuda* box[28] (*fudabasami*) (Length eighteen cm and width six cm)
- a shoulder bag (*zudabukuro*)

In addition, I will walk with the pilgrim's staff I received from Yamamoto Sōgan, and my hair will be cut short, tied back and hang down.

The goods to be carried are writing paper, ink, pen, books, a change of clothes, a small knife, my name seal, and some odds

---

23 This is the custom of *osettai,* the giving of food, money or services to pilgrims.
24 Often made of wicker
25 The *oizuru* is worn on the back to protect it from the rubbing of the baggage carried on the back
26 These are said to improve circulation.
27 These protect the hands from sunburn.
28 This holds the slips of paper on which the pilgrim's name and address is written. Pilgrims deposit these slips of papers in boxes at the various temples.

and ends. These are the basic things. Carrying the bag and *fuda* box and so on suspended from me will be no problem but I am worrying and worrying about carrying the *kōri* on my back and thinking only about how to do this. It would be really good if someone would carry it for me, but thinking about this makes me feel like crying.

However, the next day, unusually excited and becoming quite a hoyden, I ran about, to and from my room, the kitchen, and the reception area, making preparations.

"Do settle down, won't you. I'll talk to you about the pilgrimage," said the priest where I live.[29] Both the priest and the old man here[30] are people who have made many pilgrimages.

The old man's wife incessantly repeated, "Listen to what people say[31]—and never, never, travel at night." While I was listening respectfully, I became somewhat disheartened.

"Granny, will people let me stay anywhere I go?"

"Sure they will because a young woman like you walking alone.... Just be careful not to get sick...."

The old man said, "Let a sweet child go on a trip;[32] you should also stay in a *kichinyado*[33] once in a while."

---

29 She lived in Sennen-ji temple in Kumamoto city.
30 The old man was a cooper. Takamure sometimes helped him sell his wares on the street. She walked the streets with him as he shouted out his services. Then he would spread out a number of tubs for rice and washing in a corner of the street. One time Takamure's friend saw her; the friend was embarrassed but Takamure says she was not. He and his wife were "bohemian" according to Takamure (*Ohenro*, 26, 27) and they were not at the temple when she returned from her pilgrimage.
31 Takamure uses the word "らくばなし" (rakubanashi) which I have been unable to track down or translate with assurance. Prof. Kishie Shinsuke of Tokushima University suggests that it may have a religious connotation as raku means bliss, pleasure, joy. "Gokuraku", for example, means the highest joy and is the name of the Pure Land of Amida.
32 This is a Japanese proverb meaning if you really love your child, rather than keeping it near you, you should send it travelling so that it learns about the harsh reality of the world. The meaning is somewhat similar to "Spare the rod and spoil the child."
33 In the Edo era, *kichinyado* were lodgings for travelers that charged fees (賃 *chin*) for wood to burn (木 *ki*). Travellers either brought their own food or purchased raw ingredients and cooked their own meals. At the time of Takamure's pilgrimage, *kichinyado* had become cheap lodging houses for

However, I was surprised to hear that around ten people sleep together under one mosquito net. Also, I began to feel like crying hearing that there were people who flare up in anger at the slightest provocation and I wondered what I would do if that happened. But, I even had the audacity to think "It sounds interesting—why not check out such inns for the experience?"

Then, I heard about how sometimes people staying at an inn put in money and the food received by a guest is in proportion to the amount of money that the person put in.

Article 3: FROM ŌZU

June fourth. I awoke at one in the morning and couldn't get back to sleep. When the wind blew and the leaves of the trees rustled, I wondered if it were raining. The sky was slightly overcast, but it didn't rain.

The old woman got up early on my behalf and boiled water, cooked rice, and made *onigiri*[34] for me. Even then, it still seemed like a dream. Going on a pilgrimage? How strange reality is!

At eight in the morning a rickshaw came. Even though I was thinking how funny the hat, pilgrim staff and so on looked, the die was cast.

"Take good care of your health," said the old woman, her old eyes already full of tears.

With my eyes downcast I barely managed to say, "Yes, I'll be back again soon. You too, Granny, don't get sick yourself."

My tears spilled over and ran down, and I couldn't get out another word.

Going down the slope I came to Shinsaka and went right through Tatemachi of Tsuboi.[35]

"That's a real pilgrim!"

Every now and then the comments of the townspeople caught my ear, "Come outside for a minute. There's a cute pilgrim." My face turned bright red.

---

people such as street minstrels and travellers with little money.
34 rice balls
35 All are in present day Kumamoto City.

Some people even questioned the rickshaw puller, "Is it a child in a procession?[36] Whose daughter is this young lady?"

I got out of the rickshaw at the Ozeki Bridge.[37] Here, the old rickshaw man retied my *waraji* sandals for me again.

From there to Ōzu,[38] I kept my eyes cast down most of the time. At a school along the way students streamed out to the gate and, because they said various things, I was embarrassed. Ah, the time of wandering has come at last. It is a reality; it is already a definite reality. However, I still can't shake the feeling that I am in a dream. The great Aso mountain range stands desolately before my eyes. How beautiful it is!

Ōzu was a longer town than I had expected.

"Probably fifteen; maybe sixteen? Oh the pity of it."

"How pathetic!"[39]

"How daring her parents are."[40]

And so on—here also comments were heaped upon me from houses on both sides. In my embarrassment I put a handkerchief over my face and, as I passed hastily along, from one house on the right hand side a voice called, "Hello, pilgrim, let me give you this."

I felt so embarrassed that I passed the house as though I were running away. Then I heaved a sigh of relief.

"It seems to be a female pilgrim," said a boy.

Finally I left the town behind me and, given directions by a housewife, I came to a village that I was told was Aza Hikinomizu, Ōzu town. After I had hesitated many times, I daringly went to a house at the very edge of town, and when I said with downcast eyes, "I'm on a pilgrimage trip; would you please let me stay in your house tonight," I found the villagers

---

36 *Chigo san* is the word Takamure uses. *Chigo* refers to parish children, usually aged between three and twelve, who dress in traditional clothing and parade during shrine and temple festivals.
37 In Kumamoto City.
38 Ōzu is 19 km east of Kumamoto City and half way between the city and the Aso mountains. It was just before Ōzu that she seems to have parted with Furukawa, the aspiring poet who was in love with her, although no mention is made of him here.
39 A young woman traveling alone is pitiable and they may also assume she has leprosy, a terminal illness, or terrible problems.
40 that is, to let her go on the pilgrimage alone.

were really kind.

I was showered with, "I'm impressed. Going on a pilgrimage is a pious thing for such a young girl to do. Praise be to Amida,"[41] and I became redder and redder.

However, I was told that in that house there was a sick person so I was sent with an introduction to the home of a person called Tejima Torao. There, the people said, "Well, please come in. Won't you have a cushion? Won't you have some tea?" In this warm hospitality, I just sat frozen upright not knowing what to do.

Article 4: FROM ŌZU (Continued)

All the people in this house were kind to me, and we ate supper together. How pleasant the family gathering was. A big pot heaped with rice was placed in front of us. Around it, family members were chatting and laughing freely. I soaked up the genial atmosphere of this unusual, pleasant scene with keen delight.

The bath was heated in a corner of the earthen-floored entrance area. Many people of the neighborhood had gathered there.[42]

Being told, "Take a bath," I flushed. How could I possibly take off my clothes amongst so many people?

"Oh, please, all of you bath first." I myself thought my voice was like that of a mosquito.

Saying, "How pitiful. There's probably a very profound reason,"[43] one after another they questioned me. In quick succession they said to me, "You're just like Otsuru.[44] How old

---

41 Amida is the principal deity of Pure Land Buddhists, who repeat this phrase (*nenbutsu*) frequently.
42 Even as late as 1936, it was the custom in rural Kumamoto for neighbours to share bath facilities because filling the bath with buckets from the well was difficult and firewood was expensive. Two to three households took turns filling and heating the bath for neighboring families. (Embree, John F. *Suemura: A Japanese Village*. Black Star Publishing Co. New York, 1939, p.70)
43 that is, for making the pilgrimage
44 Otsuru is a child pilgrim in a famous, tragic *bunraku* (puppet) play, *Keisei*

are you?" "What is your name?" and so on.

"My name is Ha—Hanae. I'm eighteen."[45] At last I had escaped and I heaved a great sigh. Oh, you people, I beg you not to ask me any more questions.

But, because of their sympathy, their pursuit of information became more heated. With the blood rushing to my head as though I were utterly intoxicated, I told them that when I was born my mother had vowed to Kannon,[46] "If you let this child grow up healthy, I will be sure that she makes a pilgrimage by herself." (This was because before my birth, her many children had all died.) This is the truth. My mother is a person with great faith in Kannon Bosatsu.

"How touching that such a young girl as you had the courage to decide to make the pilgrimage by yourself."

"However, never think that you are alone because the Buddha is going with you."

Being told, "Go ahead, take your time having a bath, and go to bed," I cried, without knowing why. Feeling embarrassed, I finally finished the bath and went to bed before the others.

The next day was June fifth. A fine rain was softly falling. What to do in this rainy weather? The pain in my legs was somehow unbearable. My chest also seemed a little painful. I wondered if I might be suffering heart failure from beriberi[47] and, feeling forlorn, I longed intensely for my parents in my hometown. "Father! Mother! Be happy and enjoy good health! Please give me your blessing for my journey and don't worry

---

Awa no Naruto. Dressed in pilgrim's clothes, she searches for her parents who have gone to Ōsaka but, when she finally finds them, her mother denies that she is her mother and then her father, not knowing that she is his own daughter, kills her for her money.

45 Both of these statements are untrue. Her name is Itsue and she is 24. See also Article 26. Before the pilgrimage she had published poems under the name of Hanayo. As Setouchi Harumi points out (*Jitsugetsu futari*, section 3, p. 413 [Bungei Tembō, 1976]) when she published her first book of poetry, the promotional material referred to her as "not yet 20" and for her second book, she was described as "just 20" despite the fact that she was already 27.

46 Kannon Bosatsu is the bodhisatva of great compassion, mercy, and love. Kannon was originally a male, but is now often regarded as a female deity.

47 Symptoms of beriberi include leg swelling and numbness, build up of fluid in the heart and severe muscle wasting. Patients often died.

about me!"

Article 5: FROM ŌZU TO TATENO

It was nine in the morning when I left Ōzu. With warmth in my heart and an intensely joyful feeling, I walked along the rainy road wrapped in my heavy rain gear, thinking only one thing, "How kind the people of the world are." Along the way I encountered a group of people on horseback. I stuck out just my face from the rain hood but, because the hood tended to slip down and cover my eyes, every time I sort of lifted it up, the white vest, *fuda* bag, hat and staff showed. And then the people on horseback said one after another as they passed by, "Goodness gracious, it's a pilgrim!" "What a pity!" and so on.

Because the rain stopped before long, I held the rain gear and staff in my right hand and in my left hand I held a map and *The Young Woman of the Fjord* by Björnson,[48] which someone had given me.[49] Stepping lightheartedly, I walked along softly humming the song of Sasurai[50] to myself.

Before long, I became pretty tired. The damp air after the rain was a bit chilly down my neck. The woods near and far loomed dimly as though a pale haze had become motionless, and watery sunlight poured down as though weaving dreams.

The weight of the luggage on my back was unbearable.[51] When I thought about it, I felt more and more tired. Soon, I could no longer endure the pain in my neck and shoulders. All of a sudden it occurred to me that I could throw away this box.

---

48 Björnstjerne Martinus Björnson (1832-1910), a Norwegian, won the third Nobel Prize for literature in 1903. He wrote poetry, dramas, epics, and novels. Through the international press he championed persecuted people and oppressed nations, and worked on behalf of peace and international justice.
49 Might she have received this from Furukawa ?
50 This is a famous popular song with music by Nakayama Shimpei and lyrics by the poet, Kitahara Hakushū. Both words and tune are sad and forlorn. The first verse says "Under the aurora borealis shall I go on or turn back? Russia is the northenmost country and boundless. The sunset's afterglow is in the west; day breaks in the east; a bell sounds in mid-air."
51 If the weight was unbearable, why did she not find it so on the first day when she walked to Ozū? Furukawa must have been carrying it. As Horiba points out, this seems to prove that Furukawa accompanied her the first day.

Wrapping all the things in it in a *furoshiki*,[52] I stealthily discarded the box and the frame for carrying it by the side of the road. "But the old man where I lived[53] made this box for me painstakingly. The frame also...." Thinking like that, I couldn't bear to discard them. Several times I reconsidered and picked them up but then, thinking again of the hardship of carrying them on my back for a long time.... In my heart I said to the old man, "I'm sorry, please forgive me," and then, after all, I decided to discard them.

But, in that box I put a piece of paper on which I'd pencilled words with a meaning like this:

"Taishō 7,[54] June 5. I have made up my mind and am throwing away this box. Although I really can't bear to throw it away, how can I, who am too frail, bear to continue on a long trip carrying it on my back? I wonder who will pick up this box and where that person will be from. Whoever you are, please cherish this box on my behalf. A woman on the Shikoku pilgrimage, Takamure Itsue."

Just when I was about to leave with no further ado, another group of people mounted on horses came along. They were wearing western clothes and had beards; judging from their appearance, they seemed to be people not from this area. Perhaps they were a mountain climbing party from somewhere. Again, I was flustered, thinking they would be sure to say something embarrassing to me, and then they stopped their horses as I expected and said arrogantly, "Hey! Miss! Are you alone? Where are you going? Are you traveling alone even though you're young?"

Then they said, "In mountains like these, isn't this kind of child by herself probably a ghost?" When I heard the word "ghost", it was I who became afraid. I headed hurriedly towards Tateno. I was completely exhausted. The scenery in this place is beautiful and, in particular, the feeling of being on a plateau seemed to permeate my heart. However, because I was

---

52 A square of cloth in which things are wrapped and carried.
53 The cooper. It was a woven bamboo basket covered with paper.
54 1918

unbearably tired, along the way I leaned on fences, leaned on trees, sat on rocks, and trudged along weakly relying on my staff.

Finally—Tateno. I was about to step into the outer crater of Aso.[55] Someone's *tanka*[56] suddenly occurred to me.

"May there be a light burning in the station at Tateno on the border between the counties of Aso and Kikuchi."

Article 6: AT THE SUGARU WATERFALL

A person who said he was returning from Ōzu became my travelling companion, and while I was dragging my weary feet along, said, "Just below is the celebrated Sugaru waterfall.[57] Why don't you go to see it? I'll show you the way."

I cheered up right away, and when we had descended a pebbly road, we immediately came out in front of a cottage-like house. Later I learned that such a small house had been built temporarily because the previous house had burned down. In the house a dignified looking couple and a young man were reading a newspaper. Because I was afraid that my travel-worn appearance was uncouth, I made a slight bow and seated myself on a bench in the elegant summerhouse which stood a short distance from the cottage.

The renowned Sugaru waterfall was more peaceful than I'd expected. The spray gathered, became clouds and smoke, and gradually flowed down. Whether it was wind or thunder, there was a mournful sound. For a while I was completely entranced, lost in a dream world, as though my eyes were seeing but not seeing, as though my ears were hearing but not hearing.

"Won't you have some tea?" It seems I was called any number of times. However, because I was silent, they finally came to get me.

The wife was kindhearted. Said she, "How touching! You are making a pilgrimage like this although there is nothing wrong with you. Please go right ahead and wash your feet."

She treated me so kindly in every conceivable way that I

---

55 Mount Aso is surrounded by a large outer crater 24 kilometres wide.
56 A poem of 31 syllables in the form of 5, 7, 5, 7, 7.
57 Now known as Sukaruga Falls (height 60 metres)

didn't know what to say. Her husband was sweet and warm, albeit strict, and the young man, who must have been their son, was superior to others of the area. They appeared to be of high birth. I decided to stay there that night because they begged me to.

With great respect I can say that the man's name was Umehara Hiroichi and that place was Setamura Village, Kikuchi County, Tateno.[58] He said, "I feel great empathy for you because I have sent my daughter and son to Kumamoto to study, and they are about your age." How dear and profound were his words and attitude; I was as delighted as if I had met my father in my own hometown.

In the evening we talked of various things and listened to the lonesome sound of the waterfall. Then, disregarding their telling me that going down to the falls was dangerous, I took a stroll and sang in a low voice. I thought of far-away Kumamoto and my father and mother, longed for my younger brothers and sister, thought of a certain person, lamented my situation and, seeing the lonely contours of the darkening, grassy mountains, felt immense sorrow. For some time, my fragile heart was clouded by the sadness of the vagabond life.

Article 7: FROM TATENO TO SAKANASHI

June sixth. I left Tateno, and went deeper and deeper into the outer crater ring of the volcano and proceeded across the central part of the Aso Valley. I thought the free-ranging herds of cattle here and there on the grassy plains were unusual.

When I crossed a bridge called the Akasebashi, carpenters were working at a house near the approach to the bridge. Said they, "Even the daughter of a good family cannot escape illness. It's probably punishment for sins in a previous world."[59]

When I walked on with a wry smile, three joyful looking beggar children came along from the opposite direction. I heard them singing, "Because we will not be born twice in this world,

---

58 This is now Otsu-chō.
59 They assume that she has leprosy or other serious disease.

we pray to you, Kanzeon,[60] for help."

Following right after the children came their parents, extremely triumphantly. No wonder—a bag with a large number of things received from begging was dangling dirtily. You shameless people! How pathetic you are—but I feel that we are birds of a feather.

Even they looked at me as they passed as though they felt we were on familiar terms. Afraid that they might speak to me, I shrank back and narrowly avoided that danger.

Today I had a very shameful experience when I was replacing my straw sandals at a shop. The woman shopkeeper there took a good look at me and politely said, "Excuse me, but won't you please take my gift?" Then, while I was watching, wondering what she was going to do, she came with rice on a tray. Oh, it was terrible! I thought that I have to accept it now or it will seem strange, but in my bag there was a collection of poems, notebooks and pens.

I didn't know what to do and was flustered and, seeing this, she said, "Well then, I will give you a bag," and kindly put a great deal of rice into a funny sack that is perhaps called a beggar's scrip or something. It was really unbearable but thinking I would be rude if I didn't take it, I finally accepted it, but then the agony of walking for several *chō*[61] with it dangling down. Hoping someone might pick it up if I discarded it on the grass beside the road, I put it there but I was afraid that the storekeeper might be offended if she saw it. At that very moment a mendicant priest came along. I wanted to take advantage of this fortunate encounter, but I could not utter a word. Finally I flung it down and ran away as fast as I could. Oh, I was sorry, but it was the only thing I could do.

In the early afternoon I arrived at Bōchū. When I passed in front of the gate of the Hekisui Elementary School, two teachers came out. Students streamed out and followed me. It made me thoroughly sick.

I entered the town of Sakanashi[62] tending to keep my head

---

60 Kanzeon is another name for Kannon Bosatsu.
61 A *chō* is an old Japanese measurement of length equal to 109 meters.
62 Sakanishi is 6 km from Bōchū

down. As usual I seemed to attract people's attention. One young man even poked his head under my hat and said wonderingly, "Hey, it's a girl who's still young!"

As I followed the road toward the village, the sun was already setting. Because I was utterly exhausted I sat on a rock beside the road and watched the brilliant red setting sun, while my tears rolled down uncontrollably. Where on earth shall I stay? The sun is sinking minute by minute.

Oh—where is my destination?

Article 8: PEOPLE REGARD ME WITH SUSPICION (Part 1)

When I was at my wit's end, forlorn and downcast, two people who looked like villagers happened along, and asked, "Hello, young pilgrim, what on earth is the matter?"

Then they said, "If you're worrying about a place to stay, there's no need to. There's a temple right up there. It's a famous temple. Go and ask there." They kindly explained the route in detail. When I went along the road they had told me about, I found the temple easily. It was a dignified temple called Jōdo-ji with a large *zelkova* tree[63] in its grounds.

It seemed the temple was very busy and in a muddle just then but the warm and gentle temple priest (When I say that, he may sound old, but he was still really young.) readily gave me permission to stay there. At this place also was his dear, sweet wife[64] who looked after me warmly. As usual, I was asked about my reasons for making the pilgrimage and was dismayed but when I told her of my heart's desire, she said, "I see," and that night I slept cosily.

The next day was June seventh, the whole sky was clear and the morning sun shone serenely. No sooner had I washed my face than one of the two villagers whom I had met the day before

---

63 *Zelkova serrata* (*Ulmaceae*) is a deciduous tree native to Japan. It is noted for its graceful symmetry and for its fresh green leaves in the spring, which turn yellow, red, and orange in the fall.

64 The word used, 坊守（ぼうもり）can mean either priest's wife or assistant priest. In the Jōdo school of Buddhism, it is used to indicate the resident priest's wife. I have assumed here and in Article 11 that Takamure is speaking of a wife.

came. He seemed to be consulting seriously with the temple priest. It was about me. They were saying, "From all appearances she is the daughter of a good family who met with some misfortune and left home without telling them. If that's the case, we would like to help her somehow."

Finally, they called me and again my situation was inquired into. A young woman traveling alone—is that so suspicious? Leaving home thoughtlessly, it had never occurred to me that I would encounter such a situation. It couldn't be helped —now it had become time to tell the true situation.

"Really? But you are much too young," they said.

Ah—poor me! May I instantly age and die! How can I deal with their painful suspicions?

However, with that, the matter rested. Then I was told that because there were people who had been to Shikoku the year before, I should rest here today and listen to what they had to say. I readily agreed to that proposal, which was more than I could have hoped for. While I was doing my washing and taking a leisurely rest, a messenger came expressly from the home of the person who had been at the temple and invited me to his home. I went there immediately because one should not disregard the kindness of others. It was a water mill and I was told that the host was Ino Kakuma.

Many people had gathered and I was served tea and entertained well in various ways. Moreover, the couple mentioned earlier who had made the Shikoku pilgrimage were sent for and came from a town more than three *chō*[65] away, although they were very busy, and kindly told me every detail of their experiences.

Article 9: PEOPLE REGARD ME WITH SUSPICION (Part 2)

I was alarmed when I heard their talk. Even travel expenses are a concern; they say I need as much as fifty or sixty yen.[66] In addition, they said that young girls have been killed or raped here and there in the mountains; moreover, the present

---

65 Three *chō* is equivalent to about a third of a kilometer.
66 Takamure had been given only 10 yen by the Kumamoto newspaper.

season is the worst for that sort of thing.

　　I lost heart. But it doesn't matter. Life and death are of no concern. I want to acquire faith and a sense of wonder; I want to acquire joy or frenzied passion. Somehow or other, while I am suffering in agony and wailing loudly, I may arrive at an incomparably majestic and lofty faith.

　　The path I should follow in life is none other than this: I should be an honourable, dignified, and noble woman. If I cannot become that, then I don't mind dying instead. Come persecution! Why should I be alarmed? I must experience the difficulties of the Shikoku eighty-eight temple pilgrimage, however hard they may be.

　　As I was coming back to the temple having firmly made up my mind, I again met on the road one of the two whom I'd met before. He told me his name was Ishida Mantarō. He too tried to persuade me to return to Kumamoto.

　　Many thanks for your goodwill! But—who knows my heart and mind? Moon and sun—shine! Shine and be with me! My heart is truly pure. When night came, the wind began to blow a little. I sat at the table with the priest and his wife and ate dinner, served with much warmth, and heard about various things. This temple is the seventeenth temple of the Kyūshū pilgrimage route[67] but it is extremely dilapidated because it has burned down twice. However, it is said to be a famous temple and when the Kannon of Sakanashi, is mentioned, everyone in the neighbourhood knows the temple. This Kannon image is kept hidden.[68]

　　　How dear to my heart this temple seems! It really feels like a sacred place. While we were thus talking, someone knocked on the door. I wondered if I were hearing the wind, but I wasn't. Soon there was the voice of a visitor, and in came a person who seemed to be a leading figure in the community. The very first thing he said was "Is this person the pilgrim?" and I felt quite overwhelmed. Oh no! To my surprise, yet another person has come because of me.

---

67 This is not a well-known pilgrimage route.
68 This is not uncommon; most of the Shikoku pilgrimage temples have principal images which are kept hidden from the public.

Just like everyone else, he said, "Young, too young." Ah, how I abhor my youth!

In the end, he finished with "Well take care, won't you. Please be particularly careful on the pilgrimage."

The next day was June eighth and finally the time came to part from the priest and his wife. As you might expect, tears welled in my eyes when I thought that meeting them had also been fate. Unusually solemnly, the priest said, "Actually, I also am still wondering about you. When I look at your behaviour carefully, I have to believe that you are the daughter of an uncommonly fine family. Is what you said really the truth?"

"Yes, it really is. Some day the time will come when you will understand."

"Then I'm relieved, but please take really good care of your health. If you ever come here again, please think of us as family and give us a visit. There's absolutely no need to thank us. Just accomplish your purpose."

As I was listening, my tears began to fall. Ah, people are so kind to such an unworthy person as I! How fortunate I am! Sakamoto Genrei of Jōdo-ji Temple, Sakanashi Village, Aso County[69]—this is a name I should remember forever and never forget.

Article 10: FROM SAKANASHI TO TAKETA (Part 1)

In the morning I was seen off, left Jōdo-ji temple, and came to the steep Sakanashi hill. Along the way I was invited to rest for a while at a teahouse. There, the mistress said to me, "You must be the pilgrim who stayed in the temple last night."

"Yes, I am."

"The people of the village have been talking about you here a lot."

When I had climbed to the top of the slope, the range of Mount Aso was already hazy in the southwest. Farewell, great Aso, I am sorry to leave you. Namino, as its name indicates, was a grassy hill with meandering waves of grass[70] extending

---

69 This is a Sōtō sect temple.
70 Namino means 'a field of waves'

gracefully to the right and left.

A light rain began to fall. With my rain gear over my shoulders I walked quietly. Oh, up until now my mind has been very unpleasantly wavering. I have felt bashful, sad, and despondent and thus each rumour about me has weighed greatly on my mind. But, now, suddenly, transcending all the joy and sorrow of this world in a very beautiful and sublime way, I feel the delight of a heart and mind steeped in indescribable pleasantness.

For human beings, vanity is the most intolerable thing; worrying about causing others offence is the most complicated. Existent and non-existent, visible and invisible, audible and inaudible, how joyful is the artlessly pure and independent mind. In such a mind, a most precious and abundant love arises. Life exists within the vastness of the universe. Detached but not detached, I love everything intensely. For me there is not the slightest uneasiness or sorrow. When the sun sets, I sleep; when the dawn breaks, I walk.

It has been pretty hard for me to abandon arrogance and abstain from frivolous pride. Elatedly, I have done calligraphy in front of others. How disgraceful was my mind; how deplorable it was. If I have to write, I'll write; if I have to read aloud, I'll read. Just let me be as I am.

However, there is one thing I can say: nearly one hundred percent of people do not understand the person that I am. I don't care. If they have doubts about me, it doesn't matter. However, it's annoying that problems arise because of their doubts. So what if I'm young? So what if I'm a woman? So what if I'm traveling alone?

My mind takes pleasure in the boundless universe and yearns for noble, undoubting faith—people won't believe that. They only think that I was in some really wretched situation and then set forth on a trip like this. They are such deplorable, pitiable people. Really, delusion is ingrained in their heads. They have an infinitesimal world. Their faith is a faith of delusion. Why don't they look heavenward? Why can't they study Kōbō Daishi? Why do they say they are too awed to do so? In short, they have minds that are very base. Thus their faith cannot really be called true faith. At this very moment I fervently believe that the Buddha is all important.

Set your mind free, be free—It's difficult to deal with people who, when I say that, immediately regard the idea as dangerous. Oh, when I think about Kōbō Daishi and Saint Nichiren,[71] they were all great people.

Article 11: FROM SAKANASHI TO TAKETA (Part 2)

I have finally set foot in Ōita Prefecture. The border marker said fifteen *ri,* seventeen *chō,* forty-three *ken*[72] from the zero marker in Kumamoto Prefecture and fifteen *ri,* eleven *chō,* fifteen *ken*[73] from the zero marker in Ōita Prefecture. On one side was Ōaza Ozono, Namino Village, Aso County, Kumamoto Prefecture; on the other side was Ōaza Otsuka, Sugō Village, Naoiri County, Ōita Prefecture. When I thought about the fact that it was the border between the provinces of Higo and Bungo,[74] for some reason or other, my eyes glistened with tears. Alas, my hometown is further and further away.

> Again and again,
> Craning my neck, I try
> To see Kumamoto City but cannot.
> I cry endlessly.

While I was resting in the shade of a tree because I had become very tired, a rickety horse-drawn carriage came along. The driver said, "Miss, please get in. You don't need to pay any money." When the driver brandished his whip, the horse ran along with lightning speed, and we entered the town of Taketa in a flash. It is the site of Taketa Junior High School.[75] It is a rather

---

71 (1222-1282) Buddhist monk and founder of the Nichiren school of Japanese Buddhism.
72 60.88 km. One *ri* is 3.93 kilometers
73 60.18 km.
74 Now Kumamoto Prefecture and Ōita Prefecture respectively.
75 The reason for mentioning this is probably that the school was once attended by Taki Rentarō (1879-1903), composer of the famous melody, "Kōjō no tsuki" (The Moon Over the Ruined Castle). The ruined Oka Castle in

prosperous town. As soon as I got down from the carriage, I was given directions and I went to Shin Kōyasan Temple (Zuisenji).

When I arrived, the wife of the priest there said, "Although you've come all the way here, we cannot let you stay. You look to be fifteen or sixteen. I don't think you can possibly be alone. You don't look like someone who is walking alone. You had better go somewhere like the inn below."[76]

The sun had already set. Saying nothing, I stood sorrowfully on the stone steps of the temple. The priest's wife shut the *shoji*[77] and showed herself no more.

Alas! Where will I go? Goodbye temple! Priest's wife! I bear you no resentment. I'll just go until I can go no further, until I collapse.

With my eyes cast down, I walked through the outskirts of the town, dimly lit by twilight. On one side of the road ran a river. "Don't be frightened; don't be troubled," I said to myself. "What can darkness do to you?" With my eyes raised heavenward and a joyful heart, I walked several *chō* and suddenly there was a voice behind me. "Pilgrim, where are you going?"

When I turned around, there was a young woman. "Oh my!" she said, "Well then, come to my house and I'll give you lodging."

It's a curious world, isn't it—some people reject me and some people help me.[78] I went along, thinking quietly and smiling softly and reached that house where I stayed one night. Everyone in the family was friendly. It was the home of Furuya Yoshijiro, 727 Kyōda Okamoto Village[79] Naoiri County, Ōita Prefecture.

Because rain began to fall fiercely, they very kindly said, "Why don't you stay today as well?" I have decided to take advantage of their kindness and stay another night. What a lonely

---

Taketa is famous throughout Japan as the inspiration for this song, one of Japan's most representative. Taki read the poem of the same name written by Doi Bansui and is said to have thought of Oka Castle in Taketa.
76 According to Takamure (*Ohenro*, p. 36), they thought she was eloping.
77 Sliding paper doors.
78 Takamure may be thinking of the Japanese saying "捨てる神あれば拾う神あり" which the Kenkyūsha dictionary translates as "The world is as kind as it is cruel."
79 Now part of Taketa City

day it seems. When I think about it, how very strange are my varied fortunes as I stride thus, step by step, toward an unknown future. What will my life be like fifty days from now, thirty days from now, ten days from now, even one day from now? I am now day dreaming about the time when I will take the steamboat from Ōita. The rain is falling harder and harder.

Article 12: FROM TAKETA TO NAKAIDA (Part 1)

Everyone at this house was kind. Because it was raining again today they asked me to take it easy so I did just that, and spent a relaxing day.

About nine in the morning on the tenth, I was bade farewell and departed and finally entered Kamiida Village in Ōno County.[80] The sky is very threatening, but I don't care. I am only delighting in the fact that my heart and mind are completely bountiful and undisturbed.

Well, I don't know where I'll stay today but if nobody puts me up, I'll just walk on. However, the fact that I will be asked various questions from now on is intolerably bothersome. My undisciplined mind is thrown into confusion by this in a multitude of ways. I have not yet achieved mental equilibrium!

While I was resting for a while with my hat off, three small children happened by and seeing me, they bowed politely and said, "We're on our way home now." Questioning them, I learned they were first grade students at Kamiida Primary School. Their speech was rather clear. I can imagine the regular drilling they've had.

In Ōita, the things I admire are things such as the wooden sign posts erected without fail by the road, and the fact that children are good mannered and clear in their speech. To be sure, there are many mountains and it is completely mountainous on both sides of the road. But the schools are all well regulated.

On this journey I have thought long and hard about the steps towards achieving an ideal and superior character; they are first, to be liberated, and second, to love. These are the two. The

---

80 This town first became Asaji and then, in 2005, became part of Bungōono city

first step is to divest oneself completely of such things as showy embellishments and impurities and return to one's original true nature; the second is to add a warm, beautiful, sacred, glossy lustre. If "lustre" is not appropriate, shall I say "radiance"?

When I passed in front of Yōrō Elementary School, the pupils there also bowed to me appropriately. In addition, their demeanour was very calm.

When I left the village behind, the sun was shining in such a lonely way. My Kumamoto lies in the direction of that familiar setting sun.

Where would I sleep tonight? This had become a matter of some concern. When I was trudging through the pitch-dark village, a white-robed pilgrim came toward me from the opposite direction. She was a woman in her forties. She said she was from Amakusa[81] and that she was on her way back from Shikoku. Listening to her talk about various things, it seemed that finding a place to stay is difficult. She said they hardly let pilgrims stay. In addition, she said that she had been begging because the forty or fifty yen she had was not enough for the cost of the trip.

I felt just a little bit discouraged. To tell the truth, my wallet is already almost empty. Never mind, I have an idea: I will spend all the money I have in Beppu and go around Shikoku without any. That's it—that's what I will do. Living and dying will be up to Divine Providence.

But, my parents in my hometown…. No, if I just have faith, what can frighten me? Nothing! I will go; I must go. Without any money, I must go. May the eighty-eight sacred temples of the pilgrimage be resplendent for me!

Article 13: FROM TAKETA TO NAKAIDA (Part 2)

While I was walking more firmly determined and suddenly filled with courage, the sun sank completely. Unexpectedly, from one small cottage there was a voice saying, "Pilgrim, won't you please take a rest?"

When I turned around, there was an old man of over seventy. He said, "Stay here tonight," and so I stayed.

---

81 An area in Kumamoto Prefecture composed of 120 islands of various sizes.

The old man's name was Itō Miyaji of Nakaida, Higashi Ōno Village, Ōno County.[82] He was a very pious man and from his appearance seemed extremely kind hearted. Kindness after kindness—so many that I felt unworthy. Seeing that my sedge hat had nothing written on it, he asked a neighbor to write on it for me.[83]

I had a bath and went to bed early. I slept peacefully. All of a sudden, I was awakened by his voice, "Miss! Miss!" and when I woke up startled, he said, "You are an attendant of Kannon Sama, aren't you?"

It was a strange question. I replied, "No, I'm not."

"Yes you are; it's useless to hide it. The connection between you and Kannon Sama is very deep. If it weren't, there'd be no reason for this miraculous thing that happened now."

"This miraculous thing that happened now?"

"This is what happened. It was probably about thirty minutes after I had gone to bed when, like a dream, although I was not yet asleep, a little child of seven or eight wearing a crown and another person, whose appearance wasn't clear, came down somewhere above my head, and promptly vanished. For sure, it was Kannon Sama."

Kannon Sama and I—we certainly have a deep connection. Because the boys born before me died one after the other, my mother made a vow to Kiyomizu Kannon[84] and I am the one who was born as a result of those prayers. It also seems astounding that I was born on Kannon Sama's day, the eighteenth of the month. Anyway, after that, and for other reasons as well, my mother became a very devout believer and we celebrate the eighteenth of the month without fail.

---

82 This is now Higashi Makigami Aza Makibaru, Ōaza Ushiroda, Ōno Town, Ōno County.

83 Pilgrims have *dōgyō ninin* written on their hats, meaning fellow wayfarer or two people travelling together. The two people are the pilgrim and Kōbō Daishi. The hat also has a poem written on it which Statler translates as follows: For the benighted the illusions of the world/ For the enlightened the knowledge that all is vanity./ In the beginning there was no east and west,/ Where then is there a north or south? (Statler, p.32)

84 Her mother, praying for a daughter, worshipped the Kiyomizu Kannon image in a small temple in Aso, Nangōdani, Kumamoto Prefecture. (Monnet, 67-8) See also Article 98.

I had not spoken even one word about matters such as these, but the old man was scrutinizing me carefully and said, "When I look at you this way, you are somehow very different from other people. From the beginning, judging from your general behavior, I thought you were much too wise."

Being told that I seemed to have the strength of about thirty people,[85] I was surprised. The strength of thirty people? Far from that! It's a shame but I don't have the strength of even *half* a person.

The wind is blowing a little hard but I will leave here today anyway. I'll go to Beppu by steam train, stay in an inn, and board a steamship there; then my wallet will be completely empty. At long last the test of my willpower is approaching.

Article 14: MY STRANGE FATE

June thirteenth. Rain is falling today as well. I am still in the home of the old man in Nakaida, Higashi Ōnomura Village, Ōno County that I wrote about in the last article. What is more, fate has unfolded interestingly. That is to say that it has unexpectedly come about that I am making the pilgrimage together with this old man of seventy-three. My connection with Kannon that I wrote of last time contributed much to this and another miracle (?)[86] was discovered.

This was because of a chat we had. The old man said, "I met a strange person during the Shin Shikoku pilgrimage.[87] An old man of about sixty, bald-headed, not wearing pilgrim robes at all, but wearing something rather nice and possibly striped over his pale yellow kimono, gave me detailed advice about my sedge hat and staff and other things, and then just vanished. When I talked about this with people at the inn they said that it was certainly Daishi *sama*,[88] so I want to meet him once again, no

---

85 Kannon Bosatsu is believed to appear in thirty different manifestations in order to help people.
86 Takamure's question mark.
87 There are various Shin Shikoku pilgrimage routes that have been developed for people who cannot go to Shikoku itself, including one in northern Kyūshū.
88 "Sama" is an honorific.

matter what!"

Hearing this, I thought, "How very strange!" because surely I had also met a person of about that age and with that kind of appearance. After leaving Tateno he was my travelling companion for just a little while, kindly talking to me about various matters concerning Shikoku, but we soon parted, and until now I had not even remembered him at all.

It was interesting. When I very briefly told the old man about it, thinking, of course, that it must surely have been by chance, he said, "What a blessing, what a blessing! What with the appearance of Kannon last night and what you have just told me, it's clear now that you are an extraordinary person. I am unworthy but, if this old man does not make the pilgrimage with you, protecting you, then he will have no excuse to offer the Buddha. Please stay here for another ten days or more, because I will certainly accompany you."

How inflated it has become! I was surprised and could do nothing but sit in stunned amazement. With this, even my plan to travel on foot alone seems to have come to naught. There seems to be no choice. The old man said, "I have no money, so we'll beg as we go. Bearing that in mind, you must have fortitude."

Come fate, whatever you are. I will go in the hands of fate, sleeping with an easy mind.

Rain is falling in a desolate way as before. In this area the mountains are beautiful and the grassy hills nestling in soft lines are gentle. Among the hills are some very fertile valleys. With the fine rain now softly misting the green grass which is growing luxuriantly on the surrounding cliffs and seeming about to avalanche down on to the tiny valley bottom below, it looks like a scene in a painting by Sesshu.[89]

The people of this locality called me "Elder sister" and "Sis". I had an interesting experience. A neighborhood child was playing with my pilgrimage staff. Using local dialect he asked, "Is this *one gan no*?" I didn't understand. However, not replying something would have been rude. When I replied, "No, it's not heavy," he made a peculiar face That was natural because he had

---

[89] Sesshu, (1420-1506) was a Japanese painter and Zen Buddhist priest. He is considered to be one of the foremost figures in Japanese art.

asked, "Is this yours?"

The pronunciation of the people of the area is generally sticky as though their mouths are twisted. Compared to their pronunciation, the tone of my clipped Kumamoto dialect seems out of tune and strange.[90]

Because the next day was a seasonal festival,[91] in the evening an old woman of the neighborhood made rice cakes and kindly brought them to me. There were various and sundry kinds: some were wrapped in oak leaves, some wrapped in flat leaves, and then some were very big, made of wheat flour to which sake had been added, with a little bean paste inside. Because she kept repeating, "Eat! Eat !" I clutched a huge rice cake and finally ate it although I thought I would die.

PILGRIMAGE POEMS BY TAKAMURE ITSUE[92]

In the evening how
The setting sun lingers
On the mountains ranging
All the way to Bungo.

In the wind I stand
Longing intently for my parents.
In Bungo Province
Hot water flows.[93]

I will not be frightened
I will not be doubtful
I who travel the world
Alone and lonely.

---

90 It is impossible to understand what Takamure means here. According to Prof. Kishie of Tokushima University, the intonation of Ōita dialect has more variation than that of Kumamoto dialect; the latter is montonous and flat.
91 Boy's Day, now held on May 5 by the solar calendar.
92 Takamure is considered to be a gifted poet; these translations do not reveal her true ability.
93 Hot spring water.

Dear blue sky and
Roots of trees and grass
When the sun sets
You'll become my inn.

In the midst of a grassy field
In the late afternoon sun
The sight of colts
Running free and whinnying.

Lonesome is the trail
In the evening
In the valley that is the border
Between Higo and Bungo.

When I feel the heaviness
Of the long sleeves of my violet kimono[94]
I regret my youth
For a moment

The loneliness of the pilgrim—
Dressed in pilgrimage robes
I cast down my staff and stand
On Mount Aso in the twilight.

Article 15: ADMIRERS

The night of the thirteenth, the crescent moon shone forlornly on the valley. Having been invited to take a bath at one home, I walked there silently amidst the lights of throngs of flying fireflies. I thought earnestly about the mystery of fate. "Oh, my town of Kumamoto! Is this moonlight shining solemnly upon you also?"

From journey to journey—I am like Edgar Allan Poe. I seem to be a child of fate who is destined to spend this ephemeral life either as a wandering exile or as a nun in a mountain temple.

---

[94] The kimono sleeves of an unmarried girl are long.

I was at my wit's end, being made to drink tea, being made to eat *dango*,[95] being made to listen to talk, and being questioned—so much so that I was even forced to consider the reprehensible idea that it would be better if all the people in the world were mute and blind.

Moreover, there is not one single person here who can understand me. With eagle eyes, everyone endeavours to understand me, to see into me but .... That is reasonable; even I don't understand how the crazy psychological state of this eccentric person keeps changing.

I certainly lack conventional sense. Actually, I don't think I am at all strange, but when I see people straining their eyes and looking at me doubtfully, there can be no doubt that I lack conventional sense. However, I am embarrassed because the people around here seem to greatly overestimate me. It seems that my every action has become the target of their watchful gaze, but what was laughable and made me feel embarrassed was the old man of the house, greatly impressed, saying one day when I was reading a book in a corner, "You seem to have practiced *kendō*.[96] This is immediately clear because of the unusual way you are vigilant and keep a sharp eye out." Actually, at that time, the eyes of the person being praised were not steady but were moving restlessly about.

On the fourteenth, the Shingon priest in charge of the neighborhood temple unexpectedly paid a visit and I listened to him chant the Kōmyō Shingon. "On abokya beiroshanou[97] manihandoma jimbara harabaritaya un."[98]

The priest very enthusiastically interpreted it for me. "When a person chants '*On abokya*,' all the Buddhist gods and

---

95 A dumpling, cake, or other round food made from rice flour and water.
96 A Japanese martial art in which two opponents fight with bamboo sticks.
97 The priest leaves out *maka-bodara* at this point.
98 The priest chants it in Sanskrit. The *Kōmyō Shingon,* the Mantra of Light, is said to encompass the entire power of Dainichi Nyorai, the principal deity of Shingon Buddhism. It is said that when the *Kōmyō Shingon* is recited with single-minded focus and concentration and egoless intent, the Great Radiant Light of Wisdom of the Buddha will embrace the reciter (or the person for whom it is recited), dispersing the illusions that hinder our development, and returning the mind to its original state of purity and Buddha-nature.

saints come down from heaven, and when he chants '*Beiroshanou*,' the person becomes Dainichi Nyorai preaching."

He said moreover, "Whole heartedness means one single heart; faith means to extend your heart; when you reach out with your whole heart and have faith from the bottom of your heart, your future will surely be promising. As for the word 'future', the characters for it are written as 'come at the end'[99] and the characters for the world after death are written 'born afterward'.[100] The future and the next life are truly very important."

Hearing this, the old man, wept copious hot tears. I myself, flabbergasted and not knowing what to do, kept my eyes down and sat very respectfully.

Article 16: A LITTLE QUEEN

Perhaps first, before anything else, I want to ask all of you if you have ever eaten kneaded rice flour.[101] (and eaten it just dipped in soy sauce).[102] This morning, June eighteenth, I ate that.

Here is what I always do: after I get up, I finish my ablutions and go for a walk, choosing a place where there is no one, such as the hills, the forest, an earthen bridge, and so on. Then when I return, it's soon time to eat.

After realizing that it was utterly useless no matter how much I insisted, "Let me do the cooking" and "Let's eat together", I let the kind old man here do as he wanted.

Well, this morning, that customary stroll took a little longer than usual—this was because I suddenly had an unbearable desire to see the mountains of Kumamoto and climbed the high mountain behind the house. From there, Mount Aso was faintly visible. Then, at last I returned and saw the old man furtively eating something in a corner. When he saw me, he said, in an extremely flustered way, "I'm so sorry; I'm eating

---

99 He has mistaken 'end' （末）and 'not yet' （未）. The characters for future are written 'not yet come'. （未来）.
100 His interpretation is incorrect again.
101 Rice flour mixed with water and kneaded.
102 Readers would have eaten it made into various kinds of *dango*.

before you."[103]

When I said lightly, "Oh no, think nothing of it," and went into the house, it was very strange. The food that the old man was eating was soft and sticky, white, like a melted *dango*. I very much wanted to ask about it, but couldn't possibly do so. Over and over again I wondered to myself what it was. In the end, I couldn't restrain myself, and when I asked, blushing, "What is that?" He replied, "This is rice flour but it's not for your eyes."

Rice flour? I wanted to try eating it. Because of this curiosity of mine, I have eaten rice flour. I'm glad that I can boast to all my readers about this.

Also, since then, I don't know how many times I have taken strange baths. These experiences together have sufficient merit for me to take pride in them. Maybe someone will say, "A frog in a well doesn't know the great ocean".[104] Stop saying that. Perhaps it is merely that a precious fish in the ocean doesn't know the inside of a tiny well.

Writing that, even I was amused. How could I say such a thing as if I knew what a precious fish is like? To tell the truth, I want to write a "queen" instead of a "precious fish". These days my life is entirely like that of a little queen. If I eat a sweet one morning and say "Oh delicious," after that I am assailed with that sweet. Each evening I am invited to someone's house to have a bath. Moreover, I am the first to bathe, and because all the others must wait until I've bathed, it is too much.

At this point, what is bothering me is the fact that a lecture I gave is on the verge of becoming an issue. The cause of the trouble was my killing time one evening when the moon was hazy by gathering the children of the neighborhood together and telling them about hell as described in some *wasan*.

At this rate, all countless living beings may gather to

---

103 I wonder if the old man was cooking rice for Takamure, which was more expensive, then later eating kneaded rice flour by himself. However, it seems that Takamure did not consider this possibility.

104 This is from a Chinese fable. A frog living in a shallow well saw the circumscribed world of the well and thought that was all there was. A turtle from the East Sea described the East Sea to the frog shocking the frog into a realization of his own insignificance. The Japanese proverb is "The frog in the well does not know the ocean." (*I no naka no kawazu taikai o shirazu*.)

listen to my stories, including not only the village young men and girls, but also the old men and women of the village. It's a depressing thought. Of course, I may preach, "Thus I heard, that the Buddha once preached on Mount Kyōdara"[105] and so on—and people will again be enthralled by my preaching. Oh, how trivial that is!

As the Lotus Sutra says, "If your arms and legs are bound with manacles and fetters, evoke the power of Kannon, and you will be freed."[106] Yes—return to my true nature. Offer a fervent prayer regarding my whole-hearted desires. Do not be vain. Do not be false. I must think about this quietly.

Well, if it can't be helped, so be it. From the bottom of my heart I want to destroy their base faith and tell them where our highest ideals should be. What is religion anyway? Someone said, "It is the fervent aspiration toward the highest ideals in people's minds and the path leading to their achievement."

Article 17: THE LITTLE QUEEN

Lately, I've been earnestly considering the pressure of the void—that is to say, the limitless pressure arising from doubt, insecurity, dread, and anguish concerning the worlds of life and death. At one time I boasted and said that life and death are inconsequential.

Nevertheless, when I think about it now, it must doubtless have been the voice of some indistinct, hazy emotion. At this point, I vividly recall the life of Tolstoy. Drifting and tormented, at times he marvelled at the serfs' simplistic life of faith and, seeing it, was painfully moved. However, in the end, he was

---

105 According to Buddhist cosmology, Mount Kyōdara is one of the seven golden mountains (mountain ranges) that encircle Mount Meru in the center of the world.
106 This is from the 25th chapter of the Lotus Sutra which is regarded by the Tendai School of Buddhism as the final and most authentic teaching of the Buddha. At the beginning of the chapter the Buddha says, "If countless millions of living beings, suffering pain and torment, should hear of this Kannon Bosatsu and single mindedly call upon his name, Kannon will instantly perceive their cries and voices, and all will be able to obtain deliverance."

unable to take hold of great philosophical principles to convert to.

To be able to believe—that must be a blessing. Actually, since setting foot in this province of Bungo, what I have especially felt is the faith, this truly devout, truly consistent, truly earnest and truly secure faith, that believers in Kōbō Daishi have. To be sure, I have both admired and envied them. Nevertheless, the disappointment I felt when I realized that they are, in the end, people belonging to a different world from mine, has made my persistent loneliness more apparent. Of course those people cannot accept me as the solitary person I am. In short, the Itsue whom they see is an Itsue changed into one of them.

Various difficulties have arisen concerning that point. Regarding my present pilgrimage trip, I have been subjected to really unbearably annoying doubts and misconceptions. Is my pilgrimage because of a vow or because of an incurable illness or because of some misconduct—people will not accept any reason other than one of those three. Then, when I stay at one place for a long time, as I have now, all of a sudden my actions and my opinions expressed without forethought are greatly prized and this time I'm exalted as "the Buddha reborn". From one extreme to the other—even though I try not to, I can't help smiling wryly. Must a trip by a young woman alone be a matter of so much suspicion and wonder? Everywhere I've gone people have said, "You don't look like a person who would become a pilgrim." I wonder why.

People's thinking is too materialistic, too concerned with actualities, not in the least noble and eternal. In short, people do not understand poetry. The faith that arises in the mind of this kind of person is shaped only by a hope for rewards and an idolizing of miracles; they appear to be that kind of person. From miracles to faith—this progression is clear if you look back at the early days of missionary work among all ignorant and benighted sentient beings, not only the missionary work of Buddhism but that of Christianity and other religions as well. Of course, this was essentially a matter of expedience.

The *Daishi Wasan* says "the salvation of the Shingon[107] school of Buddhism is promised to anybody, regardless of their

---

107 The Shingon school of Buddhism was founded by Kōbō Daishi.

potential for enlightenment, whether they are a saint or an ordinary person. However, for people with poor potential, the easy way to practice Buddhism is to chant the Kōmyō Shingon earnestly in daily life and before they know it, age-old evils will completely disappear, and their entry into the bliss of Paradise will be ensured." (I have omitted the rest.) Thus, the ignorant in their ignorant state, just as they are, can be saved. Chanting that *nembutsu*[108] is excellent if seen as a means to an end.

Of course, if we look at it from the point of view of the founder of the Jōdō school of Buddhism, Saint Honen,[109] after many years of anguish and sorrow he seems to have suddenly discovered a shaft of sacred light in the Kangyo-sho,[110] which was authored by Saint Zendō at the end of the Tang Dynasty. Although he seems to have felt nothing but joy and faith through reciting the *nembutsu* and scooping up quiet, solemn, tranquil peace of mind into his unfathomable and infinite heart, this is not the case for those with poor potential.

Even so, in any case, blessed are those who have faith—I reiterate this here. Then, because of these thoughts, I decided to research *sutras* or *wasan* very seriously. When I said this to the old man, he willingly bustled about with the result that, in the twinkling of an eye, a mountain-like pile of such documents appeared on the table.

Article 18: I WANT TO RUN AWAY

Having stayed here several days I now seem to have become the focus of everyone's attention. Horse-drawn carriages pass right in front of me and as they go by, people say things like

---

108 Invocation of the name of the Buddha. In the majority of cases the word *nembutsu* refers to invoking the name of Amida in order to be reborn in his Pure Land.
109 1132-1212
110 *The Commentary on the Meditation Sutra*, written by the Chinese Pure Land Master, Shan-tao (Zendo). In this work, he made a number of radical advances in Pure Land thought which laid the foundations for the subsequent development of Pure Land Buddhism in China and Japan. Shan-tao was Honen's greatest influence because he developed the nembutsu as the reciting of Amida's name rather than the visualization of him in his Pure Land.

"That's her!" I always cry out to myself "Be calm, my heart!" but in vain.

One evening the old man came back home beaming and said, "You know, your contributions have been published in the newspaper.[111] People are all saying you must be an illustrious young woman scholar."

I flushed a little and thought, "So, they've appeared." To relieve my boredom, I'd written some articles for the Ōita newspaper.

So what! There's no need to make a big fuss about it. Ignoring the matter, I was again devoting myself to the sutras when a gentleman of about fifty and his neat and tidy daughter, such as are not usually seen around here, dropped by saying they had just returned from Beppu.[112]

The woman said, "Are you the 'Young woman on a pilgrimage trip'?"[113]

In an extremely subdued voice I replied, "Yes," and sat upright.

"Eh? Is that right? Well, just as I imagined, you are a woman. You know you've caused a big commotion in Beppu. They're saying this is certainly not the writing of a woman. They say it must be a male reporter at the newspaper who is ghost writing such things. But, if it is a woman, it's really strange ….. There's been much heated controversy."

"Really, was there such a reaction to my writing?"

I blushed redder and redder. She said, "Well, please come to see us, how about tomorrow? Our place is just over there."

With these kind words, she headed home; I watched her retreating figure blankly. My natural tendency is to be a recluse; she had said how about tomorrow but I wasn't inclined to go.

However, when I was leaning on my desk (actually an old

---

111 She had submitted articles to the *Ōita Shinbun* and nine were published on June 13-16, June 22, June 23, June 25-27. The contents of the articles were virtually the same as in the articles published in the *Kyūshū Nichi Nichi Shinbun*.
112 A port city in Kyūshū with many hot spring resorts. There are ferries to Honshū and Shikoku.
113 Her articles were titled "The travels of a young woman pilgrim in Ōita for the first time".

box), ruminating in my usual fashion, the young lady came to see me without waiting for me to call and I felt embarrassed. She said her name was Ōtsuka Fumiko. I didn't intend to but I spoke pretentiously, and afterwards felt so awful that I couldn't stand it.

The next day the old man was out and when I was sitting musing, many horse-drawn freight carriages, passenger carriages, and passers-by went by, with the people straining their eyes and saying things like, "It's the person who was in the paper." I was so embarrassed that I didn't know what to do with myself. Among those passing, there were even some drivers who expressly stopped their horses and went to the trouble of giving an explanation to their passengers. Do they think I am an animal in the zoo? Thanks to their attentions, in this heat and dripping with sweat, I had to conceal myself—barely—behind a folding screen. How very miserable my life has become! From now on during the day, I will make a point of going out somewhere such as the hill over there or the forest in the neighbourhood.

Evenings are better; moreover, this house, in particular, has an indescribable charm in the twilight. While I was thinking about such things, a drunken man of about forty came into the house saying, "Excuse me, are you the pilgrim?" and "Please tell my fortune." When I nervously told him, "I don't know anything about that kind of thing," he came back with "You can't say you aren't able to do it." Then, just when I was totally confounded, I was so lucky because a somewhat crippled man came in, supporting himself with sticks on both sides of his body, and said, "Please buy a fortune from me!"[114]

The more I looked at this man, the more sympathy I felt for him. How inconvenient his life must be. He said that his home was in Saganoseki, Kita Amabe County, Ōita Prefecture, and that he was called Etō Kaichirō. The fortune telling problem solved, the first man left and then the second man stayed a while and we talked.

---

[114] In earlier times fortune venders or small boys sold *tsujiura*, slips of paper with fortune-telling messages, on the street and from door to door. The second man seems to be a *tsujiura* seller.

Article 19: THE CURIOUS SIGHT OF THE *SAA* AND THE RELOCATION OF THE YELLOW SEA

June nineteenth. While I was eating breakfast, an unusual procession of people carrying some sort of wooden tub on their heads went past on the road in front of the house. All were young women. They had very splendid physiques and thumped along laughing noisily and merrily, supporting the tubs lightly with their hands. When I asked the old man what was going on, he said they were 'Saa'. 'Saa' is a curious name. When I asked where they were from, he said they were from Usuki.[115] When I asked what they were selling, he said they were selling fish.

He also said, "Those people are the descendants of Heike fugitives.[116] I have heard that they said, 'Saa,[117] come on, we must flee right away; all is lost' and, they fled, stuffing freshly steamed rice into bags because they didn't have time to make rice balls. So look—the bags they carry on their hips—even now the bags contain cooked rice that was just scooped in. The strange name of *Saa* came about because of this."

"There are rural aspects in the capital."[118] I was impressed by the Saa and wondered if this saying were applicable.

After eating breakfast, I went for a walk wearing a light *yukata*[119] and a hat with a green ribbon—even I thought my appearance odd. I approached the mountain path where there was usually no one else. All of a sudden, from the opposite direction, a somewhat fine looking person wearing western clothes came walking along. He was probably about forty-two or three. You

---

115 Usuki in Ōita prefecture is famous for rock carvings of Buddhist images.
116 After the Taira-Minamoto war between the Taira clan (Heike) and the Minamoto clan (Genji) ended in 1185, the Heike were forced to flee because the Genji had won. There are many legends about Heike moving to distant, isolated places where they could escape detection.
117 "*saa*" is a common interjection in Japanese with multiple meanings such as "please", "come on", "come", "here", "well", "I'm ready", and "now".
118 京に田舎あり（きょうにいなかあり） Even sophisticated urban people sometimes do rustic, crude things. Although the Heike were very sophisticated members of the Kyōto court, even they, in their haste to flee, simply scooped cooked rice into bags.
119 An unlined summer kimono.

could say he looked as though he had returned from Hawaii.

I was surprised when he addressed me, "Miss!"

"Miss, you're not from around here, are you?"

"Really? You're on a pilgrimage? That's an admirable idea." Because he kept staring at me and talking, it was creepy.

"You say you're going with an old man? How old? Seventy-three—that's a great mistake. Don't go with him. I'm thinking of making the pilgrimage myself in two or three days. If you want, I can help you." Gradually his true colours began to appear.

"The other day I returned from traveling abroad. When I went abroad, I saw how vast the world is! From Yokohama I went straight to …." Without my realizing it, I was listening intently, my eyes shining. "Besides, en route there, there is an unusual place. It's called the Yellow Sea; in this one place, right in the middle of the Pacific Ocean, the color of the water is tinged with yellow." This surprised me—the Yellow Sea had moved.[120]

He also said, "I have an interesting thing with me here. If you like it, I may give it to you. Oh, yes. Anyway, come with me. Even tomorrow would be fine. Look, this is it."

When I looked, it was a gilded watch. "This cost more than a hundred yen. That's because it's diamond." He was more and more outrageous.

He said, "I'm sure that America is a substantial country because it's on the gold standard. Japan is insignificant because it's on the silver standard."[121] The more he spoke, the more deplorable he seemed.

Article 20: FIFTEEN YEARS OLD OR FORTY ?

"What do you say? I can take care of you. Where are you from? I see, Kumamoto; I pity you. I'll take care of you even if it costs me my life. How old are you? Fifteen? Poor child! There's nothing to be concerned about. Throw away a ring like that, I'll buy you a better one."

---

120 The Yellow Sea is bordered by China, North Korea, and South Korea. It merges with the East China Sea to the south.
121 At this time both Japan and the USA were on the gold standard.

I said, "No, this one cost more than a hundred yen. And, it's a diamond one like your watch. Look—it's a gold diamond—extremely unusual isn't it? But it's also a little strange that the Yellow Sea has changed its location." Uncharacteristically, I chattered flippantly and suddenly my face went red. The expression on the face of the man in western clothes was a sight to see; his eyes glittered and rolled. Spitting out, "What did you say? What kind of person are you?" he walked away flustered. What a strange man he was.

In Shikoku there are many whom local people call corrupt pilgrims[122] who, when they see that a young woman is traveling alone, skilfully sweet talk her so that the woman falls into their trap; I've heard that such cases are frequent. However, as you would expect, the women who are thus tricked are mostly uneducated. Such cases as those make me think seriously about the necessity of women's education. I have certainly become disgusted with half-baked education. There is no person more unpleasant than a woman with a smattering of knowledge who has lost her humility. Thus, a further breakthrough in women's education is required. To step back is cowardly.

In the afternoon, because I was so bored, I told the old man so and he borrowed the *Shi Kyō*[123] from the gentleman who had called on his way back from Beppu. (At that time he had offered to lend it to me.) Upon his return he said, "He thinks you are forty years old. I said to him 'Where did you get such a wrong idea?'" When he said this I was abashed. The world has all kinds!

Around here they are already transplanting rice. I wonder how it is in my homeland of Kumamoto?

Later, at about four o'clock, a person from a nearby village came and said that our going to Shikoku was very opportune because there was a woman who wanted to be taken. He asked us to take her. He said she was an old blind woman of about fifty who had her heart set on going to Shikoku and on that

---

122 She uses ぐれ, from ぐれる, to do wrong.
123 The *Shi Kyō* (In Chinese called the *Shi Jing* or *Shi Ching* –*The Book of Odes*) is a collection of 305 Chinese poems believed to date from the 12th to the 7th century BC. It was very influential in establishing Chinese lyrical poetry.

alone.

I said, "Please let her come with us. I'll lead her by the hand." After thinking for a while, the old man said, "Let me see. Anyway, tomorrow I'll meet her." That was how the matter was left.

The old man's intention is to train us to endure camping outdoors and in the mountains and all ascetic practices. I have also thought that way from the beginning. The *kichinyado* where lice and germs swarm will be terrible but, when we camp out and cook rice in a pot hanging from the branch of a tree and so on, how enjoyable that will be.

Because the old man was scouring a bamboo tube, I asked, "What is that?" and he said it was a container for salt. Will we be going with it dangling down?[124] At last a beggar's life is unfolding. I wrote a poem—

> Dear blue sky and
> Roots of trees and grass,
> When the sun sets
> You'll become my lodging.[125]

I'll go! I'll go walking peacefully and quietly, leading the blind woman by the hand. On our way the green leaves will be fragrant and the birds will sing of the future. Ah, a solemn evening at a pilgrimage temple in the mountains with the old man and the old woman standing before the red, setting sun. In addition, my lonely figure—

We will surely be silent. Teardrops will be rolling down my cheeks.

Article 21: VARIOUS VISITORS

June twentieth. Since morning, it's been hectic.

First, a priest came. Then came a fortune teller, and a person whose name I didn't learn, and some worshippers. Then

---

124 The salt was used to massage her feet. Each night the old man massaged her feet when they arrived at their lodging.
125 This is also found in Article 14.

came a school headmaster, some female teachers, and a would-be member of the prefectural legislature. It's been really intolerable.

In particular, the worshippers were quite extraordinary. They said, "Following your footsteps we have come from quite far away. With the concentration of your mind, please heal these diseases that you see."

They appeared to be an old woman of over seventy and a housewife in her early forties and I felt overwhelming pity for them. (Due to the circumstances, I omit their names and addresses.)

Indeed, the old woman had a boil on her leg,[126] and the housewife, one on her neck. They certainly looked painful. "We've heard that you're not an ordinary person." I wondered what on earth I should do. Every time they said this and that, I was downhearted and felt like crying. In the first place, although I explained to them "I'm not that kind of person," they just wouldn't accept what I said.

There was nothing I could do, so I immediately pretended to be the God of Boils and said, "It is important for people to have faith. As soon as you return home tonight say three times 'Get better, boil!' and pray to the gods then go to bed. Never ever doubt my words! Also, consult a doctor in your neighbourhood. This too is a revelation from the God of Boils." Although I did not say that in so many words, I at least told them something to that effect, blushing and turning pale many times.

But thank heavens, they prostrated themselves like flat spiders, completely submissively. Ah, unexpectedly I have gained one profession! After I return to Kumamoto, I shall immediately become the God of Boils.

Next, Mr. Mori Isamu, headmaster of Ida Primary School, took the trouble to visit me bringing with him two women teachers, Koizumi Chiyo and Takeuchi Chitaru. I was really appreciative and we talked animatedly about various things. Their thoughts concerning religion and people's ways of living were quite interesting.

"Clear, but not clear; unclear, yet not unclear. At any rate,

---

126 The word used is *odeki (=dekimono)*, which the dictionary defines as tumour, boil, or ulcer.

the bright, radiant fire of the ideal is burning at the bottom of my vague hope. Such a thing as reality or existence is not so disturbing or lonely. But there exists the pressure of the so-called void.[127] Naturally, of course, I don't intend to deny reality; no, I'm willing to acknowledge it.

"Become a nun? Well, I may. However, if you think that it is only for that purpose that I am now living and acting in this manner, then you are mistaken."

And so on—I spoke out of character, pretentiously, and afterwards felt unspeakable disgust, remorse and loneliness. And, what did I look like while I was rather heated, rather excited, my face red and my eyes sparkling, my young blood dancing?

We had talked for some hours and it became late, so we took leave of one another, saying, "Be sure to keep in touch in the future as well."

Like a dream, the night is moonlit. Ah…the universe! Life! Solitude!

What on earth is my present situation? And what kind of future will it bring about?

Article 22: A SOLDIER'S WIDOW OR A HATOYAMA-STYLE WOMAN?

On the morning of June twenty-second while I was taking a walk, I visited Mr. Ōtsuka who is somewhat well-known in this village for his old, established family, as well as for being a scholar of Chinese classics. Here, again, I was told that there have been any number of conflicting rumours about me.

First of all, suppositions vary depending upon whether people have seen me or not. Those who have not seen me say things like, "She is undoubtedly the widow of a soldier. Or, perhaps she is a Hatoyama-style woman?[128] Maybe she is

---

127 Takamure discusses this idea in greater detail in Article 17. "Void" may also be "empty space".
128 Hatoyama Haruko (1861-1938), born into a samurai family in Matsumoto, was educated and subsequently taught at what later became Ochanomizu Women's University. She was well-known as a writer on women's education who contributed articles to such magazines as *Fujin no*

investigating women's living conditions in every district and will use the results for her great advancement in the future."

Those who have seen me say, "We just can't figure her out. She certainly seems to be a daughter who has run away from her family due to some misconduct. And some man with her has been ghostwriting those newspaper articles."

These are extremely self centred imaginings. Then, finally, they want to meet me and talk to me in person. However they hesitate, fearing what will happen if they are written about in the newspaper. Thus, a great number of people of this kind deliberately make up some excuse and go back and forth in front of the place I'm staying.

"Today she was leaning against a pillar."

"Today she was sitting on the raised floor in the entrance."

"Were her legs dangling?"

"No, her feet were on the floor below."[129]

"How about her footwear?"

"Straw sandals."

"Hey, today she smiled."

They think of me as some kind of show. Also, the letter carrier scrutinizes my mail. He says, "Today something came from the newspaper company in Kumamoto...."

Mr. Ōtsuka told me, "At any rate, people are making an issue of you and talking about you. You must be particularly careful in what you do ...." I was deeply grateful. I was told that some people have clipped out my newspaper articles. And, when I stopped contributing to the Ōita newspaper for a while, letters poured in fussing about this and that, like the commotion of a festival. Yet, it is not clear whether the object of worship is a dog, a cat, or even the God of Boils. However, I feel sorry for those making the fuss because the object of worship is simply stunned and surprised by the turn of events.

In the afternoon Miss Takeuchi of Ida Elementary School, who had come to see me the other day, visited me and naturally our topic of conversation flew to the field of education. I guess

---

tomo. Her great grandson, Yukio, became prime minister of Japan in 2009.
129 In a traditional Japanese home the entrance area is lower than the floor.

she is probably a fairly prominent woman teacher in this area. We never stopped talking about such problems of women teachers as styles of lesson plans, supplementary lessons,[130] and so on.

"At any rate, the policy of the authorities is too stopgap. I have to think so because they are not really trying to help women teachers through and through but are intent at this time on making effective use of them as quickly as possible.[131] This is proven by the fact that, although short courses for women teachers and self-improvement groups are held on a grand scale, their contents are too one-sided. Take, for instance, needlework or household management—it seems they pay attention only to developing the so-called strong points of women teachers, considering this the only solution for the problem of the low standard of female teachers. I heard that in my area a headmaster once said that practice is more important than theory for female teachers. Not only that, but nobody found this remark offensive and female teachers themselves were convinced of its truth. What a mistake it is! The authorities have no intention of helping female teachers in all aspects; they are only trying to improve them in some limited areas ...."

As usual, I exhibited bitter pretentiousness. We parted saying that we hoped for a continuing association. Later, I felt a little sorry for her.

The sun is setting, and in a moment the shades of evening are closing. I am standing watching the sun set, leaning against a pillar, my heart and mind filled with indescribable grief.

Ah, my heart and mind! Always be calm, always be noble; don't be disturbed, remain gentle and modest. Oh, I want to go to those awe-inspiring pilgrimage temples soon!

After musing for a long time, I found the moonlight had become hazy. Someone came and addressed me saying, "It's you isn't it, the person who copies any and all sutras." When I looked closely, it was the priest.

Then he said "If you read indiscriminately, you will be

---

130 These were lessons outside regular class time which teachers gave when there was not time to cover topics in the regular school day or when extra lessons were needed in preparation for entrance exams for upper levels of education.
131 Takamure had worked as an assistant in her father's elementary school.

punished and it will be impossible to memorize as much. You should be careful."

Thank you very much!

Article 23: AN IMPERTINENT SHIROMON[132]

If I don't first explain the meaning of *shiromon*, I wonder if you will be able to understand. As a matter of fact, I can't explain it; even the person who was called a *shiromon* doesn't know its meaning, but because I thought it was amusing when a woman called me a *shiromon,* I immediately took up the term.

Incidentally, this shiromon has become very saucy these days. One moonlit night I wanted to lead the old man to salvation and asked him, "Old man, when you gaze at the moon, what are you thinking about?"

The old man was dumbfounded and could make no reply. So I said elatedly "Those very people who can get a sacred, lonely, tearful feeling, a kind of indescribable feeling from the very depths of the moonlight shining all around, boundlessly brimming, can return to life with a high and precious faith. By all means savour the profound tranquillity of the moonlight."

Hearing that, the old man repeated, "I'm so thankful, I'm so thankful". So I became elated and thought, "If you want to save people, be ambiguous. Ambiguity is obscurity. Obscurity is mystery; mystery excites divine inspiration; divine inspiration creates faith."

Another time a certain priest came and asked me, "What are you reading?" Because *shiromon* at that very time was reading the *Eki Kyō* (the *I Ching* divination book),[133] I told him

---

132 Shiromon is derived from shiromono (代物) and means such things as merchandise to be traded, price of the goods sold, a beautiful woman, a fellow, a guy, a character, a customer, a person. It tends to have a negative connotation when applied to a person and can mean the equivalent of 'a difficult customer' or a person of questionable character.

133 The *I Ching* (The Book of Changes) is a three thousand year old Chinese oracular system. In Japanese it is called the Eki Kyō and the priest thinks that Kyō (経) indicates a sutra because sutras are called "kyō". He is an ignorant man. Important books in both Confucianism and Buddhism are called kyō.

so. Then he said, "Ah, a sutra. At any rate, that's admirable but do you understand it? I'd like to ask again what in the world you are thinking when you read a sutra?" This priest comes to see me from time to time and it is amusing that he makes blunders like this.

I answered with an extremely serious attitude, "I read because I am seeking enlightenment."

"I see, Kōmyō. Then I will lend you the Kōmyō Shingon, the Mantra of Light."[134] He makes no sense at all. Moreover, this priest won't leave.

"I hear you contributed something to the newspaper. Was it a comic *haiku* or a *tanka*?[135] Mine have also been published. Please write your poem for me on this paper."

He doesn't give up easily. There was nothing I could do. So I said, "All right! I'll write," and dashed off,

> It doesn't matter
> That I'm desperate.
> Nobody knows
> The future.
> Tonight, paradise;
> Tomorrow, hell.

Then I explained, saying, "This poem can also be sung."

Struck speechless, the priest left. At this point, the cheekiness of the *shiromon* was radiating a light like the burning sun.

These days the *shiromon* has begun to feel deeply depressed. I have already stayed here for ten days and am bored out of my mind. Since I am a music lover by nature, I asked around saying that I wanted to play some instrument, a *samisen* or anything would do, at midnight in the moonlight when no one was around and I was all by myself. I was soon able to borrow a

---

134 This is the Shining Light mantra of the Shingon sect. Because Takamure uses the term Kōmyō to mean enlightenment, the priest confuses her desire for enlightenment with the Kōmyō mantra.

135 Haiku and tanka are two types of short Japanese poetry. Haiku have 17 syllables and tanka have 31.

half-broken *biwa*.[136]

How glad I was. I couldn't wait until it became dark. Finally the time came and I sat erect and cleared my throat. The old man insisted upon my playing Kōbō Daishi's *Mountain Opening Wasan*, so I had to do it. I played and sang mournfully, "Verily, I've heard that the Japanese bead tree is fragrant even when it is in bud and that genius displays itself even in childhood.[137] It was in the midst of the summer of the fifth year of the Hōki era.[138] The voice of the *hototogisu*[139] was calling out behind green leaves ...."

Because I was improvising the words, it was very difficult. I went on, "He was born at Byōbugaura, Sanshū,"[140] and then made a mess of it. However, the old man was deeply impressed and said, "It sounds very much like a war story."

I was mortified! With this, the insolence of the *shiromon* ended. A person shouldn't be an impudent *shiromon*—writing this now I feel unbearably disgusted with myself.

Ah, I will put down my pen. The wind seems to be blowing rather hard.

Article 24: A PILGRIMAGE ROMANCE (Part 1)

Actually, I don't know whether I should write this or not. But, you misunderstand me if you have the idea that I deal with

---

136 The *biwa* and *samisen* (or *shamisen*) are Japanese stringed instruments. The *biwa* was used in singing tales of wars and the *samisan* was used by entertainers in the pleasure quarters. Takamure was musically gifted and could play many instruments such as violin, flute, mandolin, and organ. She had perfect pitch but because of childhood pneumonia, did not usually sing. Her brother thought that she might become a musician when she grew up. (*Waga Takamure Itsue*, p.58)

137 The *sendan* tree (Japanese bead tree) (*melia azedarach*) has purple flowers and, in the winter, yellow berries which grow along the branches like beads. She is quoting the Japanese proverb, *sendan wa futaba yori kanbashi* which means 'Genius displays itself even in childhood' as was the case with Kōbō Daishi.

138 774AD

139 A Japanese cuckoo.

140 Byōbugauru is now Zentsuji and Sanshū is now Kagawa Prefecture, one of the four prefectures on the island of Shikoku.

such matters as I describe here for no reason other than mere interest's sake. Of course, I'm writing after sufficiently pious and humble consideration and with an attitude that is pious and humble, and that's the truth.

    One day a letter appeared. In childish handwriting was written more or less as follows: "I am a youth of fifteen. Seeing you off with the people of the town, I had a really indescribable feeling when you passed in front of my house. How old are you? And where do you come from in Kumamoto? I was really surprised to read your pieces in the newspaper. I also have resolved to go to Shikoku. What month and what day will you depart? Although you are a beauty, I am not thinking of making you my wife." (Thank you very much! However, he really wrote this way and it was too much.) "Please be sure to answer this letter because I am eagerly awaiting your reply."

I wondered what to do. Should I reply or not?

In the end, I wrote this on a postcard and sent it: "I had the honour of reading your letter. I sincerely pray that you are in good health."

The residence of that person was four or five *ri* from where I am staying. As soon as I sent it off, a letter came back saying, "I would like to meet you."

As a matter of fact, because I had received visitors that day as well, I forgot until sundown about that letter which I'd stashed unread in a box. Then, just when I was hastily reading it, someone came, saying, "Anyone home?" and put a letter-like thing down in the entrance way, and went away as though fleeing. Surprised, I picked it up and looked at it. It read "I have just come here."

Well then, he was certainly waiting outside. Without thinking, I stood up and went outside.

He wasn't there; no one was there. There was nothing I could do about that. I went inside and while I was eating dinner and so on, it became completely dark. But, breaking through the clouds, the light of the moon shone forth on the surrounding landscape so it looked as though it had sunk to the bottom of a mist in an old masterpiece.

Timidly I peeked outside furtively and went early to bed.

Then, after a long time had elapsed, a sorrowful whistle sounded. My intuition immediately told me it was he. I was somewhat flustered, but felt guilty staying inside doing nothing when he had come from far away. Therefore, impulsively, I opened the door and went out to see. As I had surmised, the lad was standing there, his whole body bathed in faint moonlight. This time he was not running away.

"Come here," I said in a loud voice but he would not come. I didn't want to go near him because that would be strange. However, I had to. Assuming the manner of an older sister (which came naturally to me), I spoke to him. "Are you Mr. _____?"

Then he perked up and said, "Yes, I am."
He asked, "When do you leave for Shikoku?"
"Sorry, I don't know yet."
"Will you leave soon?"
"No, it will be a while yet."
"Well, I ....."
"Are you going home?"
"Yes, and I...."

Thus we finally parted. After that I was sent another letter and a magazine. It was a boy's magazine to which he had contributed. While I have been writing this, another letter has arrived. I don't know what the future holds but I long to depart without replying. Farewell, young man.

Article 25: A PILGRIMAGE ROMANCE (Part 2)

Although I haven't mentioned it before, the old man here has lost one eye. So he is a masseur[141] by occupation.

Incidentally, these days a young man comes here almost every day it seems. Although I say "a young man", he is still almost a child. And, although he takes the trouble to come, he never receives treatment here. He comes to say, "Please come to our house again today."

I know that young man well. Of course I have not yet exchanged one word with him, but I have repeatedly been invited

---

141 Traditionally, blind people in Japan became masseurs, acupuncturists, or musicians.

and gone to his house to have a bath. Whenever I go, I see him in the window of his room intently reading by the light of a kerosene lamp.

One evening, as usual, I, the old man, and a woman from nearby, the three of us, went to his house. The moon was as bright as day. Right there a shimmering, deeply carved river flows, winding between rocky cliffs in a mountain valley. Under the reddish light of a lamp people were talking together noisily. They told me to join them. Because I thought refusing would be rude, I sat there obediently drinking tea that I did not want to drink, listening to conversations that I did not want to hear, and became utterly disgusted. So I snuck away and went down to stand alone by the moonlit riverside.

When I think about Kumamoto, I am sad. You dear people whom I left behind in that beloved town! When I think about my homeland, my heart almost bursts. Also, father and mother, my sweet younger sister and brothers in my hometown, and also you people and friends who are far away! My future? My fate? The moon is shining—I am standing alone beside a river whose name I don't know in the province of Bungo. I wonder when the song, "The Banks of the Seine" rose to my lips.[142] I always cry when I sing it. There is no one else, no me, no heaven, no earth. There are only my tears and the song.

That night, I was in a pretty agitated state, but fell into a deep sleep and slept until dawn. When I awoke and was washing my face, the old man came and said that this morning he had gone to that house and that the son had written a *tanka* for me. (The old man repeatedly praised the son for liking studying and for having been able to write a *tanka* in the traditional form of thirty-one syllables.) He said that the poem took my singing last night as its theme. The *tanka* said,

> Under the moon
> A damsel sings sweetly
> I am sad because
> I'm not good enough for her.

---

142 No information could be found about this song.

Other than that there were four or five poems. I gazed at them in mute amazement.

Somehow going to take a bath at his place seemed strange. He would hear my singing and anything I said. Because of that, I stopped going to his house for a bath for a little while. Then, two or three days later, they insisted that I come, and when I went because I couldn't refuse, he was just lighting the fire for my bath. I was truly perturbed. In general, my nature is not the least bit bold when there are people around—even if they are old men or old women, so again putting on the kimono that I had started to take off, I hesitated, wondering what to do.

It was out of the question to say, "Please go away." But, because he was not a fool, he soon made a bow and left. Feeling thankful I got in the bath: and then he came back agitated, as if he had left something behind, and said hesitantly,

"When do you set off?"

"I don't know."

"You'll come back here again, won't you?"

"No, probably not."

"You won't come? What about those *tanka*...?"

"Yes, I've read them. You're very skillful." I have to admit what I said was clearly condescending. Saying nothing more, the youth left. I also soon went back.

Somehow or other I feel distressed and wretched. At any rate, I want to leave soon.

Article 26: A MYSTERIOUS BEAUTY

July the first. I have become intensely sad. I have become lonely. I am suffering agony because I want to leave here, want to be out of here as soon as possible. However, in fact, our departure has been delayed as long as this because the old man has sent a letter to a relative, Majima,[143] and says we have to wait until a reply comes. The old man has already resolved that he will set

---

143 The old man wrote to a nephew in Dalian, China, asking for money. He had to wait for his reply. In addition, the old man was given money by the villagers as a parting gift. Takamure also earned money during her stay in Nakaida by doing calligraphy. (*Ohenro*, p.39) She was skilled in writing Chinese characters (*kanji*).

out on the pilgrimage prepared to die.

For a while I did not even pick up my pen because I was depressed. During that time what kinds of things happened? A great variety of things. At least four or five letters came each day; no, they are still coming. And I also met and talked with many anguished young men.

Yesterday someone took the trouble to come from Beppu to visit me; today I received Mr. Satō, LL.B., from Ōita[144] and teachers, priests, and so forth, came.

While these things were happening, I received the following letter from a certain man in my hometown: "You who have become the talk of the town are rather curious and interested in this, aren't you? Is the smile on your face at this time a smile of satisfaction, of compassion, or of loneliness?"

That's what it is—a smile of loneliness. Even that is gradually paling and fading away.

Escaping from the uproar of the world, I am standing alone on top of a mountain in the sunset. Only then does my heart seem to be relieved. I must walk quietly, quietly. My calm smile must always be beautiful and saintly. That's it—I must not lose my faith.

People say that an article "A Mysterious Beauty etc." was written somewhere in this area. I smiled forlornly. I hear that someone or other said, "In Beppu the talk is of nothing but the pilgrim. Is it a man? Or is it a mannish old maid?"

Today a government official said to me, "The expression, 'double surprise' certainly applies to you. Everyone says you're too young."

The anguish that I feel about this is as though I've drunk poisoned water. This is because when I have been asked, "Are you eighteen?" I have replied, "Yes."

Oh well—wherever I go, problems arise if I don't keep pretending to be eighteen. It's awful. Now that things have come to this, from now on and even after I return to my hometown I will likewise have to go on being eighteen, just like Bitō Kinza[145]

---

144 In those days it was unusual, even for men, to graduate from college or university and such graduates had high social status.
145 尾藤金左. This is perhaps Bitō Kinzaemon, (?—1638), who served the

of ancient times, who was insane.

The setting sun seen from the peak is really awe-inspiring. When I think of dear Kumamoto, my tears roll down and will not stop. Kumamoto! Be in good shape! Also, you people of Kumamoto, please think of me small and pitiful standing despondently at the top of a mountain in Bungo Province.

I am writing this manuscript on the top of that mountain in the setting sun. There are footsteps. Surprised, when I raise my head, five or six young men of the village have come following behind me surreptitiously watching me. What pathetic, laughable people they are! However, even towards such people I must never lose my politeness, reverence, humility, and what is called love.

I will quietly go back. Around here it has become somewhat dark.

Article 27: YOUNG MEN WITH AGONIZING CONFLICTS[146]

Never in my life before have I been as keenly aware as I am now of how much promising young men are agonizing and suffering with regard to their future aspirations. To put it in other words, I think it can be regarded as anguish that arises subconsciously concerning "a man's responsibility".

A certain young man in his twenties is a very sincere, frank, and serious young man. Although he was born into the only good family in X Village, after various complications within the family, all assets are gone and only two people remain, he and his old grandmother, and they are making a miserable living. Moreover, this man, having aspirations he is unable to suppress, told me he had firmly resolved to leave his old grandmother in the care of a relative and go off to Tōkyō. He said he had already saved money for his trip. I whole heartedly sympathized with

---

first lord of Kumamoto, Lord Hosokawa. I have been unable to find any reference to his continuing to claim to be 18 or to his being insane.
146 Before they met, Hashimoto wrote her a letter in which he said, "I'm at a mountain school living a melancholy and orphaned life, a young man immersed and buried in studying social science and literature." (*Waga Takamure Itsue*, p. 6) Perhaps this contributed to her interest in the young men of this article.

him.

How can an inexperienced girl like me possibly resolve such a complex issue? I don't know if I am too conservative, but in my own opinion, I'd like to be content where I am and live happily ever after. As they say, "The trilling bush warbler comes to rest on the side of a small hill. In that spot he sings of this and that".[147] How glad and happy I felt seeing the young man so sincerely grateful for my presumptuous, banal and lukewarm comments.

Another young man was eighteen. He said that his older brother had worked his way through university and was now a diplomat working overseas. Because of this very close at hand example, the young man has also set his heart on working his way through school and on taking some kind of civil service examination but his father really dislikes that. The father insists that he succeed him in the family business.

Yet another man was also eighteen. His family had a fairly big commercial establishment but being a merchant was abhorrent to him, so he left home and became an office boy in some government office, but he says that when he read my newspaper articles, his resolve became firmer and firmer. What he aspired to be was a cabinet minister. You mustn't laugh. At present he is enrolled as an external student at Waseda University, and he says he will certainly go to Tōkyō in the near future and enter Waseda.[148]

Several other young men told me these sorts of things, and I considered the matter seriously. Is it right to go? Is it right to stay? Just have strong faith. Have lofty ideals. In addition, have a sound body. Think about the universe and life. Think about how really, really short a person's life is.

---

147 緡蛮たる黄鳥丘隅に止る。其の止るに於て云々..... This is perhaps from the earliest collection of Chinese poems, Shi Jing (Book of Songs; Shi kyō in Japanese), the book she had borrowed (Article 20). The collection was compiled about 700 BC but the songs were probably composed and sung about 1000-700 BC. I could not find the exact quote.

148 External students studied by correspondence, often from transcripts of lectures. When they passed a test, they could enter the university as a regular student.

Article 28: TO ŌITA CITY

Having stayed here for many days, I am in agony every day. However, because I thought the old man might get even more worried if I told him this, I managed to wait until he finished what he had to do. When it finally became time for our departure, my heart danced, as you might expect. Everything seemed to be blessing me, the things that I saw with my eyes, the things that I heard with my ears, so much so that I produced a poem like this:

> Streams of sunlight
> In the rose-fragrant sky;
> How delightful is
> My morning departure.

July ninth. The luggage was all neatly organized   I was carrying only a pale green Chiyoda bag[149] slung from my left shoulder across to the right side; no matter what I said, the old man would not let me carry any luggage. I wore a white pilgrim vest over a rough Takijima[150] unlined kimono and I carried my sedge hat and staff in my hand, while on my head I wore a hat with a crimson ribbon, and on my feet, *waraji* straw sandals. Smiling happily, my steps were light hearted but, as one would expect, in my heart I was reluctant to leave. Farewell, dear familiar mountains and village of Nakaida, that I've become accustomed to seeing for so many days and where I've become accustomed to living! In addition, farewell to you villagers from whom I have received until the very moment of my leaving, kind and warm hearted help, greater than one would expect from blood relatives! Ah, I cannot even bear to look back. That is because the old ladies of the neighbourhood have come crying to see me off. Time! Fly away instantly! No, instead of that, put me out of my misery by concealing those familiar mountains and beloved people. Oh, I am too cowardly. Look heavenward!

---

149 Chiyoda is an area in the center of Tokyo which may indicate that the bag is fashionable. No information could be found.
150 Vertical stripes composed of lines graduating from narrow to wide.

Ah, the sky on such an auspicious day! Because I had become a person of grave silence, a person of holy contemplation, I even completely forgot about that old man walking behind me step by step carrying much luggage on his old back.

After more than two *ri* we reached the town of Inukai. It is quite a long, narrow town. It was close to one in the afternoon, so we imposed on the hospitality of an acquaintance of the old man, a Mr. Morita, and ate lunch at his home. Then, after lunch, as we were wiping sweat from ourselves, we were told that two men on bicycles had come following me. I wondered what this was about. While I was feeling surprised, two gentlemen dressed in western clothes came and their greetings to me were so deferential and polite that I felt more and more unworthy. According to them, they had come all the way from a village more than two *ri* from Nakaida and over four *ri* from this village. Not only had they come a long way but they said, as they wiped the sweat off them, that they'd been asking for me along the way. I wondered what I should say and was choked for words. Here, the writing of souvenir messages on folding fans commenced again.

A large number of people came to the railway station to see us off. (Steam trains come as far as here.) In the few minutes before the train left, people were still thrusting fans at me for me to write on. I asked the old man to take care of the farewell gifts and souvenirs we had received and I reclined feebly on a bench, utterly exhausted.

Someone went to buy a blue ticket[151] for us and came back; whereupon we got on the train. Changing to *zori*, I heaved a sigh of relief and leaned on the window.

Farewell, my dear Ōno County! How beautiful are the mountains standing crowded together in front of my train window! How delightful is my freedom!

"When you ride this train you'll go a thousand *ri* in just an instant."[152] A song of my elementary school days rose to my lips.

---

151 There were three classes of coaches and the tickets for second class passengers were blue in color.
152 In the Meiji era and later, there were many railway songs written about

I was delighted and happy; my eyes shone and my heart throbbed.

In less than an hour, we arrived at Ōita Station and when we came out of the wicket, rickshaws were waiting. As we went along people's eyes shone. However, my heart and mind were relatively calm. Our two rickshaws carrying two strange looking people, the old man and me, must have quite whetted people's curiosity—but I can't be sure of that. My eyes were still sparkling because of my curiosity and delight at my first sight of Ōita.

Article 29: IN SHOKUJŌ-MACHI

The rickshaws arrived at the house of Mr. Abe Muneaki in Shokujō-machi. It was the house of a relative of the old man.[153] I was very grateful for their hospitality and their extremely warm welcome made me even more grateful. In the evening I went to the Ōitakan Theater to see a moving picture, mainly because the old man had strongly recommended it. To the old man's way of thinking, I am much too shy; he wonders if it is harmful to my health. Although I was utterly exhausted and ready to collapse, it would have been awkward to disregard his kind suggestion, so I went out. However, wherever I go, I am alone. Groups of people and solitary me— this was the only thing I thought of the whole time and I paid scant attention to the movie I had come to see.

I went to bed at eleven-something and got up at six. The weather was a worry. The morning breeze, chilly but somewhat warm at the same time, blew the loose hair at the back of my neck, which I found unpleasant.

Going for a walk combined with some shopping, I asked a child, "Where is the Ōita Newspaper Company?" and was told, "It's right over there."

On the spur of the moment the impulse arose to go there and I asked the old man to go to the reception desk for me. They insisted that we come in, and we were sent upstairs to the reception room. It was still before eight in the morning.

---

the stations along the various railway lines. This verse may be from one of these *tetsudō shōka* but it could not be found in the many versions searched.
153 Abe was the husband of the old man's younger sister.

I spoke with a young reporter by the name of Satō. He was a kind, friendly, cheerful man. As usual, I tended to look down saying nothing with my face repeatedly turning red; my manner seemed cold. I consider myself too faint-hearted but I can't help it. We were there twenty or thirty minutes, and when I said I would leave, he told me to please wait for a while because the company president and the chief editor would come in due time. However, in the end, I excused myself and left.

Then we walked around looking at Takemachi, the heart of this city. It's really prosperous but it's a pity that the streets are a little narrow. Before long, rain began to fall. We were at our wit's end and ended up taking a rickshaw.

I had just returned home, wiped off the perspiration, and was changing my kimono when I had a visitor. I went at once to the drawing room and found it was Mr. Satō whom I had met a while ago.

After talking of this and that, he asked to take a photograph of me. Firmly refusing, I narrowly escaped.[154] In any case it was embarrassing—I am nothing more than an inexperienced pilgrim on a journey.

After seeing him off, when I returned to my room I felt a little sick and, telling the old lady so, I asked her to put out my bedding. The rain has become worse and worse. Tomorrow's weather is a concern.

Article 30: FROM THE RICKSHAW

The next day, the eleventh, it was still raining. When I was about to go out because I had a little shopping to do, I found that the place where I am staying had a rickshaw ready for my use. First I headed in the direction of Takeda, then turned left and came to Ōmichi. On the way, I came across several places in the area that had flooded because of the rain since yesterday. (In front of the courthouse I stopped for a moment at the home of the lawyer, Mr. Satō,[155] and sent in the rickshaw man with my name card and a message saying that I would pay a visit later. Both the

---

154 The interview with her was published in the Ōita newspaper on July 11th.
155 He had visited her when she was staying in Nakaida. (Article 26).

husband and wife came to the gate and kindly urged me to come into their house, for even just a little while, since we were here, but I politely declined. Then the rickshaw flew in the direction of Ōmichi.)

At Ōmichi there is a large rice-polishing mill. The wife of the owner had kindly visited me yesterday and asked me to be sure to come to her house. Apart from that, our talk of various things for some reason made me feel close to her, so I decided to drop by for a minute just to present my greetings. Here, also, everyone came out and asked me to stay for a while, but I insisted on leaving. I then decided to brave the rain and do some Ōita sightseeing. The rickshaw turned around and headed in the direction of the harbour construction area. On the way there was a temple called Itoku-ji. The old pine tree inside the gate was a really beautiful sight with its branches curving tastefully and extending in all four directions. The rickshaw soon entered Okinohama. I understand that the people living in this area are mainly fishermen.

We went a little way onto the beach and I got down from the rickshaw. As the lead coloured waves made muddy by the rain rose and rolled in from offshore, the sound was tremendous. The Kunisaki Peninsula[156] was visible before me but today I could not see the mountains on Shikoku. I was told that on a fine day one can see beautiful undulating mountain ranges there.

Being warned repeatedly, "You're asking for a cold!" I eventually got back in the rickshaw and we finally went to the harbour construction area. There are no special views or facilities to speak of but at least the future of the city of Ōita is to be envied because the sea is right in front of it. It is said that in the last two or three years a lot of development has actually been seen.

The rickshaw flew through the licensed quarters.[157] As I was going along observing both sides of the road feeling somewhat curious, there were several prostitutes at one hairdresser's. When I said, "I'd like to talk to them" the rickshaw

---

156 The Kunisaki Peninsula is in Kyūshū.
157 Brothel district

driver said, "God forbid!" and ran through the area at great speed.[158]

Passing in front of a spinning company and the gate of the Seventy-second Regiment, we came to Nishi Ōita and, plunging into Takemachi again, we flew to the prefectural office and as we left the prefectural Girls' High School behind, somehow I felt tired. When we came out into an area of rice fields, the buildings of the Women's Normal School looked really stately. We turned back and arrived at the house where I am staying.

When I was lying down because I was tired, someone brought me a newspaper. The headline "Young Woman Pilgrim" seemed really pretentious. The article said, "When I met the woman whom people think is a man because of her writing, to my surprise I found her to be gentle and entirely feminine...." Without being aware of it, I have become a questionable person and a woman who is the talk of the town.

Smile quietly and think pensively. Look heavenward and cherish life! And love everything passionately! It is true that I am young. I want to poeticize; I want to weep; I want to burn madly! And I want to stroll leisurely along a moonlit path and stand on a mountain in the setting sun.

This afternoon, at this house also, I was confronted with the trying experience of writing calligraphy.

Article 31: SHOKUJŌ-MACHI IS FLOODED

July twelfth. Because of the rain of the past few days, nearly all of this neighbourhood is flooded and today, since morning, there has been a great commotion. Firemen came; soldiers went; policemen passed. Just for fun, young men, children and young women, windblown and rain-beaten and dressed in various kinds of rainwear, frolicked in the water. They were so noisy that I was almost deafened.

"Gosh, over there boiled rice was distributed by the neighbourhood because they couldn't cook."

---

158 Hiratsuka Raicho and Okade Koukichi were once taken to a brothel by the latter's uncle, a painter. This caused a great scandal. Perhaps this event motivated Takamure.

"The house is about to float away."

"A boat has come as that far."

In the afternoon the rain gradually turned to drizzle and the water had greatly subsided, but the sky still looked threatening. A blind man wrote a *haiku*[159] in Braille commemorating my visit and sent it to me. It said, "Rain of early summer, make way for the songs of the pilgrim!"[160]

Yes, I should live only as a pilgrim. Mixed with the rain, how exalted, beautiful and plaintive are the resounding *goeika* hymns. Somehow or other, for me there is nothing more oppressive than being trapped. I yearn to be a person who not only sings the praises of "freedom" but also practices it in its true meaning.

Concerning this, if I explain tangibly using an extremely familiar example, you will understand. First, our clothing—a favourite teaching of moralists that is often heard is that it should be plain and sturdy. And yet, what is the real sitation? In fact, they are saying that the inclination to like beautiful things is bad.

No, let's not be so rigid. In any case, I am keenly aware that control through one fixed form of clothing greatly hinders us from freely displaying our individual beauty. Stop saying things like, "People will laugh at you if you don't do your hair this way" or "Your clothing is weird". We are young people. We are the possessors of beauty. Where is the inconsistency, where is the contradiction between giving full scope to one's personality and the displaying of beauty? However, I am not a person who regards freedom and self-indulgence as identical.[161]

Enough of this idle chatter. The rain has not yet stopped.

---

159 A short poem of 17 syllables divided into three groups of 5, 7, and 5 syllables and the inclusion of a seasonal theme. It was a farewell gift to her.
160 In a note, the editor of *Musume Junrei-ki,* Horiba, says, "Takamure included this haiku[巡礼の歌通されよ五月雨]in three of her later works, "*Ohenro*" (Pilgrim) [Showa 13], "*Konjaku no uta*" (Poems of the past and present) [Showa 34] and *"Hi no kuni no onna no nikki"* (Diary of a woman from the country of fire) [Showa 40]. It became "Rain of early summer, let the song of the pilgrim flow." [巡礼の歌流されよ五月雨] Horiba feels that the wording in Article 31 should be considered to be a typographical mistake.
161 At the Kumamoto Normal School she had broken school rules by using makeup and having showy hairstyles and fashionable clothing and had been criticized for this.

Because I had become bored, I sorted the mail that had come while I was staying in Ōno County. There were thirty-one postcards and twenty-six letters; I'm sure there were more but I couldn't find them. In addition, I could not clearly remember the number of people with whom I had talked (the visitors who had come especially to see me), but according to my journal, the number of such people amounted to seventy-five or six. The majority of these people were unwilling to be written about in the newspaper.

Ah, the dream-like past! Even during that turbulent period I was able to strive not to lose my identity—of that at least I am glad. More than that, I found a loneliness in me that I could never lose. In this loneliness there is also a powerful love formed that burns fervently: that is to say, love for my hometown, love for my friends and others, love for everything.

Seeing that I looked bored, the old man at once rushed to the bookstore. Because I had said any of *Bunshō Sekai* (*Writers' World*), *Chūō Kōron* (*The Central Review*), or *Taiyō* (*The Sun*) would be fine, the old man brought me *Taiyō* saying it was the biggest.[162]

No sooner had I said in a low voice, "I'd like to read *Bunshō Sekai* too", than the old man disappeared. In an instant I saw him appear with what I had wished for in his hand. My heart leapt.

I will begin by reading *Taiyō*. The lead article is "The New Asian Doctrine" by Dr. Ukita.[163] I must read it so I'll put

---

162 These are all intellectual magazines. *Bunshō Sekai* was originally established for contributors but became the center of the naturalism movement. *Taiyō* had articles on politics and society and literary reviews written by leading critics. *Chūō Kōron*, a general interest magazine that published articles on politics, literature, education, religion and economics, was important in the democratic movement in the Taishō era. It remains an important monthly magazine. The man who was courting her in Kumamoto, H, (Furukawa) published poems in *Bunshō Sekai* in August and October of that year. Did she hope to find his work?
163 Ukita Kazutani (1859-1946) was born in Kumamoto, and educated at Doshisha and Yale universities. He taught at what is now Waseda University. His social criticism from a Christian point of view was influential in the ideas of "Taishō democracy". At the time of Takamure's pilgrimage, he was editor in chief of *Taiyō*.

down my pen.

Article 32: A DUEL BETWEEN PEOPLE OF DIFFERENT BELIEFS

When evening fell, the rain finally stopped. It was a quiet twilight. For a long time I stood at the window, meditating. When the old lady here called, "There's someone who wants to meet you," I came to.

The visitor was at once shown into the reception room downstairs, and I listened to his talk. All of it concerned religion.

I said, "Well then, you see the self as non-existent and the Buddha as almighty, don't you?"

He replied, "No, you said 'I see as non-existent, but the term, 'see' is wrong. Actually, 'seeing' doesn't exist. Without a doubt it's non-existent. The fact is it's a great mistake to speak of 'thinking' or 'seeing'. True faith should never be based on such academic-like, analytical grounds. The Buddha is the embodiment of wisdom and compassion. The Buddha understands all of us better than anyone else and bestows on us infinite, boundless love. In general, the self and the Buddha are in opposition. If the self becomes self-important, the Buddha disappears from a person's heart."

I asked him, "What does it mean 'to become self-important'?"

He said, "In short, it is the self-confident state in which one feels that with one's own strength one has been able to achieve perfection of character. This causes the self-important person to say, 'Is there such a thing as the Buddha?' I am really sorry that such a person cannot accept the precious mercy of the Buddha because of such a presumptuous way of thinking.

"Human beings can never escape from worldly desires. Through your own strength you are trying to become free from the bonds of illusion and suffering. That's the same as washing blood away with blood. You are suffering and trying to arrive at an ideal world. But that is not possible. Why don't you, with no effort, take the shortcut of devoutly believing in the Buddha? The Buddha loves you limitlessly."

Our dialogue continued thus for three or four hours but I was in no way able to feel convinced about the words, "The Buddha is loving".

What I think is that rather than speaking circuitously like this, see suddenly the true nature of the self and of everything![164] Realize afresh the mysterious spirit of the universe! The self can simultaneously be both a part of the universe and the whole of the universe. By knowing the whole through a part, by knowing a part through the whole, our actions and ideas can be strengthened and deepened. That is to say, without being bound by trivial fetters, we can love everything abundantly. Is that not probably our ideal world? The Buddha will do, God, spirit or cosmos; any of these will do. (That is to say, because I consider the Buddha and God and all of them as easy-to-understand hypothetical beings which are means to arrive at the supreme ideal world, I regard them as other names for the almighty spirit that totals the wonders and mysteries of the universe.)

I do not harbour ill will toward circuitous explanations but I simply cannot entreat the Buddha in prayer if I am told to do so. In short, although the results may be the same, our actions and our thoughts, all originate in the self. At the same time, we are able to objectify the self with a rather detached attitude. Of course, this is certainly subjective objectiveness but, to summarize, the self can be a part of the universe and at the same time all of it as well.

Gradually my words also became heated.

He said, "That's wrong," and "Then you say that you are part of the Buddha, don't you?"

"Yes."

"That's insolent. A friend of mine was a very devout believer but three of her children died and she lost her faith. Up until the second child died, she thought it was the will of the Buddha, but when three children were taken, she felt this was excessively cruel to say the least and lost her faith. Just like that woman's case, your assurance that you are part of the Buddha is also an extremely shaky passing fancy and someday the time will

---

164 This sudden enlightenment is in the Zen tradition. The visitor is a Jōdo Buddhist and Takamure seems to be arguing from the perspective of Zen.

come when it crumbles."

Sorry, but now I'm utterly bored. Discussing such matters with him is pointless. It was pitiful that the woman held a grudge because her children had died. However, I was deeply impressed by the visitor's zeal. What this man preached was *tariki shinjin,* faith in the power of Amida.[165]

It was late at night. The visitor said he surely wanted to meet me one more time and pressed me to stay here a little longer. I am truly grateful for his kindness, but I want to lose no time in departing. Please excuse my bad manners and arrogance.

I went to bed a few minutes after twelve. I am anxious about tomorrow's weather.

---

165 This is a teaching of the Jōdo School of Buddhism—the doctrine of salvation by faith. The term *tariki shinjin* suggests the idea of seeking rebirth in the Pure Land of Amida by relying completely on Amida.

Section 2: Heading to Shikoku at Long Last

- Don't mention her mans
- 88 temples
- 33 days if walked at marathon p/day
- Shikoku pilgrims: 100,000-300,000 (2,500-5,000 walk)
- "rites of passage" in various cultures:
  1) Separation: stripping a participant of their existing identity
  2) A "liminal" stage (betwixt and between): often with a uniform and "blank" dress code that unifies all participants and marks them as inhabiting "sacred time"
  3) Reintegration: The pilgrim then emerges from the ritual transformed into a new status in their community, sometimes with a new title (like "Hajji ___") and a new identity

Article 33: TO YAWATAHAMA

We weighed anchor on July 14th at three in the morning and are finally en route to Iyo[166] aboard the steamship *Uwajima Maru*. In the cabin, really, it is unbearably ghastly. A woman with a fan on her chest and her mouth twisted, a woman on her stomach with her legs bent upwards, a child who looks as though he is being squeezed and crushed small and flat, every one of them, moreover, looking dirty and sleeping voraciously. Since a little while ago, the man beside me, who looks like a fierce devil, has stretched out his foot towards me—how many times have I been frightened out of my senses?

If even this cabin is like this, how much worse it must be in third class. It is almost no different from a group of wild animals living together. Forlornly sitting upright on a *tatami* mat[167] in a corner, I shudder to think of the scene when all the people sleeping uncouthly like this stand up at the same time.

The night is dark, the clouds low, the water black, and the wind heavy. This is the very moment of parting from my Kyūshū. Farewell Kumamoto! Stay safe and sound! I will be on the other side of the sea for a while.

I couldn't help falling uncomfortably asleep and when I awoke, we had already arrived at Saganoseki.[168] Dawn made the sea regain its sparkle, and a lead-coloured mist softly dampened my cheeks. The ship began to move forward calmly.

What a beautiful sight—the distant sea was hazy, the color changing from leaden white to milky white, to silvery white; the sky, the water, the mountains, the ship, and the people also, everything completely melted into a silvery world.

Shikoku has appeared! Shikoku has appeared! Are those not the mountains of Shikoku towering before me? Is it Kyūshū

---

166 Now Ehime Prefecture
167 A *tatami* mat has a thick straw base and a soft rush covering. Traditionally Japanese people kneel on mats rather than sit in chairs. Even now some ferries have *tatami* matted rooms where passengers eat, sleep, and chat in small groups.
168 The Saganoseki peninsula is at the eastern extremity of Kyūshū and is the nearest point to Shikoku. The Bungo Channel lies between the islands of Kyūshū and Shikoku.

or Shikoku, Shikoku or Kyūshū? Am I in the land of my birth or on a journey—on a journey or in the land of my birth? There was not even enough time for me to get excited as we proceeded from Sadamisaki Cape[169] to Yawatahama[170] and landed probably about eleven in the morning.

We immediately visited Daikokusan Kichizō-ji[171] in Yawatahama. When I presented my name card, I was welcomed so politely that I was embarrassed.

The priest, Reverend Kaneda, happened to be absent but, by some strange coincidence, the people at this temple were all from Kumamoto Prefecture and somehow this made me feel nostalgic. This temple is the thirty-seventh Shikoku pilgrimage temple but not many people know this.

That is to say, the thirty-seventh temple, Fujiisan Iwamoto-ji in Kubokawa in Kōchi Prefecture is certainly, indeed, Kōbō Daishi's historic site. However at Kichizō-ji the principal image of the Buddha and the printing blocks for the pilgrims' *nōkyō cho*[172] have been handed down from long ago. I was told that in Shikoku there are two temples numbered thirty-seven and the story of the origin of this is as follows.

Originally, the temple's name, Daikokusan Kichizō-ji, was taken from the name of a person, Daikokuya Kichizō, and even at present the mere mention of Daikokuya in this area reminds everybody of a wealthy family well known as being in the upper bracket of taxpayers.[173] More than thirty years ago, at night in bed, this Kichizō heard the sound of a bell at an unexpected time. He ignored it and did nothing, although he thought it strange. The next morning, when he got up early as

---

169 Sada Cape (Sadamisaki) is a peninsula jutting out on the west side of Shikoku.
170 Yawatahama in Iyo was one of the two ports where pilgrims arrived to begin their pilgrimage. The other port was Muya in Awa (now Tokushima Prefecture) near the first temple.
171 A Zen temple in the area but not one of the 88 pilgrimage temples.
172 Each pilgrim carries a small *nōkyō cho* book, which is stamped and inscribed at each temple.
173 Under the Meiji constitution, the election law stated that those who paid direct national tax (income tax) of over a certain amount per year were eligible for the House of Lords. These people were called "high taxpayers" or "upper bracket taxpayers" (多額納税者、たがくのうせ"いしゃ).

was his wont, someone in the household brought him something that had been found in the family altar room. He saw there were thirty-seven pilgrim cards to be offered at the eighty-eight temples, but with no name or address written on them, so he thought it was the intention of the Buddha to tell him to do something for the thirty-seventh pilgrimage temple. When he inquired about the aforementioned Iwamoto-ji, he found that the temple had gone miserably down hill. Making arrangements to purchase the principal image and the wood blocks for printing the pilgrims' *nōkyō cho* for three thousand five hundred yen, he immediately established this Kichizō-ji. Later it went as far as a lawsuit but it was called off. At any rate, it is the case that up until now, Kichizō-ji has continued to maintain its claim to be the thirty-seventh pilgrimage temple. Having been given the explanation, I nodded and wondered if it were true.

This is a pretty big temple with many priests in training as well. As they insisted that we must stay the night, we decided to accept their kind offer. The room, even every nook and cranny, was scrupulously clean and fresh. When I had wiped the sweat off me, changed my clothing and was drinking tea, I felt an indescribably pleasant wind blowing through the temple precinct from across the sea.

The following morning my dreams were interrupted by the solemn voices of priests chanting sutras and I immediately began to get ready. They kindly said, "If you are not in a hurry to set off, why don't you stay for two or three days?" Although we expressed our gratitude for their kindness, we were seen to the gate, dressed at last as pilgrims in simple garments, hat and staff in our hands, wearing straw sandals on our feet and carrying our *nōkyō cho* and Buddhist images on our backs. Then, continuing to look back, we were off on our journey.

Ah, during the twenty or thirty days that I stayed in Ōita Prefecture, I felt as though I were a noxious liquid stagnating in the middle of muddy water. At this very moment, lonely and pure, I am making a pilgrimage through unknown mountains.

I wonder where tonight's lodging will be?

Article 34: SLEEPING OUTSIDE ON A MOONLIT NIGHT

One can make the pilgrimage in the regular numerical order or in reverse order. We decided to go in the reverse order.[174] First, we had to head to temple forty-three, Meiseki-ji,[175] but we mistook the road badly and ended up going in the entirely opposite direction.[176] Since we were there, we decided to follow the difficult path called Okubo Pass. The road is well-known as being steep and the heat was unbearable. I was so tired that I could not take one more step. I was a weakling and the seventy-three year old man[177] helped me, picking mountain lilies for me as we went along until at long last we reached the summit. The next part was downhill so I was cheerful. Also the wind was blowing pleasantly. Then I saw a spring with cool, clear, utterly pure water. I ran to it and scooped up the water with my hands. Then I immersed the lilies I was carrying and when I was resting for a while in the shade of some trees, fatigue hit me and I dozed off lying in the midst of some grasses, the names of which I did not know. When I woke up, I had been covered with a blanket. This surprised me and I sat up; the sun in the west was shining straight into my face. When I looked to the side, the old man was also sleeping. Oh, how lonely the scene seemed.

I put my blanket gently over the old man and for a long time sat despondently with my head down. Crows flew by over my head. Crows, where are you heading? If you cross the mountains, cross the sea, cross the mountains again and cross some fields, you will come to my hometown. Oh, I envy you. Waiting for me in my hometown are my dear father and mother and ..... I started to cry and couldn't write any more.

---

174 The reverse order is considered to have greater religious merit as the hills are steeper when going counter clockwise.
175 The temple's full name is Genkōzan Meiseki-ji. The first name of a temple is the name of a legendary or imaginary mountain associated with the Buddha and the second name is the local name.
176 As the signposts along the route are intended for pilgrims traveling in numerical order from 1-88, it is not always easy to find one's way when travelling in the reverse direction.
177 Before 1945 Japanese people considered a newborn baby to be one year old; therefore, by western calculation, the old man is seventy-two and Takamure is twenty-three.

After the old man was awake, we descended the mountain in unwavering silence. After we had passed through a village and crossed a river, the sun had completely set. As for tonight's lodging—already, I could not move another step. When I sat on a rock beside the path, the crescent moon shone hazily on my whole body.

Oh, I was tired! In the end we decided to sleep outdoors and went a little way up a grassy slope and immediately lay down. I slept deeply and soundly as though I were drugged—suddenly I woke up feeling frightened by something. All sorts of bugs were crawling over me, from my hands and feet to my face; this was intolerably unpleasant. In addition, my hair and clothing were damp with dew.

The moon is lonely and the wind sorrowful—is this my body sitting here? How is Kumamoto in this moon and wind?

I wonder if traveling hundreds of *ri* from now on is something that feeble Itsue can do? As I go I'll cry. No, as I go I'll pick flowers and sing.

The lilies that I offered to the Buddha last night have already wilted. I will not think, I will not cry; if I try to sleep, naturally I am bound to miss my hometown. In the end, I sat up all night without sleeping. Before long the moon went down ....

Although I wanted to wash my face, unfortunately there was no water convenient. The old man brought me water in a saucepan, water that he had found somewhere. He told me to wash with this. What a novel and brilliant idea—a saucepan for a wash basin! I made do with it. I ate a small amount of bread and then had to stand up in spite of my aching feet. Lord Buddha! Please help me!

The road was straight and while I walked I read *Confessions* written by Chikazumi,[178] Bachelor of Arts in Literature, that I had received in Ōita. Tiredness gave rise to tiredness, and when I raised my eyes, it seemed as though the world had turned yellow and was spinning round and round.

---

178 Chikazumi Jōkan was a Jōdo Shinshū (Shin) Buddhist scholar in the Meiji and Taishō eras, who studied in Berlin at the beginning of the 19th century. He is said to have helped bring a certain social awareness to Shin Buddhism. Having a Bachelor of Arts degree in the Meiji era was very unusual.

We reached Unomachi with a feeling of "at last". From here to Mount Meiseki is ten *chō* and we sighed with relief when we were allowed to rest in a house.

Article 35: TO MEISEKI-JI

Leaning heavily on my pilgrim staff and winding my way along a mountain path, I finally reached the pilgrimage temple. The temple, Genkōzan Meiseki-ji is the forty-third pilgrimage temple. (It is in Ōaza Akeshi, Tanosujimura Village, Higashiuwa County, Ehime Prefecture.) The temple *goeika* hymn[179] says, "We hear that Thousand Armed Kannon made a vow and was miraculously able to lift a great huge rock."[180] The principal image, Thousand-Armed Kanzeon,[181] is reputed to be an ancient Chinese work. In addition, there are Buddhist statues which are the work of Unkei and Tankei.[182]

They say that this temple was originally a prayer hall for Emperor Kimmei[183] founded by Saint Jugen, a disciple five generations later of En-no-Gyōja Ozuno,[184] and that Kōbō Daishi,

---

179 Each of the pilgrimage temples has its own hymn, or *goeika*, of 31 syllables that pilgrims used to sing as they approached the temple. These hymns were written for lay people to convey Buddhist teachings and many refer to a legend of the temple. They usually have both a surface meaning and a deeper, religious meaning.
180 A temple legend says that Thousand Armed Kannon (Senju Kannon) shut herself up here disguised as a young woman holding a great rock. Miyata (*A Pilgrimage Guide to the 88 Temples of Shikoku Island Japan*, p.92) translates the *goeika* as "The famed power of Senju Kannon easily lifts up a giant rock."
181 This form of Kannon (Kanzeon) is said to have 1000 hands and 1000 eyes. Thus a longer version of the name is Senju-sengen Kanjizai Bosatsu 千手千眼観自在菩薩 or, more commonly, Senju-sengen Kannon 千手千眼観音. The form emphasizes the compassion that sees suffering (with 1000 eyes) and acts to relieve it (with 1000 hands).
182 Unkei 1148 (?)-1223 (?) was a famous maker of Buddhist images who, in 1189, invented the use of glass eyes in Buddha statues. Tankei (1173-1256) was his eldest son. The Shitenō (four guardian kings protecting the four directions) at Meiseki-ji are said to be the work of the father and son.
183 (530-557). The temple was built by imperial order as a place to pray for the peace of the country and the health of the emperor.
184 Semi-legendary religious figure of the late seventh century and founder of Shugendō (religious group which does ascetic practices in mountains in order

acting on the orders of Emperor Saga, restored it.

Scooping up crystal clear water,[185] I worshipped with a peaceful mind. I finished and when I stood in the gate of the temple, it was already twilight and the sparrows were singing sadly.

Ah, how strange it is that I am here. The sun is about to set; the sun is about to set. After meditating for a long time, I was urged on by the old man and going down the mountain several *chō* we passed the gate of the prefectural agricultural school. Reaching the town we turned left; the light of the crescent moon shone faintly on our shabby travel clothing.

Someone shouted, "Stay here." When we looked, it was a dirty *kichinyado*. Good heavens! If we stay in this kind of place, it's the very kind of place where we will be bitten to death by lice. Sleeping outside is probably better than that. Thinking that it would be preferable to go to Botsumoku-ji, the forty-second temple, I don't know how many *ri* we walked, how many *chō* we went, relying upon the brightness of the moon. When we asked our way at a house, once more we had made a mistake and once more we had to go over a mountain. There was nothing else to do, and we followed the mountain trail. The moon had already gone down, the wind was ghastly and blew down my neck chilling me. Moreover, the extremely rocky trail was steep and dangerous, and I couldn't help worrying about the old man. From time to time the two of us chanted "*Om abokya beiroshano*",[186] jangled a bell and beat a gong.

At a rather high place that we reached there was a little hut with clear, cold water gushing out beside it. "Let's stay here." I don't know which of us uttered those words. Taking advantage of a bench placed outdoors, I lay down without even removing my gaiters.

When I woke up, it was a few minutes after five. My legs ached and there was absolutely no way I could stand up, so I sort of crawled to the spring and washed. When I was refastening my

---

to attain holy or magic powers). It is said that En-no-Gyōja used spells to bind devils and evil spirits who refused to do his bidding.
185 Worshippers purify themselves by scooping up water, washing their hands, and rinsing their mouths.
186 This is the beginning of the *Kōmyō Shingon* (the Light Mantra).

gaiters, the door opened and an old man and woman appeared and stared at us quizzically. When we told them everything, they soon became talkative and made us tea, put out cushions, and so on. We finished breakfast (bread and water and salt), washed our handkerchiefs and *tabi* and while we were waiting for them to dry, it began to rain.

From here to Butsumoku-ji, the forty-second temple, there was more than a *ri* of mountain trail. Braving the rain and treading cautiously with my painful feet, I followed the trail. I was tired, I was so tired, but when I felt like crying, there were red strawberries on the cliff beside the path. When I picked and ate them, I felt better. From then on I went along straining my eyes searching for strawberries. I couldn't help raising my voice and, altering the words of the Firefly Song, singing out, "Strawberries! Strawberries! Come here and shed light on the window in which I am reading."[187] Somehow I became cheerful. After that, there were also beautiful flowers.

We visited the *Miokuri Daishi Dō*[188] and offered flowers. From there, when we had descended the Hanagasaka Slope for sixteen *chō*, there were mulberry fields and people's houses. When we had gone through that area, we reached Butsumoku-ji; I was completely covered with sweat.

Article 36: TOWARDS UWAJIMA

The goeika hymn of the forty-second temple, Ikkazan Butsumoku-ji says, "If even grass and trees can become Buddhas at Buddha Tree Temple, even more can demons, beasts, men and heavenly beings. The principal image is Dainichi Nyorai,[189] said to be the work of Kōbō Daishi. They say that when he was travelling and preaching, he saw something shining on a branch

---

187 There is a popular Japanese song set to the tune of Auld Lang Syne called *Hotaru no hikari* (Light of Fireflies). This farewell song is sung by students at graduation ceremonies and by Japanese people at the closing ceremonies for sumo matches, song contests, and so on. The song begins, "The days when we read books by the light of fireflies and snow by the window have passed...."
188 Dō designates a temple building, sometimes large, sometimes small. Miokuri Daishi means Kōbō Daishi who is seeing someone off.
189 The principal deity of Shingon Buddhism.

of a camphor tree in the middle of the mountains. He took it in his hands and looked at it and when he saw that it was the wish-granting jewel he had thrown from China[190] long, long ago, he carved a figure of the Buddha from the camphor tree, placed the jewel between the eyebrows, and this is the principal image of this temple.

We rested for a while and then set out for the next temple, number forty-one, Inarizan Ryūkō-ji. It was twenty-six *chō* away. The temple *goeika* says, "We hear that this deity swears to preserve the Esoteric teachings[191] disseminated by the three countries."[192]

The principal image is Jūichimen (Eleven-Faced) Kanzeon.[193] Kōbō Daishi made an agreement with the Inari deity[194] and established this temple to protect the four regions of Shikoku. The Inari god is enshrined in a place which is above the temple.

After a while we descended and going more than two *ri* we arrived at Uwajima port. It seemed quite prosperous. In particular, the atmosphere of a port town could be sensed in the flamboyant sounds of the *shamisen*[195] and the red lights of the lanterns.[196] When we arrived there, my feet could not have walked another step.

There, when we asked for lodging at an inn, we were told that they refused pilgrims. What should we do? Was there no house in the whole world where we could stay? While we were standing on the road uncertain what to do, a young man beside the road kindly told us we could stay at his house. It was an

---

190 He studied Buddhism in China from 804-806.
191 i.e., Mikkyō or Esoteric Buddhism. These secret teachings cannot be revealed to those who are not initiated. Shingon Buddhsim, which was established in Japan by Kōbō Daishi, is a form of Esoteric Buddhism.
192 India, China and Japan
193 The Eleven Headed Kannon is a form of Kannon Bosatsu with eleven miniature faces around the top of the head.
194 Inari is the god of agriculture, rice, and fertility in Shintō. This deity became popular during the Edo era. According to Miyata, p.90, legend says that Kōbō Daishi met the Inari god here in the form of an old white-haired man.
195 A three-stringed lute plucked by a triangular shaped pick.
196 Drinking places were marked by red lanterns.

extremely quiet, nice house that the man and his young wife lived in, just the two of them.

Because it rained both the next day and the day after that, we were persuaded to stay on. The day before we expected to leave, we worshipped at the Warei Shrine[197] in the evening. The bridge just in front of the shrine was full of people enjoying the cool of the evening. As I was leaning against the railing feeling lonely, I couldn't help remembering my hometown and it was unbearable. Ah, the earthen bridges[198] of past days when I counted the lights of distant villages with my brothers—the shade of the willow trees along the river bank where I walked happily with my mother—I thought of these things and my tears streamed down. Father! Mother! Brothers! Sister! All of you, be in good health!

When I happened to look in mid-air, there was something white describing an arc from one bank to another. I wondered what it was. I was struck by the strangeness of it but, when I looked hard, it was nothing other than a rainbow.[199] Just behind it in the distant sky shone the moon; I thought to myself that it was a rainbow of a moonlit evening.

The next day we set off about ten. We offered our *fuda* at Ryūkō-in, which is a *bangai*[200] and the *oku-no-in*[201] of the fortieth temple. Then we immediately headed to the fortieth temple, Heijōzan Kanjizai-ji. The distance was about ten *ri*. In those ten *ri* there is the difficult section of Kashiwazaka[202] and it seemed that, no matter what, it would take two days to cover the distance.

---

197 The shrine deity protects sea farers. There is a well-known festival in July and the entrance arch/gate is said to be the largest in Japan.
198 The simplest type of earthen bridge is made of bundles of small logs laid on top of longer logs, and then covered with several inches of gravel and soil. Because of the weight of the earth, the bridges usually have only a slight arch, if any.
199 In the novel, *Black Rain* by Ibuse Masuji, a white rainbow is said to be a bad omen. (p. 293)
200 An unofficial temple of the pilgrimage circuit. *Bangai* literally means unnumbered.
201 The inner sanctuary and most sacred part of a temple. It is usually a separate building containing the most sacred object of worship.
202 Walking pilgrims no longer take the Kashiwazaka route. It was 22 *chō* uphill, 8 *chō* across, and 16 *chō* downhill.

From Uwajima we came to a settlement called Kakinoki in the village of Kunomura and from there we were on the old road. Plunging into ravines and climbing to summits, the lonely road continued far. I wonder where this long journey will take me.

Article 37: LONGING FOR MY FATHER AND MOTHER

Recently I have completely lost my appetite. No matter how hard I try, I cannot swallow cold hard rice with unrefined salt in it. However, I say nothing because the old man made it, but I seek some slight solace by going on reading, even when walking along the road. For me, reading is like a drink of water from a crystal clear spring. Chatting and not reading is like having my soul rot away minute by minute; it is unendurable even for an instant.

When I sometimes sigh, "Ah," the old man is surprised. Then he asks me various questions. "Is that because your faith has become weaker?"

I always remain silent. There is nothing else to do. Making any sort of response would be unbearably unpleasant.

From the deepest recesses of a settlement called Hatachimura, we finally came to the steep slope. There was a small clear river there. The old man said we would stay here. Just as he had said, in the middle of some bushes on the left, we spread our blankets in a pebbly, grassy field and sat down. For some days, my long, long silence has been continuing, lonely and quiet.

I recalled Doppo's *Gen-oji*.[203] Without a word, I scooped up water; without a word, I sat on a rock; without a word, I looked up at the sky. The moon was already shining overhead and everything—the nearby quiet mountains, forest stream, path —had already sunk into the sleep of infinite night.

The old man was also already asleep. By myself, I sat

---

[203] Kunikida Doppo (1871-1908) was a poet and novelist. *Gen-oji* was his first short story (translated as *Uncle Gen*) and tells the tragic story of an old fisherman who has lost his family and finally commits suicide. Doppo also started the magazine *Fujin-Gaho* (Women's Illustrated) in 1905.

upright in the moonlight for a long, long time until I don't know when; my thoughts were in my far-away hometown. Ah, you mountains that I miss, you earthen bridges, you wooden fences, you thin groves of trees, you lazily floating clouds. Still more I miss you, my dearly beloved father and mother, young brothers, and young sister. I guess I've grown up without your realizing it; I guess I've left on this trip without your being aware of it.

> We children
> Wait for father
> In a sunlit field
> Under a cobalt blue sky.

This was a poem I wrote in days gone by. I am unbearably yearning for the innocent era when, tired of waiting for my father's return from town, where he had gone, I frequently went to meet him on the way.

Oh, father and mother, I want to meet you now! Tonight again Itsue must sleep in the grass.

Please let me sleep now ....

It was difficult to stop my tears. When I was standing despondently with my sleeves against my chest, the open yellow flowers on the beach beneath my eyes looked tender, noble, and extremely humble in the moonlight. Are they evening primroses?[204] When I thought so, I was so nostalgic that I felt like leaping into the air. Oh evening primroses, are you blooming just to console the frail pilgrim Itsue? Even when I unsteadily lay down in the grass, I was wide-awake and could not sleep.

All of a sudden, I remembered an evening when I was small and my mother said, "Be a good child and try to think about going all by yourself on a distant and lonely mountain path. If you do that, you soon become sleepy, you know." Now I am trying to do that. I want to sleep peacefully, but mosquitoes are swarming noisily about my hands, feet and face, so no matter how hard I try, I can't fall asleep. Covering myself with my kimono I looked at the moon through the material and, stifling the sound, cried and cried. Ah what does the future hold for me?

---

204 Tsukimisō (Oenothera tetraptera)

Tomorrow, relying on my staff, I must finally go over the hill that is famous as a difficult slope.[205]

Article 38: SPENDING THE NIGHT IN THE MAIN HALL OF A TEMPLE

July twenty-second. The misty rain was dreary. Wrapped in our rain gear we set out, finally about to come to the famous hill of Kashiwazaka.[206] I walked, dragging my still aching feet. In spite of my feet continuing to ache and my whole body and spirit being engulfed in a cramped world that was hot and sweaty nearly to the point of suffocation, I seemed to be being driven along. The wind gradually became horrible. Along with that, slanting rain began to pelt down.

All of a sudden, I was surprised and delighted. "The sea! Look!" Near my right foot stretched the silvery-white ocean. It was just like a miracle. Passing through the thickly wooded mountains, my heart stank of sweat, but coming here, I saw the sea, like an enticing trap, into which it seemed that I would fly if I took one leap. My joyful surprise became uneasiness; uneasiness became admiration, admiration became rapture. For a while, I was stunned and stood stock still being blown by the wind. Suddenly, a person tapped me on the shoulder from behind and said, "Don't give up; you'll soon be there." Surprised, when I turned around, a single traveller, travelling light, smiled and went past.

The raindrops had become slightly larger. When the sun streamed through the clouds a little, then all the clouds, the clouds flying low above the sea, the clouds rising from the depths of the mountains, the clouds to the right, left, in front and behind, became silver in color simultaneously. Then that silver melted and became thousands of streaks of rain. The beauty of this scene was really beyond description.

The path crept along the side of the mountain and came out on the peak, then wound around several forests and finally headed downhill. This place was Kashiwazaka. There was a

---

205 Pilgrims learned from others about *nanhan* or difficult slopes.
206 This means Oak Hill.

steep slope for twenty-six *chō* and the wind began to blow really fiercely. Both sweat and heat were completely blown away and even my hat and sleeves were blown upward by the blustery wind. It was fun! Driven by the wind I flew down the slope. The old man, coming down leaning heavily on his staff, watched me with a worried look as I flew down light heartedly, my hair blowing and fluttering like a flag in the wind.

Descending to the foot of the hill, we quenched our thirst with Ramun[207] and going along several *chō* and passing a hamlet called Kashiwamura, we came out at the village of Kikuchigawamura. On the way, the old man worried constantly because of my having eaten nothing since yesterday but I was not really hungry. However, eventually I was forced to eat a rice cake and some fruit and so on. When we reached the fortieth temple, Heijōzan Kanjizai-ji,[208] it was dusk. The temple is located where the street goes left at about the middle of the town; it is a rather large and awe-inspiring temple with a patina of age.

The temple hymn says, "My heartfelt wish is flowers blooming and animals living in the spring of self-being far from this transitory world." The principal image, Yakushi Nyorai,[209] is the work of Kōbō Daishi. It is said that this temple, founded by Kōbō Daishi, was established by imperial order to pray for the peace of the country and the health of the Emperor, and was used as a temporary palace in Emperor Heizei's reign.[210]

When the sun went down, a cool wind began to blow. Is tonight's moon a full moon? It is sending down a bright light that has permeated the various trees in the temple precinct, a light that seems to me to be like the tears of frail me longing for my

---

207 This is a traditional Japanese summer drink, a kind of clear soda similar to 7-Up. It comes in a special two-chambered bottle in which the drink is in the lower chamber and the upper chamber is stopped by a glass ball in its narrow neck. Before drinking, the lip of the bottle is hit with the palm of the hand in order to dislodge the glass ball.
208 Kanjizai is another form of Kannon Bosatsu. Kanjizai means the Boddhisatva that sees and acts freely at will. The temple hymn is related to this idea.
209 Yakushi Nyorai is the Buddha of Healing and the Buddha of the world of Pure Lapis Lazuli in the east. He heals mental and physical illnesses.
210 Emperor Heizei reigned from 806-809. This temple would have been used by him when traveling in Shikoku.

hometown. The old man bustled about, washing his feet and dealing with the luggage. I, as usual, stood blankly and looked up at the sky despondently. "We'll spend the night in prayer," the old man said. My only reply was, as it always is, "Yes."

We recited the Kōmyō Shingon until late at night. The night gradually wore on as we recited it together, I, who have fallen into a continuing deep silence, and this old man. The big, old, round pillars of the temple's main hall stand silent and lonely in the moonlight. Insects chirp, the wind echoes; everything is a dream, the world, the universe, people, me— everything is dreamlike.

Article 39: A PILGRIM'S TERRIFYING EYES (Part 1)

July twenty-third.[211] We set off early in the morning and arrived at a small harbour called Fukaura.[212] When we went and inquired at the shipping agent's, we learned of the departure of the steamship, the Yamatomaru, for Tosa[213] at ten in the morning. After waiting more than two hours we boarded the ship; as usual, the squalor inside the cabin was utterly unbearable. Because it was a small steamboat, there were only two decks, an upper and a lower one. Moreover, the passengers were packed in almost to bursting. When I was standing wondering what to do, from the cabin on the upper deck they said, "Young lady, come up here, come this way." I was startled and when I looked up, everyone was staring at me weirdly. However, I decided to go up there. From above, two or three people put out their hands to help me up. When one of them said, "Show us a smile, give us a pretty smile," many others said various things and laughed.

"What rude people they are." Rather than turning red, I stared back at them sternly and quietly left. You pitiful group of

---

211 This is the date that the Rice Riots, (*kome sōdō* 米騒動), began in Japan after the price of rice rose precipitously. The riots quickly spread throughout Japan and by mid-September between one and two million rioters had attacked rice stores all over the country. Takamure does not call attention to the riots in her newspaper articles although their magnitude and violence were unprecedented in modern Japanese history.
212 Now part of the town of Jōhen.
213 Tosa is present day Kōchi Prefecture.

people!

The sea was calm and there was no wind. However, because the sky was cloudy, the sea was also a sombre leaden color. I went into the cramped lower cabin and when I had barely sat down, the boat began to move. Here also, the eyes of everyone were shining with curiosity. Because this was unbearably bothersome, I shut my eyes and leaned on my luggage behind me.

In a short time the boat arrived at Katajima harbour in Tosa. When I was being helped up by a member of the crew, all of a sudden I realized that there was a pilgrim with frightening eyes beside me.

The pilgrim pushed aside the crew member angrily and walked straight off, looking back from time to time to stare at me. He was in his mid-forties, his frizzy red hair was dishevelled, like *yomogi* leaves,[214] and his completely suntanned face was hairy everywhere. In addition, what caught my attention most were his eyes. In the depths of his cloudy, red, feverish, bulging eyes shone an unearthly weirdness. It was a face that seemed to say there is nothing in the world other than bestial me. As for his kimono, it was pitch black with dirt and the hem was tattered and torn. Of course, his feet were bare; yet, in his hand he held the semblance of a pilgrim's staff. Strangely, rather than feeling afraid, I was curious and interested, and when he looked back and stared, I stared back at him as he left.

He soon disappeared into the midst of the crowd. Somehow I was reluctant to see him go. Various conjectures welled up in my mind as I walked along.

We passed through the town of Sukumo and when I was writing postcards at one store, people in that neighbourhood began to ask the old man about me, saying "cute" and "pretty" and so on. What was very humorous was a pretty little girl amongst them calling me "Cute pilgrim". She did not even know which one of us was cute. It's a fact that the eyes of each and every human being in this world gleam with curiosity but I

---

214 Yomogi (*artemisia princeps*) is a hardy, wild plant of the chrysanthemum family with leaves with jagged edges and white fuzz underneath. Its English name is mugwort.

couldn't help being unreasonably displeased. So I began to walk quickly.

My firm silence became still firmer. Because there was shade under some trees in front of us, we decided to pause there for a while and when I raised my eyes, eyes were shining in the middle of the clump of trees—undoubtedly the eyes of the pilgrim I saw a while ago. His bloodshot eyes, which had become more feverish and red, were turned toward my face as though he were going to pursue me to the ends of the earth.

Something is certainly going to happen! Calmly thinking this way, I looked at him smiling enticingly.

Article 40: THE PILGRIM'S TERRIFYING EYES (Part 2)

He was silent. I was silent. It was the secret strife of two silences, two pairs of eyes.

The old man did not have the slightest idea of it. When he had rested there a while he started walking. I walked quickly behind him. In an instant the route became a mountain path and going about six *chō* uphill and down, we came to where the thirty-ninth pilgrimage temple, Terayama Enkō-ji[215] is built. This is the hamlet of Ōaza Nakayama in Hiratamura Village, Hata County, Kōchi Prefecture.[216] The temple hymn says "Praise be to Yakushi Nyorai.[217] We have made a vow and come to the temple to pray for cures for various illnesses. Please deliver us."[218] The principal image is Yakushi Nyorai of Safe Deliveries, which is said to be the work of Gyōki Bosatsu.[219] That is to say, the temple was established by Saint Gyōki (in the reign of Emperor Shōmu) and Kōbō Daishi restored it as a pilgrimage temple.

For a while I forgot about the eyes I've been talking about

---

215 The temple's full name is Shakkizan Enkō-ji, Terayama-in.
216 This is now part of Sukumo city.
217 Yakushi Nyorai is the Buddha of medicine.
218 The modern temple is said to have reported that the words of the temple hymn are slightly different but the meaning is the same. (Horiba, p. 99)
219 Gyōki (688-749) was a great priest of the Nara Period. He traveled to various districts with his disciples doing social welfare work and is said to have founded many temples. He was considered to be a manifestation of Monju-bosatsu.

but when I was worshipping by myself at the Daishi Hall, suddenly, I intuitively felt something like a shudder of fear, and turning around, there he was! There he was! Moreover, my enemy was upon me with his piercing eyes very close to me, three *ken*[220] behind my back.

I wonder why I was so nonchalant facing those eyes, nonchalant enough to be able to look back steadily and glare. When I did that, his eyes flinched somewhat. However, when my eyes shifted elsewhere, his eyes began to shine fervently. Then trembling legs approached me step by step.

The stench that entered my nostrils was difficult to bear. But I stood quietly, my staff slanting, my hat tilted, and smiled. If he closed in, I would nullify his combat power by flashing a sword-like smile and also by quietly blessing him with kind words and then I would leave here purely, nobly and composedly. I waited hushed. However, it did not happen as I expected. He who had seemed to be approaching me went off somewhere in a hurry—I don't know what he was thinking.

Farewell *henro*! Be in good health!

I left there with a calm heart and went to a *kichinyado*[221] called Terayamaya—here, because it is managed by the temple, the junior priests do everything from helping to serve meals to looking after the bedding and all other things. When I sat down on the veranda, my legs began to throb painfully. We washed our feet and going up into the room, greeted the other guests staying in the same room as us, organized our luggage, and when we had finished dinner, it was already dusk. Tonight, also, the moon is bright. The wind is blowing a little but not a terrible amount.

There were nineteen people at this inn, all of them pilgrims. There were two larger rooms of six mats and two rooms of four-and-a-half mats with no sliding doors between them and they were crowded beyond description.[222] I looked

---

220 A *ken* is a little less than two meters.
221 In her later writings, Takamure said the Terayamaya was a *henroyado*, a pilgrim lodge. It seems likely that it was a *henroyado* as it was managed by the temple. In a *henroyado*, pilgrims supplied their own rice, but pickles etc. were given by the lodge.
222 There are missing characters in the text so it is not certain that there was no sliding door between them.

around curiously wondering if this was what a *kichinyado* looked like. Here, there was one group, over there, a group, and judging from appearance, some of these people were dignified, middle-aged men.

There was also a thirty-four or five year old cheerful person who said he was from Kumamoto. He said he was Mr. Gōji of Sakanashi in the Mount Aso area. How nostalgic I felt.

Even pilgrims are human beings. As one might expect, when they gather like this, polite greetings, jokes and loud laughter spring up for no reason—it is interesting. Sitting silently on the veranda I looked around timidly.

The moon is bright! Oh, I had forgotten this kind of good evening. Before I knew it, I was walking in the temple precincts lost in reverie.

Suddenly, glittering eyes from below the veranda of the main hall! Oh, are you still here? You! When you look at me, what do you think, what do you wonder? Suddenly, my feet stopped in front of him. Mustering my courage I spoke to him politely, "Are you spending the night here?" Then he muttered something and was silent. However, it was clear that he was squirming violently.

I didn't want to ask another thing.

I turned back, flinging "Well, so long," at him.

Article 41: TALES OF PILGRIMS

July twenty-fifth. Because the rain and wind have been fierce since yesterday, we are stuck at this inn for a long time. Actually, speaking of the wind today, it is really horrible. Among the places we'll be walking around in Tosa from now on I hear there are very difficult places, places that must be crossed by boat, rivers and the sea, but in this kind of storm, we won't be able to proceed at all.

As they listened to the raging winds outside, the six people staying here talked together happily, or forlornly, or helplessly, of their past or of events during the pilgrimage. Amongst them was a man who said he was from Aichi Prefecture who talked a lot about various things. He was around fifty with a red-face, thick lips, and bushy hair. He said his motive for becoming religious was that he had gone blind from gonorrhoea. Now, his prayers had been answered and he was able to see splendidly. Next, was his companion, an old lady of about sixty, thin and frail, the remains of her balding gray hair tied together. After that, an old man with protruding eyeballs, who seemed to be just skin and bones, said his birthplace was Tosa. Then there was a pale, blind man who had a dirty bald spot in his hair. Those people and the two of us looked to all appearances like a gathering of blind demons, ghosts, and monsters.

Talk moved from the kindness of Kōbō Daishi to ascetic practice. The so-called ascetic practice is begging. The pilgrims said that to be called a pious person one had to do ascetic practice at more than seven houses a day,[223] no matter how rich one was. And yet, they said, from a legal point of view, begging is prohibited.

Then the man from Aichi Prefecture spoke of a very unpleasant experience he'd had. "Well, I was on my way to Izumo to worship. I happened to be begging at one house when a policeman spotted me and I ended up being nabbed because I was unable to run away. After I was locked up in the police jail for a while, I was escorted to a place and subjected to nonsense for a week. Again, at Sukumo also, I received similar treatment and was expelled as far as the border of Iyo. So it's strange because beliefs and the law appear to be contradictory. In fact, the begging of Shikoku pilgrims has become an open secret. The easiest places for begging are Iyo and Sanuki;[224] as for Tosa, humane feelings are as thin as paper.[225] Even if all you are asking for is to be allowed to spend one night, you don't care where, there are many houses that ignore you completely. If you do beg, you won't get much on the main roads; there's a little if you go right into the heart of the countryside. But, since people give you such things as rice and millet and barley at random, it's a

---

223 In the *Sōtō Zen* school of Buddhism regulations regarding begging provided that one was to visit seven houses, without concern for whether they were rich or poor. *A Primer of Sōtō Zen: A translation of Dōgen's Shōbōgenzō Zuimonki* by Reihō Masunaga, p. 114, footnote 44.
224 Sanuki is now Kagawa prefecture.
225 A Japanese saying.

problem. You should get separate containers ready for those things and then exchange what you receive for cash."

This man said he had made the pilgrimage more than ten times and he did indeed, know a lot about it. He said further that around here rice is thirty-five *sen*[226] for one *shō*[227] and the cost of a night's lodging in an inn is twelve *sen*. Even while he was talking, however, the group didn't forget Daishi *sama* and over and over again intoned "Namu Daishi Henjō Kongō"[228] under their breath.

I wonder how the pilgrim with the glittering eyes is managing in this rain and wind; he hasn't shown himself since it began.

Article 42: VARIOUS KINDS OF PILGRIMS

Amongst themselves, pilgrims call each other "the pilgrim from Tosa", "the pilgrim from Awa"[229] "the pilgrim from Kiishū"[230] and so on. If I apply this way of identifying people to myself, then I am the pilgrim from Higo.[231] Somehow it seems like the name of a beggar. I have met many in the pilgrim groups and there are various and sundry people. However, if I were to generalize, I think it might be correct to regard them as gray, defeated people. Every one of them has sore legs, their mouths are twisted, they have wasted away to mere bones, so that they make me think of the group of beggars appearing in *The Triumph of Death*.[232]

Also, there are almost no young people to be seen. Most people are over forty. It's not that I haven't seen any young

---

226 A *sen* was 100th part of a *yen*.
227 A shō is slightly less than half a US gallon. The rice riots began when the price of rice rose to 50 sen for one shō.
228 This means I put my faith in the great teacher (Kōbō Daishi) who illuminates everything everywhere and is as hard as a diamond. (A diamond can destroy anything as the *bodhi* mind can destroy any defilement.) Pilgrims often chant these words.
229 Now Tokushima Prefecture
230 Now Wakayama Prefecture.
231 Now Kumamoto Prefecture.
232 A painting (1562) by Peter Bruegel, the Elder.

people but it is hard to tell whether any of those that I see are young or old and I cannot see a fresh young girl no matter how hard I look, to say nothing of seeing flower-like, gracious, beautiful women.

It is the same even with young men. Although I encountered one vigorous young man the other day, as a rule, it is likely impossible to hope to find in that sort of group a young man or woman with ideal refinement, scholarly attainment, lofty ideas and an understanding of poetry. Various and sundry pilgrims—I will try to write about three or four of them just as they appeared to me.

In the morning when rain was falling, a man of fifty with a dirty beard came along bringing with him a nun. His eyeballs protruded in a triangular shape and each time he spoke it was his custom to blink angrily, his eyes glittering fiercely. The nun was forty-two or three with lustreless eyes and a mouth drooping open. She was a small woman whose entire face revealed her ignorance. Straight away, the man climbed up into the room and smoked, feebly stretching out his thin, bony legs. The woman looked around at her surroundings restlessly as she rubbed her head with a small towel. In particular, she began grimly to scrutinize me.

The old man began talking to the man,
"Where are you from?"
"The province of Izu"[233]
"Your work?"
"Pilgrim."
"Your age?"
"I've forgotten."
"Your family?"
"A wife."
"Huh? This nun?"
"That's right."
"I guess it wasn't an arranged marriage?"
"That's right."

The old man was thrusting fiercely in his questioning but because he was asking seriously and enthusiastically, it was

---

233 Now Shizuoka Prefecture

amusing. The man replying was curt but serious. The nun began to question me.

"Are you a pilgrim?"

"How old are you?"

"Aren't you handicapped?"

I was a little surprised by this, but to see her reaction I answered, "I'm probably handicapped."

"I thought so; I'm also handicapped and became a nun, but because I was tricked by that man I've had a hard time. If you're handicapped, don't ever get married."

"You are plump and beautiful. Are you really handicapped?"

"You are probably a very wealthy person. I wonder how much you have."

I said, "I feel a little indisposed, so please excuse me."

At long last I escaped. The old man was still eagerly talking. Vacantly, the nun saw me off.

Article 43: VARIOUS KINDS OF PILGRIMS (2)

There was a young female pilgrim who said she was twenty-four years old. She was heart-rending—her lusterless hair rolled around combs in the *kushimaki* style,[234] her eyes hollow, her cheeks sunken, she was so emaciated that whenever she walked she looked as though she would fall down. I watched quietly to see if there some point where her young blood could be sensed, but couldn't find one. Her voice alone seemed somewhat young, although it was hoarse. She said her hometown was in Onsen County in Iyo and that since the age of eighteen she had been suffering from a chronic illness which, no matter how much she tried every possible thing, had not gotten better, and that was why she was making the pilgrimage and begging for the help of Daishi *sama*.

"I put my faith in Kōbō Daishi; I put my faith in Kōbō Daishi and the great illumination of the Daishi." As you might

---

234 Hair rolled around a comb. The *kushimaki* style began as an informal style and later became the style of downtown women in big cities, women inclined to be coarse.

expect, the sacred *wasan* chanted enthusiastically in her hoarse voice sounded touching. May she be happy.

Another person was a thirteen year old girl, with a rope-like, twisted *obi*[235] tied around her dirty, pitch black *yukata*. In the roots of her frizzy red hair bulged piles of scabs.[236] When she scratched them vigorously with her dirty fingers, the scabs peeled off and sticky, murky, bluish-red pus flowed out. The stench was really hard to bear.

This child, who knew neither where she had been born nor her mother's face, was walking together with her father. He was fifty-four or five and apparently imbecilic; whatever he was asked, he replied, "Yeah, yeah." This is hearsay, but they say that one time this man begged at a police station. Scolded by a policeman, he received two rice cakes from the police inspector and came out happily eating them.[237]

"Do you always walk with your father?"

I went up beside the girl and when I questioned her quietly, she rolled her eyes, stared at me coldly and made no reply.

"What's wrong?"

Even when I gently put my hand on her shoulder, she didn't move at all. In the end I turned red as I waited.

When this child was going out the gate, I went as far as that to see her off and when I said, "Well, goodbye," she even smiled, as I had hoped.

Oh, was I glad! Feeling deeply fond of her I watched her go until she disappeared.

The rain is never going to stop. Having borrowed an umbrella from the temple I was walking around the edge of the lotus pond when an old pilgrim woman in her early sixties approached and asked me to write a letter for her. Then we went to the main hall of the temple and I wrote in pencil on the paper she handed to me. She said, "Please write 'If you don't send me

---

235 A belt or sash.
236 It is not clear whether the girl has syphilis as the word that Takamure uses (かさ—瘡)was the vulgar word for the venereal disease as well as the word for scabs.
237 Begging was against the law. See also Articles 41 and 95.

the money, I will haunt you to death'. And please sign it from Okane, Kōbō Daishi's follower." I thought she was a terrible old lady and I tried suggesting various other wordings but in vain. Then I wrote something like, "Could you please send the money," and I read it to her, but, because the old woman couldn't understand what she heard, she thought I had written what she had told me to say and was very pleased. Said she, "They will think it will be terrible to be haunted to death."

Article 44: AT THE HERMITAGE OF SHINNEN-AN[238]

July thirty-first. Where shall I start? Each and every day I have been occupied with walking and for a long time I haven't picked up my pen. This is the fourth day since we departed from the thirty-ninth temple, Terayama Enkō-ji. During this time we have been taking the Ichinose, Ōki, Ashizurisan, Ōki, Ichinose route and are right now resting at the hermitage of Shinnen-an in Ichinose. (But, there are many villages and hamlets along the route. The distance from Ichinose to Ichinose is fifteen *ri* with fifty *chō* equal to 1 *ri*.[239]) Ashizurisan[240] temple is located at the southern tip of Sada Cape[241] that, together with Muroto Cape encloses Tosa Bay, and the thirty-eighth pilgrimage temple is a famous sacred site amongst the eighty-eight pilgrimage temples. The hymn says, "The Pure Land of Fudaraku! Whether you take the boat's oar at the cape or whether you do not, here at Mount

---

238 Shinnen Yūben wrote the first guidebook (1687) to the Shikoku pilgrimage, *Shikoku Henro Michishirube*. He also built lodging places, *henroya*, in difficult spots along the pilgrimage route. These lodges were called *Shinnen an* (Shinnen hermitages) and this one built at Ichinose, where pilgrims passed going to and from the thirty eighth temple at Ashizuri Cape, is the best known one.
239 It is 31 kilometers from Shinnen's hermitage to Temple 38. As she later comments, in this area 50 *chō* equalled one *ri* but usually 36 *chō* equalled one *ri*. As Isabella Bird, the English traveller, speaks of 56 *chō* equalling one *ri* in some areas in Japan, it is clear that there were regional variations in the measurement of distance.
240 Sadasan Kongōfuku-ji, commonly called Ashizurisan, is the thirty-eighth temple.
241 This is the old name for Ashizuri Cape. She is not referring to Sada Cape near Yawatahama.

Sata at Ashizuri Cape, leave everything to the Buddha."[242]

The main image of the temple is Senjū (Thousand-Armed) Kanzeon Bosatsu It is a famous temple founded by Kōbō Daishi and was appointed as a place for prayers for Emperor Saga.[243]

They say that in the old days going to the temple was terribly difficult; but now it is much easier because a new path is being put through. Though I say that, the narrow mountain trails are still really terrible as they go through bushes, cross rivers in valleys, and climb to summits and so on; even now the route is still considered one of the difficult paths. Nevertheless, because one is usually going up and down beside the sea, the wind is cool and pleasant. In particular, the scenery around Ōki was just like a picture. The river streams from a mountain valley, slowly and calmly cuts through a forest preserve area, and where it enters the sea, there is white sand for many *chō* and beyond that one can see the distant, deep blue ocean which is completely monotonous but like a thickly painted oil painting. Things that are blue are entirely blue and things that are white are entirely white.

After we left Ichinose, the first day we stayed overnight at Ōki, and were told that from there it was four *ri* to Ashizurisan.[244] However, it was four *ri* out of fifty *chō* equals one *ri*. In this neighbourhood it seems to be generally accepted that fifty *chō* makes one *ri*. That day I was determined that I would try to continue walking as far as my legs allowed. So, I tightened up my *zori* and crossed over mountains and more mountains, valleys and more valleys, and arriving at our destination instantly turned back. The sun had already set and we followed the hill paths in the pitch dark, at times gripping our staves and at times crawling on all fours.

Always if I go three or four *ri* I become exhausted but

---

242 As Amida Nyorai is the deity of the Pure Land of the West and Yakushi Nyorai is the deity of the Pure Land of the East, Kannon is the deity of the Potalaka in the south, known in Japanese as Fudaraku. Holy men used to set out from Ashizurimisaki for Fudaraku, which was believed to be an octagonal island-mountain paradise. Some traveled by boat and others jumped off the cliffs.
243 Emperor Saga (reigned 809-823) was, like Kōbō Daishi, a famous calligrapher. He and Kōbō Daishi had a close relationship.
244 The destination was the 38th temple at Ashizuri Cape.

miraculously that time my legs were light and my spirits were good. The old man was surprised and began to grumble. "I simply cannot walk," he said. But even though I said, "Then, let's take a rest," he said, "Since I think you want to walk, I'll walk." My heart cried out, "What do I care? Walk!"

The people in the inn at Ōki were as surprised as if they'd seen a vision when we finally returned, non-stop, without a moment's rest, at some time after nine in the evening. The reason was that they said it was really strange that I who am frail and delicate had walked eight *ri* crossing mountains and hills (If converted to the system of thirty-six *chō* equals one *ri*, this is equivalent to eleven *ri* four *chō*.) The old man also said that today seemed like a miracle in every respect, judging from the way I have walked and become weak and tired up until now. Finally, it was unanimously decided that it was due to Kannon Bosatsu guiding me.

The Kannon *sama* at Ashizurisan is strikingly miraculous; there was an actual case the year before last of a blind person becoming able to see. On the other hand, they said that when bad people go there, there are *tengu* ....[245] Everyone's talk went from this to that; in the end, it always became admiration for and adoration (?)[246] of me. At this rate, I feel that I can again establish a business as the God of Boils.

Article 45: A PILGRIM GRAVE

Here and there I saw graves of pilgrims, every one of them standing near the pilgrim path and facing it; on the new ones had been placed a pilgrim hat and staff and other things. When I think of the fate of people coming here from afar and proceeding to death in this way, I am stirred by a nebulous, sad and lonely grief, and feel as though I am walking in a misty dream.

---

245 *Tengu* are usually imagined as tall, red-faced creatures with a man's body and very long noses; although they have no wings, they can fly. They wear Japanese wooden sandals and dwell in mountains and the groves of cryptomeria trees surrounding temples. They are believed to kidnap human beings and to play pranks on them.
246 Takamure's question mark.

We were probably several *chō* from the Shinnen-an hermitage. Right near the edge of the grassy path stood an ancient, lonesome grave post. Faintly legible was Shigematsu someone-or-other, Fukuoka City, Fukuoka Prefecture

Saying "Pitiful pilgrim! Receive my humble offerings," I offered day flowers,[247] poured water, and bowed in front of the grave for a little while.

It was just dusk and the setting sun was dyeing the nearby mountains and valleys crimson. Words cannot express the tranquility that filled the air here—to the point of being frightening—making everything solemn.

Ah, a pilgrim's grave—how dear to my heart and beautiful this pilgrim's grave seems. It has been standing everlastingly silent since that time gazing at unknown numbers of groups of pilgrims passing in front. (According to the old man, his grandfather also passed away during his pilgrimage in this province of Tosa. Therefore, from now on, I intend to search for that unknown grave in a desultory fashion.)

Since we are human beings, since we are living creatures, we don't know where we will die. It is possible that even I who am writing this, will die as a pilgrim.

I hear that forty pilgrims died the other day while crossing the Shimanto River. It is said that among them, there were six people from Ōita Prefecture as well.

On the road that I must travel from now on, I will go there. Oh, Shimanto River! Let your waves be quiet! I still have parents who always feel heartfelt concern about me. I must not die. But, death as a pilgrim—that is really dear to my heart. For a while, I sat on the grass beside the grave and placing my hand on the grave post, I thought about various things as I stared intently at the setting sun.

All of a sudden I mentally shouted, "Freedom!" and almost leapt up. A life of freedom, a death of freedom—of course, freedom is not self-indulgence. Not until a person is able to endure true loneliness does he have blessed freedom. The color of freedom is the color of blood. Be young! Be noble! Be

---

247 In Japanese, *tsuyu kusa*. Wild flowers (*commelina communis*) with blue blossoms. that open early in the day.

majestic!

I will! While fighting hard against all obstacles, against all threats, I will not stop establishing my young life, a life of blood and fire, in absolute, solemn freedom. Just like this pilgrim's grave far from his home that stands speechless and solitary in a grassy field of the distant pilgrim trail, I too must also evermore wend my way across the lonely, desolate grassy field of life and death. At that time too, the blood red setting sun will probably be shining on my solitary trip.

Pilgrim's grave! Farewell, and rest in peace. From life to death—from the ever-changing to the never-changing—there is one and only one path. At this time I have come to understand that spiritual enlightenment is great acceptance of the world.

Article 46: A HANDFUL OF LEGENDS

There are a great many legends concerning Kōbō Daishi. From amongst them, I will try to present several here. The first is about the seventy-third temple, Gahaishizan Shusshaka-ji in Sanuki. This is the place where it is said that Kōbō Daishi, at the age of seven, decided to sacrifice his life for the sake of saving all people. When he was about to throw himself into the valley a thousand *jō*[248] below, an angel descended and held him back. The Buddha instantly appeared and declared "Your wish is granted." That is why this temple is called Shusshaka, "the Buddha appeared".[249]

The next story is about the twenty-first temple, Shashinzan Tairyū-ji in Awa. The *oku-no-in*[250] of this temple is a famous place. They say one crawls into a long, dark, winding cavern wearing a white gown rented from the temple and

---

248 One *jō* equals 3.03 meters.
249 The meaning of the kanji for Shussaku is "the appearing of the Buddha".
250 The *oku-no-in* is the inner sanctuary of a temple and may contain the most sacred object of worship or a sacred image. It is often a separate building behind the main temple, but in the case of the *oku-no-in* of Tairyū-ji, it is many kilometers from the main temple. Takamure is talking about Jigen-ji which is now said to be the *oku-no-in* of Kakurin-ji, the twentieth temple. Statler, *Japanese Pilgrimage,* pp.212-215, provides a vivid description of what it is like to enter the cave.

carrying a candle in one's hand. It is said that when Kōbō Daishi was doing ascetic practice here, an evil dragon came and troubled him, but that he was saved by a sacred sword that came flying out of nowhere and by means of which he sealed the dragon in the cave.

Next, they say there is a crossing of the Yoshino River[251] called the "free crossing". Long ago at this crossing, there was an avaricious boatman who adamantly refused Kōbō Daishi's request when he wanted to board the boat even though the Daishi said, "I'm in a predicament because I've just lost all my money. Won't you please take me across for free?" Kōbō Daishi then said, "If you can take me safely to the other side, I will pay you money." But the boatman, laughing mockingly, just picked up his pole. Arriving at midstream, the boat just would not move; it was as if it were a living creature and also as if it had been nailed down—the boatman was completely at a loss. Finally, the boatman was frightened of Kōbō Daishi and apologized to him, and it is said he was eventually forgiven because he promised that all pilgrims after that could travel without paying a toll.

Next, the fifty-first temple in Iyo is called Ishite-ji.[252] About this temple there is a rather long story that I have summarized as follows.

Long ago, in Matsuyama in Iyo—I'm not sure where—there was a man called Emon Saburō. He was a rich but very covetous man and was disliked by everyone in the neighbourhood. Kōbō Daishi happened to come to the area where Emon lived, and because he heard this talk, he deliberately went seven times to Emon's house to beg.[253] Even though he was driven away every time, he persisted in going again. Then, the master of the house, Saburō, in great anger, snatched the begging bowl from him and immediately threw it on the dirt floor of the entrance to the house. The broken pieces of the bowl became birds soaring up to heaven. At that time, Kōbō Daishi said, "Listen, Saburō, now your treasures are broken into eight

---
251 In Tokushima Prefecture.
252 In Matsuyama, Ehime. The temple's full name is Kumanozan Ishite-ji. Ishite-ji means "Stone in hand temple."
253 See also Article 41 regarding going seven times.

pieces!"

Even then, Saburō did not understand and ended up driving the Daishi out. He came to realize his wrongdoing because after that, his children died one by one, one day after the other. He wanted to see the Daishi, no matter what, and ask his forgiveness, so he went twenty times around the eighty-eight temples in numerical order. In the end, because he never met the Daishi, the next time he began to go around in the opposite direction. Finally, he achieved his wish, received a blessing[254] from the Daishi, and died, grasping a stone in his fist. He was reborn, with the stone in his fist, into the family of the lord of Matsuyama Castle and it is said that Ishite-ji is the temple where the stone is stored and that is the reason that the name of the temple is "Stone-in-hand" temple.

Other than these, there are a strikingly large number of legends about inedible potatoes and inedible shellfish. I'm thinking that one of these days I'll find the opportunity and write about them when I have examined all the legends of the eighty-eight temples in detail.

Article 47: TOSSING OFF WISECRACKS

Five pilgrims, six including me, were gathered on a road in the shade of some trees talking about various things. Mostly it was talk of the blessings of Kōbō Daishi. Before very long the old man, as is his custom, began to sing my praises. In the first place, he began with Kannon *sama's* appearing. Thereupon, without a second thought, everyone was deeply impressed. After that, talk of *tengu* came up. They said that a very sinful, bad person would, without fail, be flown to a far-distant temple dangling from a *tengu*. Everybody became animated and discussed this. As I listened attentively, I also was deeply impressed. At this point, thinking I was being brilliant, I said with great seriousness, "Then, old man, *tengu* airplanes are possible," but that was a terrible mistake. Although I didn't mind that their faith in me until then was dashed by this one remark, it was

---

[254] The word used is *kaji* meaning the transferring of the Buddha's power and grace, which leads to a sacred peace of mind.

pathetic because, above all, they began to question what the old man had said. People's faces changed and they said, "What a smart aleck she is!"

Along the way, when I get tired of reading and of meditation, inevitably, everything is monotonous, meaningless, and hateful. At such a time, this impertinent girl always argues with the old man. Today, also, I argued with him very heatedly. That was in the cool shade of some trees on the beach with the spray of the waves flying up into our faces every once in a while. While we were gazing at five or six boats with white sails floating dream-like on the quiet waves that we saw far away in Tosa Bay, the conversation began with the rotation of the earth. The old man said if the earth rotates, why doesn't a bucket turn over and the water spill out? That was the old man's only argument. I promptly began to explain such things as gravity and the shape and circumference of the earth. But, basically, the old man stubbornly clung to his fixed idea of up and down. He said that if the earth rotated, people would be upside down at night. I began to be somewhat short-tempered. Impatiently, my lips trembling, I sermonized for more than an hour. As I was trying with all my might, sighing with annoyance at the old man's old-fashioned brain and bitterly criticizing it, he was finally at his wit's ends. He never understood a thing. Basically the old man is not the least interested in acquiring knowledge, so arguing with him is pointless. The matter was left unsettled. I had lectured excitedly, shedding tears, and the old man's nonchalant smile when he said he had given up was unbearably distasteful to me. How disappointing it was.

Now, seizing the opportunity, every day I have been receiving training in massage from the old man. That is because, after I have become extremely skilful, I want to massage my mother proudly when I return to my hometown.

Then, when I thought I had already become very skilful, I massaged an old lady who had a pain in her chest that bothered her. Earlier, she had cured blisters on my feet. As I massaged her, I said clever things such as that there was blood congestion in her chest that caused fever and pain. She frowned and said the massage hurt.

"No, it's not effective if I don't massage so hard that it hurts," I said, and was continuing when the old man came and said I shouldn't do this kind of rough massage.

"Oops!" I thought but right away I gathered my wits and said, "This is girl-style massage that I learned at school." When I said that, the two of them were completely struck with admiration and the old lady's pain went away. In fact, I was going to say that it was pilgrim girl style massage, but if I were to say that, I was afraid that I would be found out. Therefore, in my bewilderment, I said, "girl-style massage" which I cannot help feeling was ridiculous, although I said it myself. With this I have established my two businesses: that is, as the God of Boils and as a "girl-style" masseuse.

Article 48: SURGING WAVES AND RAGING BILLOWS

July second. Going over the difficult section of Izuta, we arrived at the Shimanto River crossing. It was not as big a river as had been alleged. Disembarking from the boat we went a few *ri* and on the way we met some pilgrims. Birds of a feather flock together. When we meet, we laugh and converse together familiarly, like friends of many years standing. The majority of pilgrims are going around in numerical order. Those like us who are going in the opposite direction are very few.

As soon as we passed the small post town[255] called Irino, I heard a sound like distant thunder. When I rushed out on to the beach, with the old man behind, how delightful it was. The high white waves were dancing towards heaven and the spray was like thick clouds of smoke. How magnificent it was, how …..

For a while, saying nothing, I experienced the raging waves directly on my own body. I very nearly flew—my feet left the ground, my hair was flying .

"What are you doing?" Instantly, the old man restrained me and, shocked, I came to. Ah, what a frightening situation— even now when I think about it, I can't help shuddering at the frightening situation it was. The old man asked many detailed

---

[255] From the Nara through the Edo era, a network of officially regulated post towns was established throughout Japan to facilitate and control travel.

questions but I couldn't tell him anything. It's just that my spirit became one with those surging waves and raging billows. It was only that. Suddenly I became terrified and began to run away. But it was to no avail. Even though I went on and on, the path continued along the shore.

"Let's stay here." Finally, I laid my tired body on a grassy field in the shade of some trees. Then, with deep emotion, I looked around at the sea view. It was evening. I could not clearly discern the horizon because of the thick, enveloping silvery smoke made by the spray from the violent waves here. The waves were pounding just below my feet.

Darkness was gradually approaching. It was a white darkness. In an instant what I could see contracted and, in an instant, the utterly white darkness descended like a curtain. The stars were floating above that darkness. Oh! The Milky Way! I don't even know where I am going, but it feels like I am cascading down to the very bottom of that whiteness. The old man has already gone to bed. At first he was concerned about me but he seems to have stopped worrying.

The sea and the dusk and the sleeping figure of the remains of a wizened old man of seventy-three—I thought about death with a calm and quiet mind.

Article 49: ONE NIGHT BY THE SEASHORE

The night was gradually growing late, the darkness was growing mistier, and waves were leaping beneath my feet. Leaving my *waraji* straw sandals on, I sat on the root of a pine tree and looked around intently in every direction, listening carefully. All of a sudden I thought of chanting the *Kōmyō-shingon*.[256] (Just one thousand times.)

So, chanting it one hundred times, I plucked a blade of grass and put it in the long sleeve of my kimono and made a wholehearted effort to become composed and free from worldly thoughts, but I couldn't do it. If someone had happened to come along, I wonder what he would have thought—if the old man had awoken from his sleep, he would probably have praised me

---

256 Others might chant it more than a thousand times.

fulsomely again—only unpleasant things occurred to me and my voice became low each time.

When I had chanted it three hundred times, I suddenly thought like this: Chanting the *Nembutsu*[257] is a short cut to acceptance. That is to say, chanting the *Nembutsu* is to entrust myself just as I am to Heaven and to live with a calm mind in the flow of the moment.

In short, spiritual enlightenment is acceptance. No other road can be expected. No matter how I think about it, I think it is the lacuna of death that makes us despair. In other words, our ultimate despair is nothing other than death.

Therefore, what we always think is if we could flee from death, if we could escape death ..... However, in the physical world that is utterly hopeless. Therefore, we make an effort to transcend death through the strength of our faith.

However, as long as we live in the confines of such effort, our faith is still stiff. The mysterious wings of our great spirit are also numb.

When a person's spirit can maintain equilibrium (even though making no effort) each and every thing has already moved to a mysterious other world. That is to say, suffering and joy and despair alike are trifling matters.

Five hundred, eight hundred, one thousand....

When I had finished counting and chanting, I felt a heart warming delight. How great are calm acceptance of one's fate and whole-hearted faith because, even a common, foolish person such as I, while in such a *nembutsu*-like state, has experienced, to some extent, being able to solemnly take an unyielding attitude to surrounding stimuli and threats.

Once I wanted to ask for a thorough explanation of the *Kōmyō-shingon*. I am ashamed that I have been preoccupied with trivial matters only. Be calm, my mind! Be peaceful! Be just as you are right now!

I prayed silently for a long time and dawn began to approach. I thought I should sleep for a while but I couldn't. Before long, the moon appeared. How awe-inspiring is that light!

---

257 Invoking the name of the Buddha, often by the formula "*Namu Amida Butsu*".

If the light polishes the dew it may fall in drops. As far as I could see, the sea's surface was clouded by white mist. I began to want to walk. I began to long to walk. Tightening my straw sandals I stood up. My feet were so swollen that I couldn't bear to take even one step. But I forced myself to try to walk. In general, before long, I get used to walking. So, I decided to wake up the old man and make him set out with me. My eyes hurt because I hadn't had enough sleep.

Article 50: FAREWELL TUNNEL!

August third. I am tired, really tired, and just about everything has become so unpleasant that I don't care what the ocean is like or what the mountains are like. Where on earth has last night's spiritual awakening flown to? My mind is completely wild and it is really hard to breathe. I have become so short tempered and ready to snap that if an enemy were to confront me, I would push him out of the way.

I cause a lot of trouble to the old man also. It feels good to trouble him. How ugly my mind is. But, the monotonous path and the heat and my tiredness and the pain in my legs are utterly exasperating.

As a way to escape this torment, this unpleasantness, I deliberately look toward the sea and deliberately groan. I sing juvenile songs. I diffuse my agony and soothe my tired body in the atmosphere that results by doing so. But, that does not last long. Then I read. For me, this is a pretty effective method. But, because I have already reread the books I have two or three times, they have little interest for me. Now I want to read a collection of passionate, uninhibited, richly colourful poems.

This attitude of mine is completely selfish. Really, I don't pay the slightest attention to the old man. Sometimes when I think that he is probably very bored, I turn around and look at him. At that time I suddenly feel sorry for him and try to engage in a few words of conversation but I soon become disgusted and give up.

Oh, how mean my heart is, but everything is unbearable. Because of the heat and my weariness, I have become dog-tired and madly want intense stimulation and I am also giving free rein to my hatred that madly wants to hate, to hate and destroy. Sometimes I take a little pleasure in picking flowers, bringing back many memories that make my blood dance but this pleasure never lasts long.

Today we passed through the small town of Saga and went through the Kumai Tunnel.[258] "I can see a tunnel!" When I noticed, I was as glad as a child. At any rate, it was a pleasure to have a tunnel as one change on the monotonous path. For a time I even forgot the pain of my legs. I spoke and my voice echoed. It was fun, it was fun; I thought of songs I liked and sang them. If I do say so myself, my voice sounded nice.[259] In the end, I started talking to the old man about various things. Because my aim was to hear the echo, it didn't matter in the least that it was irrelevant chatter. The old man was simply astonished.

In the midst of my talk, the tunnel ended. I was reluctant to leave it. At the end of the tunnel, I thought I should say something but I could not think of a thing to say. I ended up yelling, "Farewell tunnel!" When I did that, it was terrible—there was someone in the tunnel about two or three *ken* behind me who said, "But where are you going?" It was strange.

When I saw the person who came out, it was a person whom I had inadvertently forgotten who had joined us a while ago in a teahouse. Because the old man had talked about various things with this man who worked at a high school and we had become acquainted, we ended up going on together.

When he asked that, I realized that he had mistakenly thought I had said "Farewell" to him and I blushed.

Article 51: A PRETTY GIRL

August fourth. We slept outside again last night and naturally I did not untie my straw sandals or gaiters. Again, I could not sleep. At midnight, my chest suddenly began to hurt. The pain rapidly became intense. The upshot was that it seemed as though I were breathing my last. I thought I was probably

---

258 Built in 1907 of red brick, the tunnel is 90 metres long.
259 Takamure was very musical.

dying but fortunately the pain stopped and I was able to sink into a deep, dark, coma-like sleep. When I awoke, it was already dawn. I immediately tried rubbing my chest but the pain had completely disappeared. However, my legs ached as they had before. I gave my face a quick wash at the nearby stream, and we decided to set out right away.

People say I am a pretty girl. But in a dim light, at a distance, or under a sedge hat, any woman looks beautiful.[260] My face, which I wash once a day or don't wash at all, is now pitch-black, and I look like a person from India. I threw away my mirror and everything heavy. However, I didn't waste the mirror. At the thirty-ninth temple, Terayama-ji, I gave it to a maidservant.

Today, we finally went to the thirty-seventh temple, Fujiisan Iwamoto-ji.[261] This temple is built in the town of Kubokawa in Takaoka County, Kōchi Prefecture. The temple hymn says, "It is the great pleasure of the deities of Niida[262] to manifest themselves as the five Shintō gods of the area and extinguish the six contaminations of eye, ear, nose, tongue, body, and mind."[263] Presumably, the temple enshrines the five Shintō gods of this area represented by statues of the five Buddhas, Amida Nyorai, Yakushi Nyorai, Jizō Bosatsu, Kanzeon Bosatsu, and Fudō Myōō.[264]

We left the temple and, suffering from the heat as we climbed the hill, we stopped overnight in a lodging house in the

---

260 This is an expression: 夜目遠目笠の内（よめとおめかさのうち）
261 The distance from the previous temple, approximately 100 km, is the greatest distance between the Shikoku pilgrimage temples. She also wrote about this temple in Article 33.
262 In this area, 仁井田 is pronounced Niida.
263 The sense organs of eyes, ear, nose, tongue, skin, and mind lead to attachment to pleasures of sight, sound, smell, taste, touch and inner experience.
264 In Japan, from about the 10th century, the relation between the native Shintō gods and the Buddhist deities was explained by the *honji suijaku* theory that the Shintō gods were incarnations of Buddhas and bodhisattvas who had manifested themselves in Japan in the form of Shintō deities. Later, Shintō theorists asserted that the Shintō deities were the true gods and the Buddhas and Buddhisatvas were only Indian manifestations of them. This is the only temple of the pilgrimage temples that has five Buddhas.

small hamlet of Hirakushi in the settlement of Niida Village. Next day, the fifth, when we were on our way to the town of Kure, also in Takaoka County,[265] the old man went to a village where there was something he wanted to do and I was lingering by myself on a grassy slope when I noticed a young and pretty girl who seemed to be eyeing me fondly. Feeling extremely tender myself, I returned her gaze.

She was a lovely young girl with beautiful hair, a young girl who seemed the embodiment of pure beauty. I like females best when they are young. Childish and pure, innocent—I want females to be like that forever.

"Come here." When I smiled and said that, she fearlessly approached me. Before long, the two of us became good friends.

"How old are you?"

"Twelve."

As I did her hair we talked about various things.

"Where do you come from?"

"The land of the setting sun."

"What does 'the land of the setting sun' mean?"

"You don't know? Well, come here in the evening today and look at the red sun as it sinks. My home is there."

"Is that so? I want to go there."

"When you grow up, by all means go there."

"Well, farewell." Because the old man was calling, I departed, leaving behind the young girl.

The girl stood for a long time seeing us off. What a dear child she was. I shouted, "Goodbye" and looked back again and again. Presently the young girl's figure vanished. For a while, I stood sad and forlorn. As I expected, she came running after us.

"Ah!" Surprised and delighted, I also began to run in her direction.

For a little while the two of us again sat there on the grass. "It is time for us to part. I'm a vagabond, an exile, but you probably don't understand what I am saying. Well, stand up. I will give you this as a memento." Untying the red cord of my hat and tucking it into the top of her kimono I resolutely started to walk.

---

265 now Nakatosa town.

"Big sister."

Oh, don't call me anymore! I felt as though I were being pulled back by my hair. I ran away, my heart bleeding, and when we had gone around the mountain, I couldn't see any trace of my dear little girl no matter how hard I tried. I collapsed there and cried my heart out. I couldn't stop crying.

Article 52: THE INTERESTING PROPRIETOR OF A TEASHOP

In a ravine several *chō* beneath the short cut leading from the village of Niida in Takaoka County, Kōchi Prefecture to the town of Kure in the same county, there was a place where a Fudō statue had been enshrined in a waterfall called, I believe, Fudō-ga-taki. Beside this place there was a house that looked like a tiny, dirty teashop in which was enshrined a statue of Kōbō Daishi, although only for form's sake. It was rather out of place.

The proprietor was a man of about fifty, unshaven and red faced, with glittering eyes that somehow seemed sinister. "Please have some tea." His voice was unexpectedly gentle and his manner was also very soft.

I sat on a bench and when I happened to look on the *tatami*, I saw a book bound in the Western style that seemed out of place in this kind of house with this kind of man. I said, "May I please look at it," and when I picked it up and examined it, it was *The Missionaries Handbook for Spreading the Faith: Complete in one volume* written by Takada Dōken.[266]

The contents looked pretty interesting. In it I found the matter of rebirth discussed. The author said rebirth is possible and presented many examples. First, he wrote about Emon Saburō but this was very different from the legend I wrote the other day.[267] I will put down the main things. Emon Saburō was said to have been born in Ebara District, Ukiana County, in the

---

266 A Sōtō Zen priest (1858-1923) who wrote many books at the end of the Meiji era and the beginning of the Taishō era explaining Buddhism to lay people. The Japanese National Library holds 35 of his books published in the Meiji era and 11 published in the Taishō era. However, 教家必携布教全篇 is not among these.

267 See Article 46

province of Iyo, and his death was on the twentieth day of the tenth month in the eighth year of Tenchō,[268] Shingai.[269] He was reborn as heir of Duke Kōno Saemon-no-suke Yasutoshi, the governor of the province and, afterwards, Emon was the governor of this very prosperous province. The temple where the stone was placed is about eight *chō* southeast of the town of Dōgo Onsen and it is said that the stone, about one *sun* eight *bu* in length,[270] is still cherished as a treasure.

The next story was about the rebirth of Ōyōmei.[271] When Ō Shujin (also known as Ōyōmei) arrived at a certain temple one day, he discovered one small building securely locked. He told a priest that he wanted to open it and take a look but the priest did not agree to his request and said, "In this room is a holy priest who fifty years ago immured himself there to meditate."

Shujin, all the more eager to see, entreated the priest and finally achieved his wish. Sure enough, there was an old priest sitting upright in the lotus position.[272] His appearance bore a really close resemblance to Shujin himself. Furthermore, on the wall was written a poem which said,

---

268 831
269 According to the sexagenary calendar adopted in 604, each year was designated by two different symbols, one from a system of ten units and the other from a set of twelve units. In ancient China, there existed two ideas, "Gogyosetsu" according to which all things consist of five elements, wood, fire, earth, gold, water; and "Onmyodo" whereby all things consist of two elements, Yin and Yang. Based on this, there are ten elements, as each of the five has Yin and Yang, and the ten are expressed by ten Chinese characters. There were also twelve calendar signs which were formed by assigning animals to twelve Chinese characters that originally expressed twelve months. In China and Japan, these ten elements and twelve animals were used to express years, days, time and direction, by combining one character each from the former and the latter types. In "Shingai", *Shin* is the eighth calendar sign and *gai* is the twelfth zodiac sign of the wild boar.
270 About 5 cm. long
271 An influential Chinese philosopher, Wang Yangming, 1472-1529 known in Japan as Ōyōmei. He emphasized understanding the world from within the mind. He is regarded as one of the greatest Chinese thinkers of the last 2000 years and greatly influenced Japanese thought in the Edo period.
272 With legs crossed and back straight.

>After this man was shut in fifty years ago
>His spirit separated from his body
>And entered Ō Shujin.
>For those who believe in Zen,
>This is not strange.

Thereupon, Shujin, recognizing this priest as his former self, buried him with due ceremony and so on.

Other than these, numerous other odd examples were given and the writer finally proclaimed, "Just as the disheveled hair of a young woman cannot be untangled and combed, the Chinese character *myō* cannot be described or explained.[273] Strange and mysterious is the truth about the universe and human beings."

When I was reading it and smiling, the owner came beside me and said with a smile, "What do you think? Is it interesting? He also said, "I have read it over and over again and think it is interesting."

He said he was from Aichi Prefecture and had made the Shikoku pilgrimage fifteen times. He said that he had come here just forty or fifty days ago. Anyway, it was strange.

Article 53: IN SUSAKI—A DESCENDANT OF MORI MOTONARI[274]

August sixth. We stayed in the town of Kure last night and left this morning. We arrived at Susaki, a small port. Thinking that we would go from here by ferry to the thirty-sixth temple, we inquired of the shipping agent and learned that it wasn't convenient right then. So we decided to stay one night in this town and are staying at a *henroyado* near the outskirts of

---

[273] 妙 (myō) has meanings such as exquisite, strange, queer, mystery, miracle, excellent, delicate, charming

[274] Mori Motonari (1497-1571) began as a small local feudal lord in Aki Province (now Hiroshima prefecture) but extended his control to include ten provinces in the Chūgoku district and parts of what are now Fukuoka Prefecture and Ehime Prefecture on the islands of Kyūshū and Shikoku respectively. He is famous for his mastery of military strategy and the use of agents to gather information.

town.

Among the nine people staying in the same inn, there is a man of forty-one or forty-two from Hiroshima Prefecture who says he is a descendant of Mori Motonari. He said, "I am a pilgrim, but I am a doctor more than a pilgrim." Meanwhile, an old man came to see him.

Frequently bowing his head, the old man said, "Doctor, I received your help just now …. So how much is your fee?"

"No, I am not a seller of medicines."

"Well, excuse me, but please take this."

"Well…. Well, since you insist, I'll accept it. And , if possible, tell the man a while ago who had brain disease to come here."

"Yes, I'll do that."

After this dialogue, the old man went away. In a little while a young man of about thirty and an old woman in her mid-fifties came. I was told he was the patient with brain disease.

After the young man had repeatedly prostrated himself for a long time, the doctor quietly began his examination. From what I saw, it seemed to bear little resemblance to a normal examination. With his fingertips, he pressed several places on the head and each time made notes in his notebook. Then, at last, there was medicine which seemed to have been mixed in advance. Without going to any trouble, he wrapped one packet of powdered medicine in two layers of paper and said, "Because I am giving you this which I brought back from America in an extremely small amount and because it doesn't exist anywhere else in Japan, you must be very careful with it. Well then, your illness is the early stage of the disease called brain congestion and even in brain congestion there are three kinds, this kind and imitation brain congestion and real brain congestion. But, because many doctors cannot distinguish between this kind and those kinds, their medicine is not effective. Now, I want you to be sure to remember that you must be certain to take this medicine at twelve fifteen." As he spoke, the young man and the woman had their heads bowed.

A little later the young man said timidly, "This is my mother, and when she showed her legs to a doctor because she was troubled by their aching, he said it was rheumatism, but ….."

The doctor got the upper hand by saying "No, I don't want you to tell me about the patient's condition. If a doctor cannot diagnose a patient's condition after examination, he's not a doctor."

Greatly obliged, the two patients flattened themselves like spiders, like stones.

Soon the same type of strange finger examination as before commenced. Then, when he gave the medicine wrapped beforehand as usual, the two of them bowed their heads again and again. After that it became a question of how much the fee was. He replied, "Because I am not a seller of medicine …." So the patients wrapped up some amount of money and apprehensively offered it with awe and reverence saying, "A small token of appreciation …." Having done this, the two went away.

After that the "doctor" took out Chinese paper and a brush saying that he had been asked for his calligraphy. While I was watching him thinking "Then, he's also good at calligraphy," he began to write something but the characters were spectral. They had neither power nor vitality. Everything was substandard, from the way he held his brush, to the manner in which he sat, to the way he kept his eyes on the paper. (I cannot be so presumptuous as to conclude that, but ….) At any rate, they were extremely twisted characters. When he had finished, he said proudly, "In Ōsaka the head of the ward asked me to write a tablet, which I had to do and I was given this brush as well as a ten yen honorarium."

All who were sitting there were impressed, each and every one of them. When I surreptitiously looked at the old man, he was listening eagerly, deeply impressed. How comical, how farcical, this whole spectacle was!

Article 54: EXERCISE EQUIPMENT IN THE MOUNTAINS

August seventh. Recently I can't help feeling distressed because I feel that my speech and behaviour have become somewhat frivolous. I must face everyone and everything with sincerity. If piety and absolute purity fly away from me, both my beauty and my radiant youth will probably perish at the same time. I must not doubt people at all, nor become wild. Continue the trip with a warm heart! Be modest, gentle, and lady-like.

    I walked along thinking about such things for a long time. That was on the prefectural road[275] leading to Kōchi City. The old man had finally begun to beg. I decided to walk slowly and wait for him but I got pretty tired of waiting. Therefore, in a certain village, I was trying to follow him stealthily but I was immediately discovered by the people there and an old lady of the place approached me holding a *dango*.[276] Because this upset me, I pretended not to notice her and began to walk rapidly, but the old lady hurried after me as if her life depended upon it, so I hurried on to a mountain path, resolutely not looking back.

    Then I felt better. When I happened to look among some big trees on the right side, there were many large vines, twisted together like a swing. When I tested it, it worked well. It was fun, it was fun, and, in addition, it felt good swinging gently to and fro because there was a cool breeze. At first I was glad to swing but in the end, I became sleepy and dozed off holding onto the vine.

    When the old man called me and I woke up, he was standing holding the aforementioned *dango*. He said that because I had run away there had been much laughter after I left. It was a very dark rice cake wrapped in a tree leaf. In Kumamoto they are not usually seen, but in this area *dango* wrapped in tree leaves are popular.

    We left there and when we had been walking for a while, there was a stream in a valley with a log across it that was used as a bridge. With my usual curiosity, I tried to walk, one two, one two, on top of the log, putting my hands out beside me for balance. It was like a balance beam and it was so much fun. After I had played there for a while, when we went twelve or thirteen *ken*, there were trees entwined together like a vaulting horse. Today, because I encountered so many pieces of exercise equipment, my feet and legs didn't hurt at all.

    We walked six or seven *ri* and entered the town of Takaoka. It was early but we decided to get a place to stay there.

---

275 Only prefectural roads were more than grass paths.
276 A cake made from pounded rice.

The wind was very strong.

When we arrived at the inn, the first thing the ladies working there said was "Old man, is this your daughter or your granddaughter?"

This is what is fired off by people wherever we go. In this way, they try to ferret out some information about me. Occasionally, a person who pretends to know says, "I guess she is the daughter of your employer?"

Article 55: PEOPLE REGARD ME WITH SUSPICION

I remember that I also wrote about these sorts of things once before when I was in Sakanashi in Aso. Since then I have passed through Ōita Prefecture, where I was the target of suspicion and felt as though I were the focus of distrust, and even in Shikoku it is the same.

Even at a teashop when we dropped in for just a moment, the old man was grilled right away.

"Is she your granddaughter?"

"No."

"I guess she's your employer."

"Yup!"

"No, absolutely not! He's an old man who's not related."

I couldn't help butting in. When I did so, the conversation became complicated.

In the town of Kure, there was even an unpleasant person who cautioned the old man, "She must surely be the daughter of a distinguished family. Old man, may I have a word with you …."

Because pretty flowers were blooming beside the prefectural road from Kure to Susaki, I stooped down a little to pick them. Three people passed by on bicycles and asked, "Where are you from?" and when I answered "Kumamoto", they said, "I guess you left there to take a trip because school is out on holiday. How old are you?"

Besides asking various things, the man said, "Excuse me, but I am a person from the town of Tatsue in Naga County, Tokushima Prefecture, and there happens to be a pilgrimage temple pretty near my house. Please be sure to drop in." He kindly gave me his name card. I just stood there blankly. I wonder why everyone asks and talks about various things?

Leaving Susaki and walking six *ri* and some *chō,* we stayed two nights in the town of Takaoka. While the old man was searching for an inn I stood forlornly on a bridge there because I was tired, leaning on my stick and looking up at the cloudy sky. Two people who looked like married ladies saw me just as they were saying, "How brash a woman riding a bicycle is."

They said, "How touching—how pretty—how pitiful with your hair cut short.[277] Is there something the matter with you?"[278]

"No."

"Oh, is that so? What a cute pilgrim you are." While the two of them were talking about various things, the figure of a woman on a bicycle passed on the other side. She was a little dark, about twenty-six or seven, clad in *hakama;*[279] I would say she was from either Ochanomizu or Mejiro.[280]

When I turned around after a while, I was surprised because there were so many people behind me. I heard the voices of old women. "Isn't she pitiful." I began to walk because I felt awkward. From the houses on both sides, everyone was saying something as though seeing me off.

I asked at one store, "Has an old man passed by here?"

"Yes, yes. Just over there." How warm and friendly her voice was.

Article 56: MY FUTURE

Rain is falling drearily. Alone, leaning against a post in an annex of the inn, I thought for a long time. From the dream-like past, from the present, to the future ….

The scenery of the whole neighbourhood where I often went to play in my childhood still haunts me; even if I try to do

---

277 At that time women were expected to have long hair.
278 They are probably assuming that she has a life-threatening illness, Hansen's disease (leprosy), family troubles or a mental disease.
279 Hakama are loose trousers tied at the waist with a cord. They were part of the school uniform for girls in the Meiji era (1868-1912).
280 Both of these were early colleges for women in Tōkyō. Ochanomizu trained women teachers.

so, I cannot forget Mount Kiharayama[281] and the Midorikawa River.[282] A little girl in spring, holding the hand of her innocent younger sister in the shade of deeply poignant blossoms in a remote village enveloped in a light and lonely mist—I was already a tearful, quiet, lonely girl. My ideal was to spend my whole life nobly and purely in a humble cottage. For several days at a time, I stood on the bank of a stream and contemplated people's ephemeral existence.

I was a totally timid girl who tended to keep her eyes downcast. At least, people who know about my past will probably remember how forlornly I smiled and how I liked to stand and walk alone. Even at school I was almost always isolated. That was lonely. However, that's the way I was. I frequently tended to say nothing all day long.

Ah, time flows along like water. My many friends have gone their separate ways and are now spending their days according to the individual destiny they chose. I wonder how my dear friend from Amakusa,[283] with whom I am no longer in touch, is doing. Oh, the memory of going to Sumiyoshi Beach in the old days and, feeling unbearably homesick far from home, holding her hand and crying my eyes out.

Now I myself—oh, now I myself—I myself have become a pilgrim on a vagabond trip.

> You island birds, let me lie down here tonight.
> I want to sleep protected by you.

That was a work of four or five days ago.

Ah, I am a pilgrim. I am an exile. My travel money will soon be gone, the future is unpromising and unclear; with such a future in front of me, I must move my tired feet.

No! I will think about nothing. If I can live in the unlimited peace and sorrow of the present, that will do. That will

---

281 Mount Kiharayama, 314 meters high, is located in the town where Takamure was born, now called Matsubase Machi.
282 The Midorikawa River is 76 km in length and runs from the border between Miyazaki and Kumamoto Prefecture to Shimabara Bay.
283 A town in Kumamoto Prefecture. Horiba identifies the friend as Matsushita Shima.

be good. The heart of a vagabond, the heart of an exile is also beautiful. If my life ends, I will collapse with a rock for my pillow.

Dear island! Dear birds! Just protect my fragile remains and let them rest in peace.

People's lives, long or short, are finite; why bear meaningless grudges or agonize for no reason? I must forever be sincere, forever be absolutely pure, forever be serious and forever keep my youthful blood.

In my past, bitter thoughts have threatened me a little. But I am myself after all. Even though I am childish, I must certainly protect and foster the me that is gentle and sweet.

Article 57: A PERSON MET BY CHANCE

August tenth. Because the rain had stopped, we went to worship at Iōzan Kiyotaki-ji,[284] which is some twenty odd *chō* from the town of Takaoka. The principal image is Yakushi Nyorai, and the temple was established by Gyōki and consecrated as a training place for the Sanmitsu Yuga[285] when Kōbō Daishi was making a preaching tour. The temple hymn says, "In Kiyotaki Temple scooping up the clear water makes our hearts pure. The spray on the rocks is like the robe of a celestial being."

As a matter of fact, writing that kind of stuff is enough to make me impatient because I am now thinking about a certain thing. What I am talking about is this. It happened when I was visiting the temple, just when I was standing alone and lonely in the temple gate. An old lady came and because she was looking at me with admiration (I didn't know why), I was feeling awkward and looking down, poking the ground and drawing lines with my staff. When she finally spoke to me she said, "Where do you come from, dear?"

---

284 Temple 35. The word, Kiyotaki, means "clear waterfall" and the temple hymn is based on this meaning.
285 By making the gestures of the Buddha with the hands (mudra), reciting the words of the Buddha (mantra) and concentrating the mind and joining it to the Buddha, a practitioner can obtain enlightenment. The acts, words, and thoughts of the Buddha are called the three mysteries or *sanmitsu*. *Yuga* (yoga) means union.

Pure Kumamoto dialect—how familiar and dear her words were. My heart involuntarily leapt and I went closer to her. I was certainly excited, so much so that my tears overflowed and all I could get out was "Granny, you're from Kumamoto, aren't you? I'm also from Kumamoto."

"Goodness!" The old lady was also terribly surprised. After that, we nostalgically exchanged names and addresses. The old lady, hearing that my family name was Takamure, said, "Then, by any chance the main family's ...." as though she had a hunch.

I had felt somewhat nostalgic hearing that her hometown was in Kamoto County, but when she said that, I was surprised. Then the conversation got right to the point. Strangely, this old woman said she had worked in my house when she was young.

"Speaking of the main line of the Ishikawa family, it was a well-known family of long standing but, because your grandfather was the samurai type and ventured boldly, one thing after another ..." she said to me emotionally as if it were happening right now.

"You are so pathetic in your straw sandals with your delicate body." Because the old woman cried easily and was soon weeping copiously, I also, in spite of myself, became sad and the two of us cried and cried, holding each other's hands.

"Granny," I said, and when I spoke that way, she said, "I'm unworthy of that. Please call me 'old woman'. You poor child! But, much as I would like to accompany you, I have a traveling companion .... And, in addition, I am visiting the temples in numerical order."[286]

When I heard her say this, crying and looking me up and down, I was so fond of her that I wanted to hug her and even though I tried hard not to cry, I couldn't stop; tears flowed down my cheeks. We couldn't stop talking about one thing after another.

Ah.... but we have already parted. We have parted. We have parted and I have returned to the inn.

About my ancestors, about my relatives—now I am thinking seriously about the things they did.

---

286 Takamure is going around in the opposite direction.

The White Chrysanthemum poem happened to occur to me.

> In the beginning
> I was the daughter of a samurai,
> And lived in a beautiful house
> South of Kumamoto castle.[287]

Because of the association of ideas, I thought of my grandfather who had devoted himself entirely to the military arts and my grandfather on my mother's side who had devoted himself to scholarly pursuits. Due to a samurai grudge of which old tales often tell, my great grandfather died a tragic death at Shirakawa[288] because he inadvertently relaxed his guard. Because of this, the family's hereditary stipend was taken back by the lord and my great uncle shut himself in on Mount Kinbōzan,[289] devoted himself to improving his skills, and, as a teacher of martial arts, restored the family name ....

Oh ... somehow or other I have become lonely. I am a pilgrim. That's right; I am a pilgrim. Picking flowers and blown by the wind, I will continue on my sorrowful trip.

Article 58: PEOPLE WITHOUT LODGING

I don't know whether there is a word for "people without lodging" or not but last night we were utterly at our wit's end. I am writing this now beside the road, sitting on a piece of rock that is wet with dew. Yesterday (August eleventh) we boarded the inlet ferry boat from a place called Fukushima, and worshipped at

---

287 This is from a collection of poems called *Kōjō Shiragiku* (White Chrysanthemums of a Dutiful Daughter) by Inoue Sonken (the pen name of Inoue Tetsujiro (1855-1944) who was born in present day Dazaifu, Fukuoka Prefecture).
288 Takamure's great grandfather drowned when with other samurai at the Shirakawa River in Kumamoto prefecture.
289 Mt. Kinbōzan, 665 metres, is in the western part of Kumamoto City. It is also called Kinpōzan. This is probably where Takamure's great uncle went. However, it is possible that he went to the head temple, Kimpusen, of the Buddhist-Shintō ascetic tradition (Shugendō), located in Yoshino District, Nara Prefecture.

the thirty-sixth temple, Tokkōzan Shōryū-ji,[290] which was over a mountain.

The principal image is Namikiri (Wave-pacifying) Fudō Myōō.[291] It is said that upon Daishi's return from abroad, this temple was opened because the *vajra*[292] he had thrown from China in order to choose a place for spreading Esoteric Buddhism had landed in the branches of a pine tree here. The temple hymn says, "I was told that the Azure Dragon living in the small spring, unfailingly protects Buddhism."[293]

When we had finished having our *nōkyō cho* stamped and inscribed, and were about to go back by the route we had come, rain began to fall a little. (Because this place is on a point of land, we had to return by crossing the inlet a second time.) Although that amount of rain didn't matter, we began to hurry but when we got half way down the mountain, it seemed as if we could go neither backward nor forward because there was such a deluge. In the time it took me to pull my rain clothes over my head, my kimono and hair were already soaking wet. I descended, feeling like crying and about the time I reached the bottom, the rain tapered off again and we crossed safely in the boat. When I was walking along putting up my straggling wet hair, a rickshaw man came along and asked, "Where are you going?"

When I said, "I'm going to temple thirty-four," he said, "Well then I'll take you because I'm also returning there."

"But the old man…"

"Oh, do you have a companion?" So saying, he entered a

---

290 The furigana in the text say "Tokkōzan" but other sources say it is "Dokkozan".
291 Fudō Myōō is a popular deity in Japan. He is the representative of Dainichi appearing in a fierce form with a sword in his right hand, a rope in his left and with a halo of flames, to protect and aid those engaged in esoteric practice, eliminating hindrances, and vanquishing evil spirits. The image here protects seafarers.
292 A *vajra (tokko/dokko)* was originally a kind of weapon used in India and is used in Esoteric Buddhism as a symbol of the Buddha mind because it is hard and can destroy any kind of defilement. The legend of the temple is that Kōbō Daishi (then called Kūkai) threw it from China while studying Esoteric Buddhism there. Other places in Japan also have legends about Kōbō Daishi throwing a *vajra* from China.
293 The Azure Dragon protects cities and the eastern side of Kyōto.

house on the right. When I passed in front of that house, a man wearing a flashy *yukata,* who looked like a gentleman, came out saying, "I'll go with you," but, because someone said something from behind, he turned back.

Again we boarded a little ferryboat, then walked on a sandy beach dragging our tired feet, and arrived at temple thirty-four, Moto-o-zan Tanema-ji. The sun had already completely set and a four or five day old crescent moon[294] was shining quietly and forlornly above the forest.

We were told that there was an inn near the temple, but when we went there, they refused us, saying, "As you see, there are already too many guests for us to deal with. We are sorry but we cannot accept you."

There was nothing we could do. Because we were going to the temple anyway, we entered the gate, worshipped at the main hall, had our *nōkyō cho* stamped and inscribed but, when we tried asking if they would allow us to spend the night there, they said that they refused all such requests.

"Then, let's walk." So saying, I laughed serenely. Already my mind had become completely composed. Whether I stay or walk, what difference does it make? It's six of one and half a dozen of the other.

Moreover, trudging along the path under this lonely night sky—I was already determined to do this and urged the old man on. But the old man was tired. "As a special favour," said the priest, and we received permission to spend the night. I didn't even take off my straw sandals and spent the night sitting bolt upright on a bench in front of the Daishi Hall, not sleeping a wink. It was a very long night.

This morning I waited for the old man to wake up and, without even washing our faces, we left the temple.

Ah, I wonder what time it is now. Today is the twelfth of the month. It's become mid-August. I wonder when I will be able to return to my beloved hometown.

---

294 Although the official calendar in Japan at this time was the Gregorian calendar, the lunar calendar was still widely used by people in the country. They were therefore very conscious of the phases of the moon.

Article 59: TANABATA[295]

Because I think I didn't write anything about temple thirty-four, Moto-o-zan, Tanema-ji, last time, I will write just a little.

The principal image is Yakushi Nyorai. In the reign of Emperor Yōmei[296] Prince Shōtoku[297] constructed Shitennō-ji[298] in compliance with an imperial decree, and had the artisans who had come from the country of Kudara[299] to build Shittenō-ji stop here on their return journey and carve the image of Yakushi Nyorai.

The temple hymn says, "This is Tanema Temple which spreads the great compassion of Amida Nyorai in the world just as the five grains[300] were spread at this temple."

After leaving there we went one *ri* and twenty-eight *chō*. Because the river had a toll bridge and the hills were rather low, we arrived at temple thirty-three, Kōfukuzan Sekkei-ji feeling not very tired.

The principal image is Yakushi Nyorai, the work of Kōbō Daishi. It was originally a Shingon temple called Shōrinzan Kōfuku-ji, but during the governorship of the Chōsōkabe clan[301] it was reconstructed and the mountain name[302] and the temple

---

295 The Festival of the Weaver, celebrates the meeting once a year of two lovers, a cowherd and a weaving girl, who are separated by the Milky Way during the rest of the year. Nowadays it is celebrated on July seventh. Children and adults write their wishes on narrow strips of papers and hang them on bamboo branches along with other decorations. They then pray that their wishes will come true.
296 (585-587)
297 (573-621) Prince Shōtoku is the great cultural hero of early Japanese history and was perhaps the most influential ruler of ancient Japan. Prince Shōtoku instituted the Seventeen Article Constitution which set out the philosophic and religious principles on which the Imperial government would be based. He was the second son of Emperor Yōmei.
298 A temple in Ōsaka, also known as Tennō-ji, founded by Prince Shōtoku in 587.
299 Kudara (Paekche) was an ancient Korean kingdom.
300 The five kinds of grains that Kōbō Daishi brought back from China and planted here—rice, wheat, millet, barnyard grass, and beans. *Tane* means seeds; *maku* means to plant/sow.
301 In the sixteenth century.
302 Buddhist temples generally have a mountain name that is the name of a

name were changed, and it was made a temple belonging to Rinzai Zen.[303] The temple hymn says, "Travelling on the road I was hungry but right now I'm happy in the dawn moonlight at Kōfuku-ji, the 'Happy Temple'."[304]

Leaving that temple, we passed through a place called Nagahama and taking a ferryboat from Tanezaki at the mouth of Urado Bay we arrived at the cape opposite and walked some twenty odd *chō* It seems that in that area the business of the Tosa Shipbuilding Company Limited is developing steadily. In a little while we entered a pine grove.[305] Passing the dunes on the right we saw the calm sea of evening.

The pine grove was extremely quiet; here and there were fishermen's houses and at the edges of the eaves, bamboo was standing tied with coloured paper. Oh, today is the sixth day of the month by the old lunar calendar, so it's *tanabata* tomorrow.

How nostalgic the scene was. When I picked up one strip of paper that had fluttered down in the wind, "*Tanabata*—the Milky Way" was written on it unsteadily but charmingly. A nostalgic childhood memory arose of writing, together with my brothers, on strips of paper, using dew taken from the leaves of taro plants,[306] and I couldn't stop my eyes from filling with tears. Ah, if I were home—I would certainly have written this year as well. Saying "These are the Weaver Maiden's clothes," I contrived cute little kimonos in various ways, hung them from bamboo leaves and my beautiful, innocent heart worshipped Heaven wholeheartedly.

Oh, I want to return to that time once again. Dropping my staff, I lingered for a while on top of a sand dune, which was coloured by the setting sun. Unless I remove shameful pretence,

---

legendary Buddhist mountain.
303 The Rinzai School of Zen Buddhism was founded by Eisai (1141-1215) after he had studied in China. The head temple is on Mount Hiei. The other Zen Schools in Japan are Sōtō Zen and Ōbaku Zen.
304 Kōfuku-ji means 'happy temple'.
305 At the time of Takamure's pilgrimage, there were thousands of pine trees. (Prof. Kazuyuki Takuma of the former Kochi Women's Junior College)
306 It is a custom to collect the dew which accumulates on the broad leaves of the taro plant and to mix this dew with charcoal to make ink. Taro dew is considered very pure.

conceitedness and all other impurities from myself, there is absolutely no possibility of escaping suffering—this miserable suffering. No matter what anyone says, I will be myself. I must never be troubled.

Oh, I want to see my father. I want to see my mother. I want to walk joyfully and beautifully with my gentle, quiet mother in the fall mountains. I remember what my mother once said to me. "I want to live with you, the two of us, on top of a quiet mountain. Moonlit evenings will be good, won't they, the white clouds flowing under our feet in the mountain valleys ...."

Oh you dearest mother in the world. I adore my mother more than anyone else in the world. This year also, my mother, who understands the charming poetry of the *tanabata* festival, is probably hanging little strips of paper on bamboo with children, smiling gently. But she is worrying about me off on a trip to a far away place.

There are birds fly towards the setting sun; how I envy them their wings.

Dear father and mother, recently I have not even written a letter; you are sure to be worrying about me. But, please never worry about me. Now I am standing safely on this seashore praying for your good health. (August twelfth)

Article 60: A PERSON WHO WANTS TO COMMIT *HARAKIRI*[307]

August thirteenth. We decided to stay at a teahouse called Fukui-ya at the end of a long, long pine grove in the village of Misatomura, Nagaoka County.[308]

When we had washed our feet and gone up to our room, there was already a guest there before us. Like us, he was a pilgrim and, as I learned later, his age was sixty-six. At first I had wondered if he were seventy or so because he seemed greatly debilitated.

"Where are you from," he asked, and when I replied that I was from Kyūshū, he questioned me again, "Where in

---

307 Suicide by disembowelment.
308 Now part of Kōchi City.

Kyūshū?"

"Kumamoto."

"Kumamoto?" He looked surprised.

"You're also from Kumamoto I suppose?"

He replied "Well, yes…." but he was extremely vague.

"Where in Kumamoto?" He kept questioning me but didn't answer my questions. At any rate, in the little while that we talked I finally came to know that he was a person from somewhere north of Kumamoto Castle, from Kikuchi, Tamana, or Kamoto or thereabouts.[309]

The wife of the innkeeper whispered softly in my ear, "Don't talk to him so much. He's a dreadful man. He says he wants to commit *harakiri* and things like that."

As I listened more and more to his talk, I learned that in the beginning he seemed to have been engaged in business in a big way; even now his relatives were fine and respectable. For that reason, he felt his own fall in circumstances was shameful, and I understood why he had not given even his name.

Three or four years had already passed since he had left Kumamoto and gone to Ōsaka. He said, "Of course, I am clinging to one slight thread of hope; somehow or other I want to be successful again and make up for my past failure. Naturally, I have broken off communication with my hometown but I've also stopped communicating with friends as well although I am concerned about my sweet wife and my brothers. I have finally come to this that you see today; I am suffering from illness— back pain— and have lost my means of livelihood. But there is nothing more difficult than killing myself. I don't know how many times I have planned to commit *harakiri* but in spite of that, each time I have flinched and so must ignominiously drag my old body on each day, a body that knows no pleasure, only suffering. Moreover, when I have worshipped at a further twenty or so temples, I will have finished the pilgrimage but I don't know what will become of me after that. I imagine death is approaching and the future is the future. I don't know at all …."

What a tragic tale it was! He seemed about to fade away,

---

[309] These are not in Kumamoto City but are cities in the northern part of Kumamoto Prefecture.

to be in the shadow of death. I urged him strongly, "Let's go back to Kumamoto together," but he just insisted, "I have lost face with all my relatives." Oh, I wonder what I should do.[310]

He was adamant about not revealing his name and even tried not to let me see the characters on his hat, but I happened to see his *fudabasami*[311] and learned what his name was. But with special consideration for his honour, I have decided not to write it here.

Many times, he sighed and said, "My younger cousin committed *harakiri* in the Shinpūren revolt.[312] Ah, if only I had died the way he did, I could have avoided this kind of shame, but there's nothing I can do about it."

Oh, I wish I could do something for him. What should I do? According to him, his younger brother was very successful. Also, he said all of his relatives were people of high status. I wish I could somehow or other inform his relatives about this person's lonely and pitiful heart. At this rate, this man may possibly yet kill himself.

From the bottom of my heart I hope that if some of his relatives see this, they will quickly do something for him. But this man says he made the pilgrimage in numerical order from temples one to ten in Awa and then jumped to the eighty-eighth temple[313] and has been going in reverse order. After he finishes here in Tosa his pilgrimage will be over when he reaches the eleventh temple, which is in Awa. Is there not some way to help him?

Saying, "Well, excuse me for leaving before you," he left the inn as though running away and there was nothing I could do but blankly watch him go. But, from now on, since I am going in

---

310 Takamure's great grandfather had also failed in business; perhaps this fact contributed to her concern for this man.
311 Box for the slips of papers that pilgrims carry.
312 In 1876 a group of samurai, the Shinpūren—the league of the divine wind—rebelled against the Westernization policy of the Meiji government. The reform program of the Meiji government had disestablished the samurai class, abolished their social privileges, drastically reduced their income, and destroyed their traditional way of life.
313 The eighty-eighth temple is in Kagawa and is relatively close to the tenth temple. It is common for pilgrims to return from the last temple via the tenth temple.

the same direction, whether I am ahead of him or behind, I always, always, intend to be praying secretly for his wellbeing. I personally hope his relatives will go to the police or some other authority but if that is not possible, they can tell me what they are thinking. I will certainly pass on messages to him.[314]

Article 61: ON THE OUTSKIRTS OF KŌCHI CITY

August fourteenth. Now I am writing this relaxing at an inn called Ōsaki-ya, which is built on the water facing an inlet in the village of Godaisan in Nagaoka County.

I wonder what the time is. Perhaps it is around eight-thirty or later. In front of me the sun has set, the sea is pitch dark, and the brilliant lights of Kōchi City have dyed the surface of the nearby water. One of those lights floated away from the others and approached me rocking to and fro; seeing it, I thought it might be a fishing boat.

I'd like to just keep watching enraptured forever, without writing a thing. Today .... I wrote only that far then, listening drowsily to the sound of the waves, I quietly dropped off to sleep.

Now I have finished breakfast and am writing this. Right below my eyes, a boat is passing. The water is leaden in color and the sea is really calm.

Yesterday, after leaving the inn in the pine grove in Misatomura, we went more than ten *chō* and climbed the mountain of temple thirty-two, Hachiyōzan Zenjibu-ji. The temple hymn says, "The Buddha's teachings are a fast boat; my unsettled heart has become calm because of Zenjibu-ji."

The principle image is the Jūichimen (Eleven-Faced) Kanzeon Bosatsu. The temple was founded by Gyōki and restored by Kōbō Daishi.

After going over a mountain, we followed a narrow raised path between rice fields for eight *chō* and coming out on a new

---

314 In the Kyūshū Nichi Nichi Newspaper of April 5th, 1919, there is a related article with the long headline of "The Old Pilgrim who Appeared in *Musume Junreiki* (The pilgrimage journal of a young woman*).*" Relatives who read the article were struck by it and requested the police to search for him and inquire into his identity because they thought the old man might be their relative. (Editor Horiba's note)

road, we went on the flat land in the Ashigatani Valley. In that area we saw that the rice plants had already turned yellow and the ears were hanging heavily. Someone said that in Tosa rice can be harvested three times a year, and that is true. However, I'm afraid that the quality is not very good. In this area I often came across old men with their hair tied up.[315]

We were told that it was one *ri* from Ashigatani to the thirty-first temple, Godaisan Chikurin-ji. Approaching the heavily wooded temple at the top of the mountain and dragging my torn straw sandals, I heard an old woman pilgrim who had just finished worshipping chanting the temple hymn. "Blessed be Monju.[316] I am told that you are the mother of all the Buddhas of the Three Worlds.[317] I myself am a child and want your milk." I felt as though I were being transported to a lonely, distant, far-away world.

The principal image is Monju Bosatsu and the temple was founded by Gyōki; the seventeen Buddhist images are all national treasures[318] and the main hall is a specially protected building. At this temple, I met the old man from Kumamoto whom I wrote about last time. Again he said, "Excuse me for leaving before you," and went down; however, for now I am feeling easier because the person I watched go seems a little less lonely—but perhaps I'm just imagining things. I'll probably meet him again tomorrow.

When we went down the mountain, we could see Kōchi City before us. Walking hurriedly along, thinking that we would go there tonight, we were hailed, "Please, you must stay here," and came to stay at this inn. This morning, after this, I intend to walk around and, at the same time, do some sightseeing.

---

315 This suggests that the area was old fashioned as in less rural areas men no longer wore their hair in the *chonmage* style. The *chonmage* style is the hair style of present day sumo wrestlers.

316 This deity is regarded as the personification or idealization of the wisdom of the Buddha.

317 These are the worlds of the past, present and future.

318 According to Miyata, there are 19 Buddhist images that are national treasures. (p.77)

Article 62: AT THE INN ON THE WATER

August 16, after four a.m. I was wakened by the sound of waves and am writing this.

Yesterday, after writing the previous article, I crossed the long Aoyagi Bridge and walked around Kōchi City. It is said to be the largest city in Shikoku. In a place called Kyōmachi I discovered a bookstore and tarried there a long time. Although I was looking for essays or collections of poems or *waka*,[319] there was nothing good. In the end, I bought a collection of poems by Tagore,[320] *Kada no sasagemono,* and finally left that store.

Perhaps because they were away for the summer holidays, I saw hardly any sign of people looking like students. Since leaving my hometown, I have keenly felt that there seem to be few students in the prefectures of Ōita, Ehime, and Kōchi. Somehow this has made me feel lonely. There seems to be no youthful fragrance and no noble tones can be heard.

Feeling acutely that my Kumamoto has now, in a sense, become a student town, as well as a solemn and serious city, my heart was struck with a kind of irrepressible happiness. You poisonous laugh of the evil practices of a vulgar, worldly, frivolous, indecent civilization, you must not disturb my sacred Kumamoto. Young men, I pray that you remain everlastingly young, everlastingly serious. Girls, like the drooping white, pensive, lovely lilies of the fields, be forever beautiful, forever modest, forever deeply caring, forever gentle, and forever pure.

One of the verses of the Tagore poem collection read, "Many a procession passes by with glamour of glory. Is it only thou who wouldst stand in the shadow silent and behind them all? And only I who would wait and weep and wear out my heart in vain longing?" When I read this, my tears streamed down.[321]

---

319 Japanese poems of 31 syllables.
320 Sir Rabindranath Tagore (1861-1941). Tagore won the Nobel Prize for Literature in 1913 for *Gitanjali* (Song Offerings). The translations here are from the original translation by Tagore himself from Bengali to English. It is the Japanese translation of this book (translated by Mitsuura Sekizō) that Takamure found in the store, Tagore's works are renowned for their lyrical beauty and spiritual poignancy.
321 Song 41. The Tagore translation is a little different from Takamure's

"From now I leave off all petty decorations. ... no more shall there be for me ... coyness and sweetness of demeanour."[322]

"I alone should sail in a boat, and never a soul in the world would know of this our pilgrimage to no country and to no end."[323]

Many small boats passed in front of me as I sank repeatedly into deep thought. The sun had already risen high in the sky.

As though in mutual agreement, the six people staying in the same room say they wonder about me and admire me. "Old man, please take good care of her. Such a well-behaved young woman, by herself, it's really pitiful. If it were Ōsaka—there are many young women rushing off there alone—but going on a pilgrimage to Shikoku nowadays .... Oh, it's admirable!"

I wonder why they all admire me so? I was rather surprised and listened blankly.

After that, when I listened attentively, their speech was very interesting because all of them had assembled together from different districts of Japan. But the intonation and tone of voice of people from other prefectures was, in general, slow and deliberate, compared with that of Kumamoto people. In particular, words such as "Nōshi" and "Aiai"[324] which I heard for the first time after I entered Shikoku, seem imbued with an irresistibly nostalgic ring.

Article 63: UP TO MISCHIEF

August nineteenth. Because the old man has some business to do, we have to remain in Kōchi City today. How in

---

version: Many a procession passes by with *noise and shouts and* glamour of glory. Is it only thou who wouldst stand in the shadow silent and behind them all? And only I who would wait and weep and wear out my heart in vain longing?
322 Song 52.
323 Song 42. The Tagore translation is different: "*Early in the day it was whispered that we* should sail in a boat, *only thou and I*, and never a soul in the world would know of this our pilgrimage to no country and to no end."
324 Noshi at the beginning of a sentence means "excuse me" and at the end of a sentence acts as a tag question. "Aiai" means yes.

the world will my future unfold? I do not know at all. However, human life is ephemeral. What is there to cry about? What is there to suffer about? What is there to agonize about? With a thoroughly innocent heart, I will confront any circumstances whatsoever, any requirements whatsoever, and go on smiling quietly.

Now, around here it is the Bon festival from today.[325] Until late at night boats have been passing below. They may be boats returning from shopping.

Because the moon was bright, I was leaning on the railing deep in thought when the sound of repeated splashing in the water surprised me. Fish! A long time passed before I realized that.

"I want to fish from here." When I thought of that, I could not contain myself. Leading the young daughter of the inn astray, I had her bring out a fishing pole and the two of us squatted furtively in a corner of the garden and dug for worms.

Finally we were ready to fish. Luckily, there was no one there and so we concentrated on dangling the line, but the fish never took it. The girl nestled close to me and craned her neck peering into the water. The moon was becoming clearer and the wind brought really indescribably cool air.

Because the girl cheekily said, "The fish aren't biting, are they? You aren't any good at fishing," I replied, "I don't care if I can't catch a fish because I'm fishing for Tai Kō."[326]

---

325 A Buddhist festival honouring the spirits of the dead, which are said to return to their homes. It is usually celebrated August 13-15, or July 13-15 by the lunar calendar. People visit their ancestors' graves, welcome the ancestors' spirits home with food and offerings, then see the spirits off.
326 Tai Kō Bō a Chinese scholar who lived in the 11th century BC, known as Taigongwang in Chinese (real name Lu Shang or Shi Shangfu) is thought to be a paragon of humble virtue and learned accomplishment. After earning a reputation as a great scholar, Taigongwang is said to have fled society to live alone spending his days fishing on the banks of the Wei River. "Taikoubou" is sometimes used to mean "skilled-angler". Many legends surround Taigongwang, including the story that when he fished his line bore neither bait nor hook. In one legend, Taikoubou was discovered by Wen Wang, the first and model king of the Zhou, who felt he needed Taigongwang's knowledge of statecraft and invited him to serve as a court minister. Taigongwang refused, thereby ensuring his place in Chinese history as a moral exemplar of

If I say it myself, that was witty, but when I looked behind me, guess what! The little girl was innocently sleeping.

Looking forlornly up at the moon, gazing at the sea, thinking of my hometown, I remembered my childhood when, every evening, I worshipped a star, believing that my dead grandmother had gone to become that star. I leaned my cheek on the railing and with the moonlight shining on my face I unintentionally fell sound asleep with the fishing pole dangling from my right hand.

When I woke up I was surprised because the old man, the landlord, and the landlady had come up behind us—I don't know when—and were laughing heartily. That didn't matter, but what in the world had happened to my fishing pole? It was no longer dangling from my hand and I was really worried because I thought it was in the water. When I whispered secretly to the daughter about this, she said she didn't know where it was and opened her eyes wide. Because she had taken out the best pole, I was really worried.

But it was all right. When I looked carefully, the pole was safely in the innkeeper's hand. "Thank heavens!" When I sighed with relief, their loud laughter and sarcastic remarks annoyed me and, most of all, made me feel unbearably embarrassed.

Finally, the daughter started to get angry. "Never mind that we were sleeping, never mind!" Then everyone laughed harder and harder. The moon shining on our two sleepy faces was becoming clearer and brighter. These days I have done many mischievous things and made them laugh all the time.

That's the way it is. Although I do things seriously human beings are creatures inclined to laugh. They had a good laugh the other day, two or three days ago, after I made musical instruments from tea bowls and proudly taught the little girl how to hit them. Then yesterday I went out rowing in a boat and that was a fiasco.

I am reminded of what my mother said to me from time to time, "When are you going to stop being naughty?" However, I am never naughty. I am never childish. Everything I do is

---

disinterestedness. The nickname Taigongwang, meaning "Grand-Duke's-Desire," originated from Wen Wang's statement, "I, the Grand Duke, have long fished for you." Clearly Takamure knows her Chinese classics.

serious. Laughing at what I do is rude.

Article 64: A TERRIBLE MAN

August twentieth. I am now trying to control my mind, which feels nauseated because of extreme unpleasantness, and am looking straight up at the sky, buffeted by an infinite number of emotions. From two or three days ago a sparsely bearded man of about thirty has been coming and hanging around the inn.

Of course, since I am so taciturn that I don't even speak to the landlady much, I didn't exchange a word with him or even see a need to look at him. But he often came to the room next to mine and did things like sing vulgar songs. Each time I heard them, I was offended.

As long as it was just that, it was fine but finally today he came into my room and said, "You must be bored every day."

"Huh?" I looked sternly at him.

He had a disagreeable, ugly, slovenly looking face. His dull eyes held a vile smile and his indiscreet mouth was open, exposing dirty teeth.

Wondering where else there could be such an ugly face, I instinctively sort of shivered and felt a chill. If I had looked more closely, it might not have seemed such an ugly face. However, what made me feel so uncomfortable was his immoral, unprincipled, easily seen through, vile attitude.

His ideas lacked any substance. First, talking about various things and grinning vacantly, he came close to me. I wondered if he were crazy. Then, as his face became instantly sweaty and his eyes became red and runny—I don't know whether with tears or pus—he suddenly bore down on me, his lips and limbs shaking.

What a horrible beast! Seized with panic more than with abhorrence, I jumped aside. Then I looked at him with my lips tightly pursed. He was an unspeakably ill-mannered and rude beast. He was a vile man. After he left, I sat upright, mastered my discomfort, and thought.

Be merciful! Be merciful. Yes, I must be sincerely merciful. When I thought like that, I came to feel that my fierce overbearing attitude that had startled him was even ridiculous. And I felt ashamed that I had become agitated and indignant, even momentarily.

Be calm! A cold wind in a lonely autumn field and the figure of a princess regally picking flowers—ah, that is my ideal.

One of my friends said, "You are not a person of this world."

If that's the case it can't be helped; I will go on clinging to my ideals until the end. (Perhaps they are only idle fancies.)

Today is the second day of Obon. I will look for *yomena* flowers[327] and with them pay my respects at the tombs of my ancestors from afar.

To change the subject, I wonder where the man from Kumamoto who wanted to commit *harakiri* is. Every day I am worried to death about him. I must quickly catch up to him.

Article 65: ESCAPING TO A FIELD

August twenty-fourth. There's no denying that the fields and mountains have really become autumn-like, looking as though they have sunk forlornly to the bottom of the yellowish sunlight. Standing on a narrow path in a bleak grassy field being blown by the wind, an indescribable feeling welling up in me makes me feel like crying. In the far distance I can see the open sea.

Today there was a great bustle at the inn because people from the Yamanouchi family, the former chief clan of Tosa,[328] had

---

327 "False asters" (*kalimeris yomena*) growing 50 to 120 centimeters high with light purple flowers blooming from July to October. They are often found in swamps.
328 During the Tokugawa period (1603- 1867), Tosa was noted for the suppression of its lower-samurai classes by its upper-samurai. The first Tokugawa Shogun confiscated Tosa from the Chosokabe and awarded it to the Yamanouchi after the decisive Battle of Sekigahara in 1600 because the Chosokabe had fought against the Tokugawa. Upper-samurai in Tosa were the original retainers of the House of Yamanouchi but lower-samurai had once served the House of Chosokabe. The new *daimyo* of Tosa established laws favouring his direct vassals. Upon occasion, his discrimination was carried to extremes: upper-samurai were permitted by law to strike down their social inferiors, but under no circumstances were lower-samurai allowed to draw

come there for an outing. The old landlady put her folded fan in front of her on the raised platform in the entrance hall and prostrated herself ceremoniously. Said she, "The lord is coming in; he is so awe-inspiring that I cannot raise my head."

Thanks to that, even we were virtually confined to our room; with walls and *fusuma*[329] on four sides (no, in one direction there was the sea), the hot stuffiness was terrible. Making matters worse, we were forbidden to walk along the corridor; this was too distressing and that is why I fled and came to this field.

Whenever I am alone I always think about what is dearest to me. Now, gazing at the distant horizon, sitting on a chunk of rock in the grass, I thought about this.

Beautifully beloved by me are young, jewel-like girls, not sullied by the dust of the world. Vulgar women who seem to be nothing more than greasy flesh are awful, even though they are young and good looking. Also, the impertinence of female students is odious. Of course I am an advocate of education for girls.

Writing this I feel the urge to become pretentious and say it is an irrefutable fact that generally speaking, there has recently been too much of a tendency towards materialism and realism. Among other things, for instance, am I prejudiced in suspecting that women's education concentrates on forming women into perfect, but small and ordinary models and pays no attention at all to the aspects of lofty ideas and profound faith?

For example, even though smeared with a plethora of vulgar ideas, we desire an eternal dignity that must never be desecrated. Reading *Genji Monogatari*,[330] noble and dear to me were the delicate innermost feelings of the women of the Heian period, adorable, fragile, poetic, and pious. Then, the tales of dignified, virtuous, heroic women which appeared in the warring period[331] also deeply and intensely inspired and impressed me. Of

---

their swords on upper-samurai.
329 A paper-covered sliding panel
330 Written in the early eleventh century *The Tale of Genji* is considered to be one of the earliest novels in the world. The author, Murasaki Shikibu, a court lady, describes the life and loves of Genji, the "Shining Prince".
331 The Warring States Period, 1467-1568. Sometimes because all healthy men had gone to war or been killed, women were the last defence of a castle

course, they all had their weak points. But they had noble grace. They had nobility not dominated by vulgar worldly desire. Towering spirits not stained by the dirt of the world and with the appearance of dearly beloved lilies of the field—ah, I want to be like that—I want to be like that.

Still more sweet and dear are motherly mothers. Mother—when I think of her, my tears flow. Oh, my dear mother in my hometown.

Old women filled with affection are also beloved and dear. In short, my ideal and my aspiration is a woman with a beautiful and tender heart, with, moreover, noble refinement.

I don't care if I live all my life in silence. I just want to be everlastingly noble. While I was writing this, the sun clouded over. I wonder if we'll have a sudden shower.

Article 66: DON'T WORRY!

August twenty-eighth. Finally, we were to leave. Because the old man had already gone to and presented a *fuda* card at temple thirty, Myōshikizan Anraku-ji,[332] and temple twenty-nine, Manizan Kokubun-ji,[333] during our stay, we went to temple twenty-eight, Hōkaizan Dainichi-ji.[334] When, coated with dust and sweat, we finally reached the temple gate, my tension lessened and tears fell down unchecked.

---

or town. For example, the wife of Mimura Kotoku, appalled by the mass suicide of the surviving women and children in her husband's besieged castle, armed herself and led eighty-three soldiers against the enemy, "whirling her *naginata* like a waterwheel." (The *naginata* is a long weapon with a sharp blade, like a halberd.) She challenged a mounted general, but he refused to fight saying that women were unfit as opponents to true warriors. He edged backwards saying under his breath, "She is a demon!" She refused to back down, but he escaped when his soldiers attacked her. She cut through her attackers and won her way back to the castle.

332 There are two temples which claim to be the thirtieth temple; the other temple is Dodozan Zenraku-ji in the outskirts of Kōchi City.

333 In 741, by decree of Emperor Shōmu two Kokubun-ji temples, one for nuns and one for monks were established in each province of Japan. They were founded to pray for abundant harvests of grain and national peace.

334 The fact that she seems to have not visited two temples may explain her apparent miscounting of temples in Article 89.

We presented our cards and when we had gone more than three *chō* from there, we came to the *okuno-in* with crystal clear water gushing out beside the building.[335]

The Buddha is Yakushi Nyorai, said to have remarkably miraculous power and to have, even recently, completely restored the hearing of a deaf person. Concerning that, I spotted some interesting offerings. "Spotted" is misleading; I really enjoyed looking at them and feeling them with my hands, my eyes open wide in amazement. They were stones, each of which had a hole in it. At first I wondered why many strange, seemingly one-eyed, stones had been offered, but later I asked and was told they were ears. They were odd offerings.[336]

We came down the mountain and in a while came out on the prefectural road. Going over a *ri*, we entered Akaoka town.[337] The town was narrow but rather long. We left there and, again going over a *ri*, we reached the post town of Yasu. Because our legs were rather tired and our heads felt rather heavy, and because the sun was already close to setting, we decided to stay one night at a certain *henroyado*. This inn, to be sure, was an unpleasant place that seemed likely to be breeding lice. I thought it would be better to camp out along the seashore but because the old man had entered quickly, I had to go in. When I was shrinking back because the *tatami* mats were somehow risky, the old man repeatedly said, "Don't worry."

Then we were told that the bath was ready and the five people staying together took turns having a bath. When it was my turn, I went to the bath but it was right in front of the toilet, a dirty crock that was clearly visible. I could stand that by looking sideways, but there was no way I could stand the hot water in the wooden bath. It was utterly pitch-black from the grimy dirt that had been washed off. It was just unbearable. But not bathing would be wrong because the old man had repeatedly said to me, "Enjoy your bath." I was utterly confounded.

The old man came along just when I was standing there

---

335 Tsumebori Yakushi Dō. The Buddha is said to have been carved by Kōbō Daishi with his fingernails.
336 Stones such as these are still offered at this temple
337 This is in Kami Gun.

perplexed and despondent. He was carrying salt in his hand. When he saw my state he said, "Why haven't you gotten in yet? Don't worry, go in. No one is looking."

"Yes, right away." I said it with my face bright red.

However, how could I get in? Finally, I was so worried that I wanted to cry. I returned to the room without getting in. After that, it was time to eat but I just couldn't eat. After one bite I couldn't swallow. The old man said softly, "Once again, you are not eating because the guests here are dirty with awful faces."

After that, because the tea was flavourless and repulsive, I decided to get freshly drawn water which fortunately there was. The filth of the dipper—this was the last straw.

When I was standing there lost in thought, feeling sorry for myself, the old man said, "Don't worry. Drink it straight from the dipper."

The old man seems to think that I am a person who worries too much.

Article 67: RESOLVED TO TRAVEL ALONE

August twenty-ninth. Today we had heavy wind and rain. Since it was merely cloudy during the early morning, we left the inn and walked three or four *ri*, but, because of lingering exhaustion from yesterday and insufficient sleep, I was intensely dizzy which I couldn't bear. At the same time, because the look of the sky was becoming threatening, we decided to stop just before the town of Aki.

The inn is built on the seashore. With a terrible and deafening roar, dreadful, fierce waves are pounding in and it seems as if they are going to chew up and utterly destroy the houses, people, trees and grass. Because the room where I am writing this is on the corner of the second floor, the place closest to the ocean, I can see a grand spectacle, which is really beyond description. Rows of waves like small mountains are approaching from the open sea, breaking upon the shore, becoming waterfalls, becoming clouds, and changing into mist.

I hear that a steamboat that capsized and sank just two or three days ago has washed up somewhere on the shore in Kiishū.

In other words, it is a violent storm. For a while my attention was caught by the ocean, but I again remembered the matter that I have been thinking about since yesterday. That is that, parting from this kind old man, I will continue the pilgrimage by myself.

The old man has really been kind to me. He has cared for such an unworthy person as myself as if I were his master and carried all my luggage on his old body, helped me with my straw sandals, and beyond this, looked after me regarding everything and anything. I always feel conscience-stricken, but because he says, "You are too reserved. Order me to do anything," I have complied with his wishes and left things as they are. But, because money has recently become a little short, the old man has been begging and obtaining food for two people, and, beyond that, carrying large pieces of luggage on his back despite this heat, and taking care of good-for-nothing me—I'm really sorry about this.

Well then, I will go together with him as far as Muya[338] in Awa, there I will see him off to cross the sea to Kiishū[339] and then I have decided I will drift along as a solitary traveler. What is more, the pathos of a solitary trip is what I long for.

At that time what will the autumn view of the shore of the Inland Sea be like? I don't care if I collapse; it will be good to just drift along, relying on my staff. A trip alone—yes—I am already firmly resolved. I have not yet spoken to the old man, but I will certainly do so, I will do so ….

Because I haven't written anything about the thirtieth, twenty-ninth, or twenty-eighth temples, a brief account follows. The principal image at temple thirty, Dodozan Anraku-ji, is Amida Nyorai, and it is said that it is a treasure brought from India, with miraculous powers.[340] The temple hymn says "The

---

338 Now part of Naruto City in Tokushima Prefecture. Muya is where pilgrims from Honshū used to arrive in Shikoku. The first temple is near Muya.
339 Mount Kōya, where Kōbō Daishi is interred, is in Wakayama Prefecture (formerly Kiishū). Pilgrims to Shikoku traditionally visit Mount Kōya both before and after their pilgrimage. This is probably why she thinks she will see him off to Wakayama.
340 For many years two temples claimed to be the thirtieth temple: Dodozan Zenraku-ji (sometimes Dotōsan Zenraku-ji) and Myōshikizan Anraku-ji. However, there is no temple named Dodozan Anraku-ji.

first shrine, which many people visit, has flourished from ancient times to the present."

The principle image at temple twenty-nine, Manizan Kokubun-ji, is Senjū (Thousand-armed) Kanzeon Bosatsu and the main hall is a national treasure. This is the Kokubun-ji of Tosa (built by the order of Emperor Shōmu).[341] The hymn says "Kokubun-ji temples, which took much treasure to build, were built in each province and will continue to exist for the benefit of the people."

Temple twenty-eight, Dainichi-ji, was founded, as was Kokubun-ji, by Gyōki, and the principal image is Dainichi Nyorai. Kōbō Daishi carved the image of Yakushi Nyorai in a standing camphor tree and dedicated it as the *oku-no-in*. The temple hymn says "If you make the pilgrimage, the Great Sun Temple will shine on your sins like sunshine on dew and frost."[342]

Article 68: TWO PILGRIMS

August thirtieth. I hear it is the two hundred and tenth day.[343] When we were leaving the town of Aki in Kōchi Prefecture,[344] on the outskirts we found that the long bridge there had collapsed. It seems that last night there was a severe storm in this area. Because there was nothing else we could do, we walked as much as two *ri* along the river, pushed our way deep into the mountains, finally crossed a bridge upstream, doubled back another two *ri,* and only then were we able to proceed further. When we had gone about one *ri*, all of a sudden I spotted two pilgrims in the shade of a large boulder.

How dear a sight, how sweet a scene—let me tell you

---

341 Two temples, one for monks and the other for nuns, were established in each province of Japan by Emperor Shōmu in 741. Each of these temples was called Kokubun-ji.
342 Dainichi, the name of the temple, means great sun.
343 Nihyaku tōka, literally 210 days, falls on the 210th day after risshun, the beginning of spring according to the traditional Japanese calendar. Risshun usually falls around February 4th, and the 210th day falls around September 1. It is considered to be the start of the typhoon season and heavy rainfall and strong winds can be expected.
344 Now Aki City.

about it, but don't blame me if I am breathless with excitement.

One person, apparently the father, had laid his utterly exhausted and completely worn out body on the roots of a pine tree. The other person was a girl, a cute, cute girl of twelve or thirteen who, having washed her father's kimono, had hung it on a branch of the tree. Not only that, but beside it she had hung a small pot over a little bit of burning firewood, and was simmering something or other. The girl was quietly and devotedly going about doing everything. When I involuntarily paused and looked at her, smiling and saying nothing, the young girl saw me and also smiled. So dear to my heart! I approached her with my heart pounding.

"You know, that bridge over there has collapsed."

"Oh my goodness, the bridge...."

On a rock facing the ocean the two of us sat together familiarly and talked. Even as we were doing that, the girl devotedly went to look after the fire under the pot.

"Farewell."

When I stood up, the young girl, holding the trunk of the pine tree, watched me go, smiling and saying nothing. When I quietly turned around, I could hear her sweet voice saying, "Daddy, the rice is ready."

I could see that lovely girl shaking her father awake with both hands. Ah, little girl, remain just like that. Don't wish for anything else. As you are noble now, be noble forever; as you are pure now, be pure forever.

POEMS OF A PILGRIM IN TOSA by Itsue

Wanting to go
On the moonlit sea
I am weeping loudly
But there is no boat to sail in.

If there is a boat to sail in,
I will go on it weeping,
But no matter how hard I look,
I won't be able to see Kumamoto.

I must seem unhappy,
Tired out from crying,
Falling asleep
With flowers in my hand.

On the dusky, evening seashore,
The birds of the island
Fly around in flocks
And are said to protect pilgrims.

Island birds!
Tonight let me
Lie down here and sleep,
Protected by you.

While I am traveling,
The mountains of Tosa look so lonely
The floating white clouds
Blanket them quietly.

On the hilltop
At the end of the pine grove,
I face the setting sun and wonder
Where is my home town?

Searching for a place to stay,
I found a temple
Sorrowfully dyed by the setting sun
That was so quiet it made me want to cry.

The fate of a pilgrim
Is unknown,
Like that of a floating water weed;
This is a lonely thought.

Article 69: TO THE EAST TEMPLE[345]

August thirty-first. Last evening we stayed at Sakamoto-ya at the foot of temple twenty-seven, Chikurinzan Kōnomine-ji. This morning we left early and went up the mountain path. We went thirty-two *chō* and reached the temple gate.

The temple is in a sacred compound on top of a high peak and was founded by Gyōki during the reign of Emperor Shōmu. Izanagi no Mikoto and Izanami no Mikoto as well as Amaterasu Ōmikami are enshrined together.[346] The principle image is the Jūichi-men (Eleven-Faced) Kanzeon Bosatsu. The temple hymn says, "Even if it is like the Hell of Swords, the peak of the gods, Kōnomine, is at the heart of the Buddha's promise."[347]

In this temple there are shellfish that one does not eat. They seem to have been stiffened by having soil stuffed in their shells.[348] One kind old nun there gave me some water to drink. My nostalgia was limitless. I thought that my only ideal is to become kind hearted; I have no other desire in my heart. My heartfelt wish is to be tenderly and beautifully kind hearted to everyone alike.

I heard that a priest in the office of this temple was a person from Shimabara in Nagasaki Prefecture called Mr. Araki Kihō. Coming down the mountain we walked several *chō* and reached the ferry landing. The current was rushing, the water muddy, and it seemed we wouldn't be able to cross, but we were fortunate to be able to reach the opposite shore without difficulty because of the expert boatman.

---

345 Temple 24 is familiarly known as the Temple of the East and temple 26 is called the Temple of the West.
346 According to Japanese myth, Izanagi and Izanami were the creator god and goddess sent down from heaven to build the earth. The other gods and goddesses were their descendants. Amaterasu was the Sun goddess, ruler of the heavens. Before the Meiji era, a fusion of Buddhism and Shintoism existed in Japan and Buddhist temples and Shinto shrines were often combined.
347 There are many kinds of hells in Japanese Buddhism. In the Hell of Swords, those who enter it are impaled on upright swords. According to the temple, this is the old hymn. The new one says, "The Buddha's blessing is on top of Mount Kōnomine.
348 Perhaps these are fossils.

After that, we reached a post town on some seashore and asked if we could stay at the inn but were not allowed to. When we reached the next post town, the sun was already setting forlornly, returning crows dotted the sky, and the sound of the wind was sad. So we rushed about seeking an inn, but it was completely hopeless and we decided to camp outdoors because there was no alternative. We were in a pine grove by the beach. Right in front was the sea and the sun was already about to sink behind a mountain, but one remaining ray of light was shining, making everything crimson. The sea was red, the forest red, the old man and I were red; we faced this solemn evening saying not a word.

Ah, what a good and beautiful place to stay, an inn of the gods! I sang, "Quietly, quietly, the sun has set again today."

Beside me, the old man faced the setting sun and put the palms of his hands together in *gassho*.[349] In an instant the sun sank completely and the evening darkness fell on the sea and enveloped us. All night long I heard the sound of the waves which tended to wake me up. When it was almost dawn, a north wind began to blow and made me cold. When the crescent moon rose in the sky, we picked up our walking sticks and stood up. Having slept in my gaiters and straw sandals, I just stood up groggily and walked unsteadily. Of course I did not wash my face.

September 1. Today we arrived at the West Temple. There was a steep slope. The West Temple is one name for the twentieth sixth-temple, Ryūzuzan Kongōchō-ji. The principle image is Yakushi Nyorai, said to have been made by Kōbō Daishi. The temple hymn says, "Where the moon sinks in the sky at the West Temple is the paradise we long for after death ."

It was one *ri* to the next temple, temple twenty-five, Hōshuzan Shinshō-ji. The temple is in Murotsu Port in a small inlet.[350] The principle image is Jizō Bosatsu[351] and the temple

---

349 *Gassho*: putting one's palms together in worship, veneration, thanks or other forms of respect.
350 It is now in Muroto City.
351 Jizō Bosatsu is one of the most beloved deities in Japan. He is the guardian of children, especially those who have died. He is regarded as the saviour of those who are suffering in the underworld. He is depicted as a monk

hymn says, "Whether the ship of the Buddha's teaching is entering or leaving the Port Temple, please let me board—I who am lost."[352]

From there we walked on a sandy beach and climbed the mountain at the southernmost tip of Muroto Cape. We were terribly tired so it took us quite a while to reach the top, where temple twenty-four, Murotozan, Hotsumisaki-ji, is. The principal image is Kokūzō Bosatsu.[353] Daishi, while doing ascetic practice here built a thatched hermitage in this place and wrote, "I hear there is a law of compassion at Muroto but when I was residing there, no day passed without the winds and waves of causation being stirred up." Acting upon the imperial decree of Emperor Gosaga,[354] the temple was dedicated as a place to pray for the peace of the country and the health of the Emperor.

This temple is the easternmost of the pilgrimage temples of Tosa. The temple hymn says, "East Temple is in the direction of the morning star's rising so why am I in black confusion?"

Article 70: A CHANCE MEETING

We descended the mountain and followed a path that was hard to discern. There was a sandy beach along the shore. The old man said that he was tired beyond endurance and I was worried, so we once again decided to camp out there. Leaning on a rock in the grass, gazing out at the distant ocean from a sand dune, there was a boundless view of waves with no swell. In an instant the sun had set.

I did not sleep. At midnight the look of the sky became threatening; there were tremendous gusts of wind and billowing spray, which made both my hair and my sleeves damp. When I noticed that, there were already big drops of rain falling. Luckily, beside that place there was a small makeshift hut that seemed to be a place for farmers to pile and store straw. We just went in. Because the roof was roughly constructed, it was terribly leaky. I

---

standing with a staff in his right hand and a round jewel in his left.
352 Local people call the temple, Tsu-dera, meaning the temple of the seaport.
353. The Boddhisatva of Space. He is so called because his wisdom is as vast as space. In esoteric Buddhism he is the object of worship of a special ritual.
354 1242-1246.

didn't even cry. Thus, I suffered through one night until dawn came. The rain also came to an end.

Again, I felt compelled to take my pilgrim staff in hand and start out. While I walked I meditated.

The thing that I am asking for is love. Up until now I have certainly been in terrible anguish. Really and truly human beings are stained with evil, are encased in evil, and, what is more, are unable to shed evil. Ah, what shall I do?

Look! In the torment resulting from worldly desires, even when my mind is firm this time, my path plunges unaware into sanctimoniousness. I think, I always think, that the path of goodness is a narrow, small, difficult-to-walk path, and that there are oceans right beside both sides: on the one side, the sea of earthly desires, on the other side, the sea of sanctimoniousness. In anguish we try to crawl up but many times a day we slip and fall down, fall down and drown. Oh, how small I am! Now I have realized how infinitesimal I am!

Look at the sky! The sky is not good, and again it is not bad. It is only empty; yes, only empty.

Oh my heart! Divest yourself of the anguish of good and evil now, and become completely empty like the sky. And, in addition, sense the love!

The vastness of thinking that I am loved by everything rather than thinking that I love everything through my own effort is heart warming. The essential thing is to shed narrow restraint, which is the self, and to return to the vast emptiness of the sky, which is freedom.[355]

I had thought that everything originated from me but this is already a dream of the past for me. I am free. I exist here happily, being loved by everything. How pleasant. How pleasant.

A night in a field in cold rain is not even the smallest hardship when I reflect that I am together with a loving person.

---

355 The word used is *jiyū* which is usually translated as "freedom". It can also be translated as "self-reliance". "... real freedom is the outcome of enlightenment. When a man realizes this, in whatever situation he may find himself he is always free in his inner life, for that pursues its own line of action. Zen is the religion of *jiyū*, "self-reliance", and *jizai*, "self-being". Suzuki, Daisetz T. *Zen and Japanese Culture*. (1959) 1990. Tokyo: Charles E. Tuttle Company.

That's just it; I am always with loving people. Ah, how joyful, how heart-warmingly joyful.

When we arrived at a village called Shirimizu, there was an inn beside the road at which we decided to stay for the night. Three pilgrims came. To my amazement, the last to come—I had not forgotten him for even a moment—was the *harakiri* man. We were both glad to see each other again. Since I had been in Kōchi for a long time I had thought it highly unlikely that I'd see him again and I was very glad that we were able to meet thus by chance.

The next day, the third, we set out early in the morning; when I got tired, I gathered shells and picked flowers. When we had passed the fishing town called Kannoura, we had already arrived at the border between Kōchi and Tokushima. Feeling somewhat more cheerful, I was leaning against some lumber beside the road, sunk in dream-like thoughts, when some groups of young men and women came sporting along.

"You're cute. Really pretty."

Several men approached me, talking rudely and raucously. I felt uneasy, so I began to walk away from there, when all of a sudden there arose laughter behind me. When I innocently turned around, one man said, "I really dislike pilgrims with a Shimada hairdo."[356]

Then all of them, with one accord, simultaneously opened their mouths and laughed. What detestable people they were.

Article 71: UNTITLED

When we arrived at the village of Shishikui, the old man began to look for free lodging in a *zenkonyado*[357] and found it. A

---

356 The Shimada style was used by unmarried girls and was a hairstyle of rich, upper class women. Her hair was tied back against her neck and was not in the Shimada style.
357 Formerly, some residents on Shikoku used to give free lodging to pilgrims. Such a home was called a *zengonyado* meaning 'good deed inn'. Pilgrims were allowed to stay because they were considered holy and giving them accommodation brought merit to the household. In addition, it was always possible that a pilgrim was actually Kōbō Daishi in disguise. Furthermore, villagers liked to hear stories of far away places such as Tōkyō

Buddha had been enshrined in an unfinished three mat room. We washed our feet, went up into the room, and sat, doing nothing. A woman of the house came, and seeing me, said, "You probably can't even cook rice."

Blushing, but also looking stern, I said, "No, I can cook it."

What a rude, suggestive person![358]

"Oh…"

Laughing suspiciously, she stared at me and I felt boundlessly uneasy. Again she spoke,

"Old man, you're her personal servant, aren't you?"

Ah, so she was not trying to make fun of me.

The next day, the fourth, we set out early in the morning; there was nothing different about that day. We stayed at Shihōbara Village. The next day, the fifth, I rested at the inn until noon. The old man went out begging. The landlady at the inn was extremely kind to me. When we departed she kindly tightened the cords on my straw sandals.

Going over ten *chō*, we reached the well-known beach of Yasakayahama in Awa. We went over a mountain and along a beach, and over another mountain and walked along the beach. My sandals and gaiters got drenched as I was walking around at the water's edge, but picking up shells I forgot about my tiredness and we reached the village of Mugi.[359] En route, in one valley, I met and was ridiculed by a group of people who looked like labourers. They said, "She's probably a geisha."

Utterly exhausted, we stayed at a filthy inn beyond Mugi. The children noisily surrounded me and in the end, even adults, carrying children on their backs, came out to see me.

On the sixth we left early in the morning and reached the town of Hiwasa. Here there is the twenty-third temple, Iōzan Yakuō-ji. The principle image is Yakushi Nyorai which Daishi, at the age of forty-two, made and enshrined with a sacred vow to save all living beings.[360] It is said that in ancient times this temple

---

and Ōsaka.
358 Takamure probably thinks the woman believes she's a geisha.
359 Now Mugi Town in Kaifu County.
360 His age, 42, was one of the "danger years" or the critical ages when misfortune is most likely to strike. These are 25 and 42 for men and 19 and 33

was once the temporary palace, Tsuchimikado-in,[361] of ex-emperor Tsuchimikado.

The temple hymn says "In the critical years when all men suffer, Yakushi Nyorai at Yakuō-ji kindly gives them medicine from a lapis lazuli pot."[362]

Tonight we will stay in an inn; tomorrow morning, early, we will depart and go towards Naka County.

Before the sun had set, we arrived at the home of Mr. Kimoto and asking for accommodation, we got a place to stay. This house is not an inn, but a farmhouse.

Article 72: LEFT ALONE

This morning there was an unexpected incident. That is to say I am writing this, alone, surrounded by people I do not know.

If that's all I write, you probably won't understand. It was completely dreamlike, a dreamlike happening; I have been left behind by the old man. The old man has gone away. Here I am at the home of Kimoto Tokuzō in Toyota, Aratano Town,[363] Naka County, in the province of Awa.

I wonder what my destiny will be. Truly it is a fluctuating destiny.

Why was I left? I don't know. I only know that the old man got angry and left.

Why did he get angry? This, I don't know. Last evening, with the intention of making the old man feel better, I talked just a little about traveling alone. He is pretty robust for the age of seventy-three. In addition, because he is already used to Shikoku and has done a lot of ascetic practice, if he goes on by himself, he can travel smoothly with no hardship. My being with him is a terribly heavy burden. I have always been concerned about that.

---

for women. 61 and 70 are considered unlucky for both sexes but reaching those ages is also a cause for celebration because of the person's longevity.
361 Tsuchimikado was Emperor Gotoba's eldest son. He ascended the throne in 1199 when he was three years old and reigned for twelve years.
362 Yakuō-ji is famous throughout Japan as a temple to ward off ill fortune, especially in the "danger years".
363 Now part of Anan City.

In addition, wherever we go, people ask if he's my grandfather or my personal servant and so on, and that makes me uneasy every time. But such matters are of no consequence and the virtuous old man's getting angry was a mystery. I wondered why. I was stunned and could not say anything. And then, in the end, the old man went away.

Surprised, I gazed at his departing figure for a long time, tears streaming down my face. Perhaps they were tears not of apprehension at being left alone, but rather because of the unhappiness of the old man who had misunderstood and left in anger, and also because of the feelings of regret that were greatly affecting my heart and mind. I had intended to finish this sorrow-filled, meandering pilgrimage alone after we had had parted, tenderly, sadly, and beautifully, at Muya. But I must try to reflect deeply. How were my truthfulness and sincerity towards the old man? Let me think. I feel beautifully, deeply and eternally grateful to the utmost degree.

Now I am completely taken aback. However, I will never forget that I am existing together with Heaven. I will go! Bravely and happily.

Ah, fall has come. The air has already become crystal clear. The wind continues to blow. The insects are chirping. My heart dances! My heart dances! Oh, this intense, mad, embracing —even breathless—love of nature. I am nature's unique belovèd child. I will go! Without a plan. From the beginning my friends have been my pilgrim staff and pilgrim hat, those very things.

September 8.

Article 73: KIND PEOPLE

Another day has come. Today is September the ninth. Surrounded now by the people of this family, who are being wholeheartedly kind to me, I am continuing to live happily and peacefully. In connection with this, I wonder what has happened to the old man. I'm extremely anxious. I wonder why he got angry; it was a piteous thing. However, I won't think about it. Everything is destined. I just wish for your good fortune and health, my dear old man.

From yesterday, the people of the village have come to look at me and I have been bothered by various questions. But it has been extremely good because the people of this house have taken over and talked for me. The grandfather of the house is a smiling, good man. When people come, he introduces me very proudly. Words can't describe my embarrassment. Last night he asked me seriously, "I'd like to go with you to Kumamoto. What do you say to that? If I am going I must get my clothes ready."

In this house there is a daughter with a beautiful smile. She has been friendly to timid, silent me and kindly helped me in various ways. Last night we slept together in the same room.

I am grateful; I am totally grateful. I am grateful to people who threaten me and make me suffer and to people who love and respect and cherish me. Oh, departed old man, I do not forget my deep and sincere gratitude to you also.

I am loved by all things. Above all, nature's love for me is particularly intense. Oh, my heart leaps in the bosom of mountains full of the wine-like fragrance of trees and in the midst of sand dunes bathed by the setting sun. I will not forget the beautiful smile in even one flowering plant, in one clod of earth.

I am glad, I am happy; where else is there this kind of happiness? I am moved to tears. You dear, red-legged birds! Fly to me, and drink these white hot tears to the last drop.

Article 74: THE OLD MAN COMES

September eleventh. Before anything else, I must write that the old man has come. It was just like a comic farce but it was odd because it was really happening.

Today was the fourth day since he had left and during this period I had continued to read quietly, meditate, and stroll about. Today, I again climbed the bamboo covered hill behind the house, and when I was idly thinking about things, the daughter of the house came wide-eyed to inform me, "The old man has come!"

"Really?"

I walked there with a curiously calm heart. He said, "I am so sorry. My conscience has been bothering me and I haven't been able to sleep since then. I went to just before the twentieth temple then turned around and came back because I simply could not proceed further. I beg you to forgive me. I am frightened of divine retribution. My thinking was completely wrong."

I was moved to tears. He must surely have been exhausted, having returned from the twentieth temple.[364] I didn't think of such a thing as forgiving or not forgiving him. Smiling silently, I listened to the old man's words. He said "Let me go with you to the end. It's natural for me to carry your luggage and when you said that you felt sorry for me I thought that was unreasonable, but I didn't intend to leave you. But then you just kept quiet and watched me leave so I couldn't help going. He repeated "I'm sorry. My thinking was completely wrong."

I thought deeply. The old man is straightforward. Really, isn't part of me underhanded? To be sure, I felt deeply sorry for the old man and I also felt heartfelt gratitude. But, that is not everything. Within me there is certainly a longing. There is a nebulous but intense yearning for the pathos of a solitary journey. The future, of course, is unknown. The future is unsafe. But, certainly, under the influence of my vague but intense imagination I am poeticizing and dramatizing the fear and sorrow of this unknown-ness and its danger and am rapturously intoxicated with the rich fragrance of the dream that emanates from that.

So, though I am not rejecting the old man *per se*, somehow or other I am rejecting any person other than myself. When I gave the reasons for separating from the old man, I did not say even one word about this. Really it is selfishness; it is self-centeredness; I should be ashamed. All right, I'll go with him. I have already stopped thinking about a solitary journey. He came back over the fields and over the mountains; I have done wrong to this old man. However, let me think about it for a while. No, it is not necessary to think. I am a wandering mendicant. I should flow along at the mercy of the wind. Thereupon, we decided to stay here another two or three days and to leave after that.

---

364 A distance of about 20 kilometres with two mountains to climb en route, one 518 metres and the other, 618 metres

You strange fate of mine! You are still tepid. Come to me burning hot! Rush to me madly! My heart's desire is to throw myself into your hands. My greatest happiness will be when my tears pour down and become a flood, when my heart bleeds and turns into flames.

Article 75: A PATHETIC FIGURE

September fourteenth. My present existence is extremely peaceful. Everyone flocks around me and with infinite good will does his or her best to comfort me in my idleness. The only thing is that from time to time the jokes made by the grandfather here are painful. Because I think I should respond to his jokes somehow, I try with all my might to think of a reply but .... Everyone laughs compassionately when I just look at the floor and blush.

The life of a farming family seems quite pleasant. But I'm surprised because it doesn't bother them that the little children make terrible jokes to their parents.

In the morning as soon as they get up they eat roasted rice or boiled rice and so on and call it "tea". And then after lunch they also eat boiled rice. The evening meal is always late at night.[365]

This morning when I thought I'd go to the toilet, I saw straw bundled in strange shapes piled up on the path and I didn't know what to do, thinking it might be bad if I stepped on them. The daughter saw the situation and seemed about to burst out laughing.

Feeling uncomfortable, I turned around and asked, "What are these?" But I just couldn't grasp the point of her reply because she was laughing so hard. When I finally returned to my room, there were bursts of laughter behind me. Later, when I asked a child about the straw, he said that it was a substitute for toilet paper. I was really surprised.

A pilgrim came begging just as I was writing this manuscript. His face, feet and hands were all swollen and purple. People snickered. What a tragic sight! I could not help averting

---

[365] Most Japanese ate at most three times a day.

my eyes. Such people have what is called the accursed disease of damnation.[366] Oh, I want to say a few words to him somehow.

How well other people are able to address him:

"Where is your home country?"

"Is the accursed disease the result of your karma?"

I am envious. I wonder why I am not brave enough to say even one kind word. While I was agonizing about speaking, the opportunity passed. What a sad figure he was, trudging away falteringly.

I went down into the yard by myself. A miniature garden has been made in a box, the *higanbana*[367] are blooming, and autumn is brimming in everything. Sighing, I thought deeply.

Should it not be my life's mission to become an extremely kind and saintly companion to people who are miserable and lonely?

Article 76: FORTUNATELY OR UNFORTUNATELY?

Fortunately or unfortunately, I have come to be treated well everywhere. More than treated well, treated with reverence. I feel terrible when I write in this way.

Why in heaven's name do people in farming families glorify a person too much? They exalt me. I wonder wherein I have such value.

"Within ten years there will certainly come a time when her name will be widely known to the world. When that happens, how privileged we will be to have had the honour of her staying with us. Up until now we have had a lot of pilgrims stay, but there has never been anyone like her." This is the sort of thing the

---

366 Hansen's disease (leprosy). Takamure appears to accept the then commonly held idea of leprosy being retribution (karma) for evil deeds done in previous lives. In Japan, the Leprosy Prevention Act (1907) required that those suffering from the disease be kept in isolation . This law was not repealed until 1996. It is estimated that around 1900 there were about 30,000 people suffering from the disease in Japan. Families often hid these people or the sick went to Shikoku hoping to be cured by making the pilgrimage.
367 This is a red spider lily which blooms in the autumn during *higan*, a seven day period at the time of the autumn equinox when Japanese people visit their ancestors' graves.

old man said they told him.

The God of Boils—whenever I remember that, it's unbearable. But I must earnestly consider things. What on earth is it about me that makes people think that way? I wonder if the impertinence of my words has flaunted my strangeness. The reverence has become rather painful. Such "reverence" of people towards me can even be considered a painfully oppressive burden.

The neighbouring old lady made a big deal of me. "You can see right into people's hearts and also tell people's fortunes." If so, perhaps I can also become a fortune teller.

Briefly I thought, "They are gullible people," and shuddered for thinking this awful way. Be that as it may. I don't know. I should follow the path that is right for me.

Today I suddenly thought like this. "Religion does not consider its ultimate aim to be leading people to goodness. Its aim is to make people return to emptiness."

September seventeenth. I received a letter from the Kyūshū Nichi Nichi newspaper saying, "Since your taking the trip alone seems somewhat dangerous, you should consider carefully whether to continue the pilgrimage or return at once." I was flooded with gratitude for their advice.

Because I had written that the old man had gone away, they were certainly quite worried about me. The return of that old man on the fourth day was just like a farce. What we call fate is a mysterious thing. Somehow I feel as though I am standing outside life and nature and staring objectively at my own figure getting entangled in various strands of fate. I've had that tendency since the days when I was young. At certain times, I feel the near madness of extremely agitated emotions, but I can soon smile and objectify this as one occurrence in the great universe. For example, even supposing I were now to encounter the fate of starving to death, somehow I would be able to both smile and objectify my own emaciated, starving figure.

Recently the children of the neighbourhood have started to become friendly. With these cute children I go picking *higanbana* on a nearby hill. Before realizing it, I have been made the children's queen.

Rain is falling—I hear the typhoon the other day caused terrible damage in Kyūshū and I'm worried about that.

Article 77: NO FERRY SERVICE

September nineteenth. The whole sky was overcast and the weather looked threatening, but we set off, and almost immediately arrived at the twenty-second temple, Hakusuizan[368] Byōdō-ji. The principle image is Yakushi Nyorai; in the temple grounds there is a well that is known as the White Water Well. It is said that when Kōbō Daishi consecrated this temple he dug a well to find water for a ritual and this kind of white water gushed up. Because of that, the mountain name of the temple came to be Hakusuizan or White Water Mountain.

The temple hymn says, "Hearing that he treats us all equally and without distinction, we know the Buddha is trustworthy."[369]

We went down from there, along the foot of the mountain, and up a steep slope, passing by a lonely post town in a valley. Then, braving the rain that began to fall just as we set out again up a mountain slope, we climbed, gasping for breath, and arrived at Ryū no Iwaya, the inner sanctuary of temple twenty-one, Shashinzan Tairyū-ji. This is a famous sacred place in Shikoku, said to be a site where Daishi did ascetic practice. They say that large numbers of people still come to worship because of the remarkable benefits of the place and the holy spring that gushed forth.

A legend says, "In ancient times when Daishi was disseminating Buddhism in this area, there was a venomous dragon causing heavy damage to men and domestic animals. Because of that, using a five *shaku*[370] long sacred sword that descended from heaven, he sealed the dragon in this rocky

---

368 Mountain of the White Water.
369 This temple hymn provides a good example of the use of puns and word plays in temple hymns. It starts with the words, "Byōdōni" which means 'equally' as well as meaning 'at the Byōdō temple'. It contains a second pun: "ara tanomoshiki" literally meaning 'Oh, how reliable!' but if read as 'Aratano' it names the town where Byōdō-ji is located.
370 1 shaku=.994 feet or 30.3 cm; 5 shaku = 1 ½ meter.

cavern." The cave is said to be fifty-five *ken* long and among the places that have been given names are the Jizō cavern, the *hanegae* rock, the box rock, the *harakai* rock, Fudō Myōō, a rock with sand adhering to it, the dragon *gongen*, a dragon looking back, a rock on which to light the fire for *goma* rituals, a Jizō made by Kōbō Daishi, the *kesagake* rock, a shelf for sutras, and so on.[371] It is said there are twenty-three famous places in the cavern. Today, unfortunately, it was raining so hard that we refrained from going in because we were concerned about the tunnels becoming flooded. We just tried to peek in a little from outside but it was pitch dark and we couldn't see a thing. It was a pity because we heard that on days when there is no water, the priest guide carries a pine torch and gives a detailed explanation as he leads one through the cave.[372]

Because the rain was falling in torrents we intended to rest a little while at the hermitage here (the sanctuary of temple twenty-one) and so we sat down. A priest and a woman and some other men and women came out, and said over and over, "Even if you start to climb the mountain now, there is no place to stay as far as the crossing place at the Nakagawa River. It's early in the day, but please stay here." In addition to that, they said that because of this rain it was highly unlikely that boats would go out on the Nakagawa River. It is a river with violent floods and with the heavy rain and wind of the other day, one hamlet along the river was entirely washed away with over a hundred people and domestic animals injured and dead.

In Shikoku, rivers are fractious and troublesome. Even when slightly heavy rain falls, the ferries stop. It's virtually no better than travel in olden times. However, at dusk when a post

---

371 It is not clear what these rocks are. The *hanegae* rock may look like an upside down feather or wing; the *harakai* rock may be a rock looking like a *hara* shell but nothing could be found about a *hara* shellfish. The dragon king is a Buddhist deity that protects Buddhism. *Gongen* indicates a Shinto manifestation of a Buddha or Bosatsu. The *goma* ritual is a Shingon ritual in which various leaves and herbs are burnt. The *kesagake* rock is a rock to hang a priest's *kesa* or robe on.
372 This seems to be Jigen-ji, which is now the *oku-no-in* of temple 20, Kakurin-ji. Visitors nowadays must wriggle through the cave's narrow passageways holding a candle aloft.

town dotted with lonely, bright lights starts to be seen in the shadows of the distant mountains as I am trudging along utterly exhausted and coloured by the setting sun and dirt, I feel such sorrowful, beautiful, nostalgic pathos that I want to cry. The pathos of travel—this is the very thing for which I have longed for many years. How my heart has throbbed envisioning such things as the teahouse at the mountain pass and the forked road. This very time I have actually been able to experience those.

I wonder how many times I have heaved sighs of admiration as I shivered and trembled, my wondering eye looking at the belovèd rivers and familiar mountains, my little heart beating rapidly, my scarlet blood surging, and my eyes flooded with tears that there are no words to describe. What is more, I am wearing a pilgrim's hat, straw sandals and gaiters. An ancient journey—thinking like this, I smiled with great satisfaction.

But the stopping of the ferry is a nuisance. If it is only for a little while it will be all right, but it will be really bothersome if this rain is very heavy for two or three days and keeps us here.

Article 78: FROM TAIRYŪ-JI TO KAKURIN-JI

September twentieth. We set off early in the morning. After scrambling up a perilously steep slope and following for more than one *ri* a narrow trail which had collapsed here and there, we reached the twenty-first temple, Shashinzan Tairyū-ji. This temple, established by Kōbō Daishi in the seventeenth year of Enryaku[373] by the imperial decree of Emperor Kanmu, is one of the most eminent and famous temples in Shikoku. The principal image is Kokūzō Bosatsu and the temple hymn says, "They say that the dragon that protected Daishi when he was doing the *Gumonji-hō* at Shashin Mountain[374] is still living in the rock cavern."

---

373 The Enryaku era was from 782-806.
374 Kōbō Daishi recited the Kokuzō Gumonji-hō (Morning Star Meditation) on this mountain (in an area called Shashin ga oka) hoping to acquire a good memory so as to be able to remember all the Buddhist sutras. In this ritual, the mantra of Kokuzō Bosatsu is recited one million times. Another possible translation of this *goeika* is "Guarding us, Daishi, at Minami no Shashin, has, by Gumonji prayer, enclosed a big dragon in a cave."

The temple precinct is neat and tranquil; at times a slight breeze wafted voices chanting Buddhist sutras.

Inside the Main Hall, there is one memorial plaque.[375] It depicts a scene of two hungry wolves with their mouths open about to pounce on a nearby old man and old woman sitting erect with their hands together in prayer. And the caption said (this is the original text) "On the evening of August 27, in the second year of Taishō,[376] when we were forced to camp out on Daishi *sama*'s mountain at Tairyū-ji, the twenty-first temple, in the province of Awa in Shikoku because the sun went down in the mountains, wolves gathered at about two a.m. Because they began howling and seemed about to attack us, we began to chant the *nembutsu* eagerly; then a bright light shone and the wolves went away somewhere. In gratitude, this votive tablet is dedicated. Donors Nakamura Bennosuke, seventy-six, and his sister, Maki, sixty-six, Imamachi, Fushimi, Kyōto, painted by Nishiura Yasaburo, Kyōto." The picture and the writing were extremely unsophisticated, but indeed interesting!

When I was smiling, scrutinizing the two old people in the picture, all of a sudden there was a voice. When I turned around, it was the voice of a woman with half her facial features rotted away, shouting and crying in prayer. She said, "Buddhas of the eighty-eight temples, I beg you please to have mercy on my miserable heart. Because of my circumstances I selfishly thought I should disobey my parents and because of this stupidity of mine I was a prodigal daughter to my parents and that is frightening even to remember. I can never make up for that. There is no excuse for it, I ...."[377] As she prayed, the woman could not stop her tears from streaming down. It was unbearable looking on; I left, hiding my own overflowing tears with my sleeve.

Going down the mountain was a matter of thirty *chō*, and we arrived at the crossing point for the Nakagawa River. The

---

375 A large, framed, wooden picture placed in a temple to commemorate some event such as being rescued from a shipwreck.
376 1913.
377 Girls were often expected to help support the family by becoming a geisha or working in a textile mill. They were sold by their parents and expected to send their earnings home to the family. Perhaps this woman had run away from such a job.

water was slightly high but not so rough and we were able to get up on the opposite bank safely. With a joyful heart, I picked up my staff but, when I was about to walk off, the boatman called to the old man to stop. He said, "Isn't she the person from Kumamoto?"

"That's right."

The boatman spoke again, "Then you're the one I've heard of. I was wondering if you were but I was hesitating. Won't you come back to the other side with me today and visit my house?"

We were speechless. We politely declined and left.

The path once again became a steep slope. When we reached the top, panting and gasping, there was the twentieth temple, Reijūsan Kakurin-ji.[378] The principal image is Jizō Bosatsu. Daishi, guided by a revelation in a holy dream, climbed this mountain and while doing ascetic practice, saw a male and a female crane at the top of an old cedar tree safeguarding a golden Buddha a little over one *sun* eight *bu* in length,[379] which he could not help endlessly revering and honouring. They say he took this small image of Jizō and carved a three *shaku* high statue[380] with his own hands, and in the bosom of that statue enclosed the small Jizō and made the statue the principal image. That is where the name Crane Forest Temple comes from. The temple hymn says, "In the heavily wooded forest of the cranes there was a Jizō Guardian that Daishi took as a sign."

PILGRIMAGE POEMS BY TAKAMURE ITSUE

In the white-clouded evening,
Seeing a light
In a mountain valley,
I wonder if I am dreaming.

---

378 Kakurin, the name of the temple, means crane forest.
379 A little over two and a half centimetres.
380 About five and a half metres.

When I pick up stones
With a young child on the rocky shore,
The setting sun
Crimsons our backs.

My face in the mirror looks beautiful
As though I were in a dream;
I enjoy making up my face
In the autumn morning.

I became so absorbed in thought
As I journeyed on the mountain path
That I didn't realize it
When the sound of the noon bell ended.

This fine morning,
I so liked the smell
Of my bed-tousled hair
That I played the flute.

In an unknown village on my travel route,
Children are running around
Forlornly at dusk
As in a dream.

Having silently extinguished the light,
I went out of the moonlit bedroom
And prayed
For a while.

Not knowing how
To relieve loneliness,
I comb down my hair
With a boxwood comb.

I was so miserable
Waking from a nightmare
That I didn't even sing a song
In the gray of the morning.

Surrounded by Mother Nature,
Why on earth do they adorn themselves
With fancy clothes or make merry
By singing songs?

When their sad dance
On the evening field ends,
I wonder
If they will vanish.

Although they are ridiculous,
You should not laugh at the group of people,
Dancing like that,
Dyed by the setting sun.

Wrapped in rose coloured waves
Sadly and dreamily
By the windswept seashore
I think of someone.

I think of the quiet woods
Where I felt sleepy
In my white-clouded sacred hometown
In the west.

Article 79: ONE NIGHT IN A BARN

When we came down the mountain from Kakurin-ji, we thought it seemed late and we were very tired, so we asked people of the village for a place to stay and were told that just over there was a *zenkonyado*, a place of free lodging for pilgrims.

Pushing our way through a grassy path covered with *higanbana,* we visited a certain farm family. There, an old man who looked kind lowered his voice and said, "Recently the police have become strict and we are harassed by being detained and fined small amounts even though the lodging that we give is free. I'm sorry, but is the barn good enough?"

When he spoke like that, the old man replied "Yes, certainly, it's fine." We were immediately guided to the place and were surprised. The room was pretty spacious but the stable adjoined it, and a certain type of stench powerfully assailed the nose.

Moreover, loosely woven straw mats had been spread on top of the rough wooden floor as a substitute for *tatami* mats and even a short time of sitting on my knees made my legs unbearably sore. If that had been all, it might not have mattered but in one corner old and new straw had been left piled up, totally mixed together, and, in addition to this, various tools covered with dust had been thrown in, making this place cramped. Even the old man hesitated, saying, "It's a poor place," but there was nothing we could do.

When we washed our feet and went up into the room, the old man lay down and I sat in the *seiza*[381] position and thought vaguely about things.

From time to time the children of the neighbourhood came and peeked in, but no longer did this make me lose my calmness of mind. I opened the door to the east and looked up at the sky serenely, listened to the noises of the insects, and was able to smile happily and humbly.

Nevertheless, the night is really lonely. The old man is soundly sleeping, and there is not a single person who is awake. Only the horse and I are awake.

From time to time, the horse makes whinnying sounds with its nose and lonely sounds with its hooves.

I open the door and bathing my whole body in the moonlight which is as bright as day, I sit upright in the *seiza* position on the painful mat. I wonder why I cannot sleep. It is unbearably distressing but there is nothing I can do about it.

The fact that the horse was awake made me feel better. I wrote some poems and ended up forgetting about my loneliness.

---

381 The traditional Japanese way of sitting in a kneeling position.

> Sad and awake late at night
> The horse and I.
> Don't cry horse,
> I am here with you.
>
> You should not cry, horse,
> Because I too am awake.
> Think of me as your master,
> Belovèd horse.

As a matter of fact, writing such things, I began to feel like crying.

While I was wondering why I couldn't sleep, my dear companion seemed to have fallen into a happy dream. There was not a sound. Ah, have I become the only thing in the world that is awake?

> I detest all creatures that are sleeping.
> Because I am sad,
> I really want to shake them awake
> And cry my heart out.
>
> Something making a sound
> Is coming towards me.
> Is it a mouse
> Or the wind rattling?

The horse was asleep and the moon was setting. I also wanted to sleep peacefully and prayed silently to Kannon *sama*, "Please let me sleep," but it did no good. In the end, I stayed up all night.

Article 80: A SHIKOKU BARRIER TEMPLE

September 21. We left before dawn, and approached temple nineteen, Manisan Tatsue-ji[382]. When you cross the well-

---

[382] The temple's name is Kyōchisan Tatsue-ji and Mani-in is its local name.

known Kokonotsu Bridge, you can soon see the large, extensive temple. This temple is designated as a checkpoint or testing place[383] among the Shikoku pilgrimage temples and from olden times has been a temple abounding in miracles.

I will try to introduce this temple a little according to what one pamphlet entitled *The Miracles of Tatsue-ji* said. Because of the Imperial order of Emperor Shōmu, the forty-fifth Emperor,[384] Gyōki Bosatsu founded this temple in the Tempyō period[385] as a place of prayer for the peace of the country and the health of the Emperor. By imperial order, Gyōki made a five centimetre tall image of Jizō from *embu dangon*[386] gold as a plea for the safe delivery of Empress Kōmyō.[387] This is well known as a Jizō for the safe delivery of children. Later, at the time he was establishing the Shikoku temples, Kōbō Daishi himself, while doing ascetic practice at Tatsue-ji, carved a large, two-meter high statue there and, secretly placing the small golden Jizō in the bosom of this big statue, made Tatsue-ji the nineteenth temple of Shikoku.

The temple was originally at a beautiful place at the foot of Shimizu Ōkoku Mountain, about three *chō* west of its present site. Even though it was a huge temple with the seven traditional buildings of a *shichidō garan*,[388] it was completely burnt in the

---

Each temple traditionally has three names: the name of a mountain significant in Buddhism, a name with religious significance, and a local name. Mani is the local name.
383 This temple is the first of the four temples in Shikoku where evil-minded people are subject to the scrutiny of the Buddha and Kōbō Daishi. If a pilgrim can move on without difficulty, he has passed the test, but if some trouble occurs, he has failed. He should then go back to where he began his pilgrimage and begin the pilgrimage once again. Pilgrims often feel apprehensive when they approach a barrier temple.
384 724-749.
385 749-758.
386 An imaginary type of gold which, according to Buddhist scripture was the most precious metal. It was believed to come from the bed of a river flowing through a forest of *enbu* trees, which are imaginary trees.
387 Wife of Emperor Shōmu.
388 The seven buildings are the hondō, kōdō, tō, shōro, kyōzō, sōbō, jikidō, or the main hall, lecture hall, pagoda, bell tower, scripture house, priest's residence, and refectory.

Tenshō period[389] by the forces of the Chōsokabe. Because of his deep religious faith Lord Hō-an, the founding head of the old Hachisuka clan of Tokushima, kindly had the temple moved and established in its present place. Although all of the buildings have not yet been reconstructed to their former condition, the temple precinct is spacious, and has magnificent buildings: the Niō Gate,[390] corridor, main hall, Daishi hall, bell tower, guest house, the residence of the head priest, kitchen, and so on. In particular, the recently repaired inner sanctuary of the main hall is remarkably grand and beautiful.

Among the notable miracles, there are two that everyone talks about: one is the origin of the white heron of the Kokonotsu Bridge and one is the hair with the scalp attached caught up in the bell rope.

The Origin of the White Heron of the Kokonotsu Bridge

The Kokonotsu Bridge, situated in Tatsue town in front of the town hall on the road to Tosa, has a deep connection with the history of Tatsue-ji. It is said that when Kōbō Daishi was here doing ascetic practice, a white heron came flying from somewhere and flew away holding in its wings the little image of Jizō Bosatsu made by Gyōki Bosatsu on the order of Emperor Shōmu. When Daishi straightaway followed its trail, the white heron came and placed the image in the area of the Kokonotsu Bridge and flew away. Because of this good omen, Daishi built the temple of Tatsue-ji and carved a new, two-metre Jizō image extremely reverently, and placed the small image as a hidden image in the bosom of the Jizō. Because of Kōbō Daishi's deep meaning, the Kokonotsu Bridge symbolizes the nine realms,[391] so those who have committed many evil acts over an extended period or been guilty of erroneous thoughts become dizzy, their legs refuse to move forward, and they cannot take even one step

---

389 1573-1586.
390 A temple gate with statues of the two guardian Niō deities, one on the right side and the other on the left.
391 The three worlds of Buddhist belief are further divided into nine realms. The desire-world has one realm; the form-world has four realms; the formless-world has four realms.

across the bridge.³⁹² At that time they say that a white heron is always seen standing quietly on the bridge. They say this is a sign that a person has done bad things. Is the fact that we were fortunately able to avoid that difficulty enough to certify us as good people?

The Origin of the Scalp and Hair on the Bell Rope

In Kyōwa 3,³⁹³ at Tōrimachi 2 chōme in the castle town of Hamada in Iwami Province (now Shimane Prefecture) there was a person called Sakuraya Ginbe. He had three daughters and sold the middle one of them, Okyō, to be a geisha in a geisha house in Hiroshima in Aki Province (now Hiroshima Prefecture) when she was eleven years old. When she was sixteen her workplace was changed to Shinmachi in Ōsaka and while she was working there she became the wife of a man named Yōsuke and for a while they lived together. However, she incurred Yōsuke's rage because of her adultery with a person called Chōzō and one day the two of them were severely beaten. Therefore, the two of them, having a grudge against Yōsuke, conspired together and murdered him. Then, hidden by the darkness of the night, they ran away and crossed over to Marugame in Sanuki.³⁹⁴ Even though they wanted to commit suicide together they did not; then they planned to make the Shikoku pilgrimage and continued on to Tatsue-ji. What was terrible about the divine punishment for adultery was that the black hair of Okyō all of a sudden stood up and curled up around the rope of the bell. Then, Chōzō really panicked and quickly called the head priest of the temple for help. The head priest questioned them severely about their sin and made them confess honestly. When the priest made them confess, to their wonder Okyō's scalp peeled off together with her hair and remained on the bell rope. It is said she barely escaped with her life.

After that, Okyō repented of her great sin and became an honest person and lived for a long time together with Chōzō in a

---

392 Tatsue-ji is one of the five spiritual checkpoints of the Shikoku pilgrimage.
393 1803
394 Now Kagawa Prefecture, one of the four prefectures on Shikoku.

place called Tanaka Mountain in the town of Tatsue. They finished their remaining years praying wholeheartedly to Jizō and it is said that this bell pull, with the hair and scalp attached, is even now treasured in the Main Hall of Tatsue-ji, but cannot be seen.[395]

  Other than these, there are numerous and various legends about the temple that I will set forth at some appropriate time in the future but will not touch upon here.

---

395 This tale has several differences from the legend as it is presently told. According to the present legend, Okyō became a nun and spent the rest of her life in prayer. Chōzō also renounced the world and spent the rest of his life working at the temple. The bell rope is displayed in a small house beside the Daishi Hall.

Section 3: Along the Inland Sea

Article 81: AT THE INLAND SEA FOR THE FIRST TIME

September 28. Writing that, I was surprised. All this while, what have I been doing? I think it has been like a dream but, also, not like a dream. From morning until evening I have been continuously walking, moving at full speed from the eighteenth temple to the first temple[396] and during this time, I passed in total safety along the mountain path of the famous temple, Shōsan-ji.[397]

Now I have already entered the province of Sanuki.[398] My heart is full of things to write about but I don't know where to start and cannot write a thing. Even though I am suffering unbearably as though I were somehow or other heavily in debt, I can't help myself.

Every day when we arrived at our lodgings, I always picked up my pen, but I was suffering from such extremely intense and tempestuous emotions that I couldn't do anything; fatigue and exhaustion wrapped around my body like evening clouds and I usually collapsed limply as though I were seriously ill. Every day without fail we walked an average of seven or eight *ri*. Around here they generally count fifty *chō* to one *ri*,[399] so although the distance we covered may seem short, it was long. But, because I was walking along thinking about various things, my eyes sparkling, fantasizing as colourfully as a peacock's tail, I didn't feel so terribly tired and, in particular, these last four or five days have seemed like only an instant because I have been engulfed in such intense, acute, painful emotions, emotions that do not let up for a moment. My mind has been so tense that I could not even react to what I saw and what I heard, and an intoxicating brew of insane feelings has been rising from my

---

396 A distance of about 110 km.
397 The twelfth temple, Shōsan-ji is considered a *nansho*, or difficult temple because it is at the top of a mountain, 800 meters above sea level.
398 present day Kagawa.
399 At this time there were different ways of measuring distance. One *chō* is approximately 109 meters. Thus, she walked an average of 38 to 43.6 km. Per day. (Counting 36 *chō* to a *ri*, the distance walked would have been 27.5 to 31.4 km.) These are all long distances in the heat and humidity of the Japanese summer.

heart's wellspring and overflowing. Of course, I don't know what the cause is.

It's just that my hometown is overwhelmingly dear and the people living there are dear; I love them, I love them wholeheartedly. But, these feelings have given rise to various convoluted waves which assail me, advancing and retreating. I have become a great deal thinner and I am so troubled by thoughts that seem to have bewitched me that my tears and breath almost choke up. Nowadays somehow it seems as though my heart is on the verge of madness. No, I bless my heart. I delight in these frenzied emotions. They are like glad tidings sent from heaven. Look! My present existence is soaked, and saturated with drops of the rich, sweet juice of poetry. Today, I am standing on this peak and have chanced to encounter one part of the Seto Inland Sea, the focal point of many years of longing. From the time that the island of Awaji was first visible, my eyes saw more clearly and I began to feel a mysterious calmness as if my heart had slipped forth from a thin silk veil.

I am glad! Calling myself glad does not express my emotions adequately. How can I describe my mind that is poised to penetrate attentively, calmly, and completely clearly this beautiful scene bit by bit, starting from its smallest elements, its minimal, infinitesimal molecules and its compound elements. None the less, the pine trees are green, the sand white, the sea deep blue, the sky sapphire, the clouds are flying, the sun gradually slanting, the birds singing and the trees sparse. Except for those words, I cannot think of any other finer expressions. In front of this superb view, I will just lower my head, close my eyes, and pray silently and sincerely.

The wind has begun to blow a little.

Article 82: YASHIMA HAS BEEN SIGHTED!

September 30. Yesterday, leaving a place called Hiketa early in the morning, we went up and down ever so many foggy mountain slopes in light rain and arrived at temple eighty-eight, Iōzan Ōkubo-ji, probably at about five in the afternoon. When the gray, scab-like clouds began to break apart a little, the rain stopped. When we passed through the temple gate it was so lonely. Even though I listened intently, there was scarcely a sound.

We came down the mountain and ventured into an inn at the foot of the stone steps. There were five people staying there, from Kyōto and Fukuoka, Ōita and Kumamoto; the talk was lively and finally pilgrim songs and hymns began to be chanted. They said that if one does not beg at more than seven houses in one day, it violates the teachings of Kōbō Daishi; there was general agreement about this and the old man was very deeply moved. Furthermore, the old man had already choked up again and again with tears of gratitude because his *fuda* bag had arrived here safely stuck somewhere on his back, although he had forgotten to put it in his baggage today. He was was quite overcome.

Thus, one night passed. When we left early in the morning, it was still raining. We kept walking along valley paths and hill trails going, as usual, over four and a half *ri*, and reached the eighty-seventh temple, Fudarakuzan Nagao-ji. After visiting the temple we rested for a while and then walked. In an instant, nearby to the north, we could see two strangely shaped mountains. One peak was steeply craggy and soared beyond the clouds; one lay low and flat and table shaped.

When we went into a house beside the path and asked, we were told that the high one was Mount Yakuri and the low one was Mount Yashima.

"Is that Yashima?" As you might expect, I gazed at it intently, my heart dancing.[400]

Ah, Yashima—tomorrow we will climb to the top of that mountain.

Article 83: YAKURI AND YASHIMA

October 1. Rain is still falling. However, I can't help feeling joyful when I think that today we will climb the two strangely shaped mountains that we can see in front of us.

---

400 In 1185 during the Genpei War, Yashima was the site of many battles between the armies of the Minamoto and Taira families.

Because the rain began to let up a bit, I took off the rain gear I had wrapped around me and held it, together with my staff, in my right hand. My only other luggage was a small bag that hung from my left shoulder to my right side. Because I was travelling light like this, I was unusually lively as I walked along.

> I am a water reed
> Blown by the wind,
> Flowing, flowing nowhere.
> In the daytime I travel,
> At night—at night I dance
> In the end I perish
> God knows where …..

Singing this, I felt like crying. However, those would not have been tears of sadness.

When I happened to raise my eyes, I found that, without my noticing it, we had reached the foot of the very steep, towering mountain where Gokenzan Yakuri-ji[401] is. I retied my *waraji* sandals and climbed. The path was wide but walking in the mud was indescribably difficult because rain was falling. In addition, it was uphill. When I took a step I slipped, and when I took the next step, it seemed that I'd fall. Persevering with great difficulty we struggled almost to the peak and from that point on it was all right. Resting for a while, we had a bird's eye view of mountains, rivers, plains, villages, hamlets, and forests.

How delightful! How magnificent! The panoramic view, having been made hazy by the light rain, had natural gradations of light and shade. It was just like a floating island in a dream. Was the dark part, mountains, the light part, the sea? At times, white clouds welled up, and here and there they filled the gorges; dissolving, they became fog, became rain, became haze, and vanished. Even though everything was tranquil, it was the coming together of the individual actions of the swirling clouds, gushing rain, and raging river that made the whole seem calm. Viewed from a broad prospective, it was deserted but if a small part were viewed closely, it was dizzyingly active. How

---

[401] Temple eighty-five.

mysterious!

For some time I was stunned and entranced, and then, being urged on, I walked again. Finally we reached the temple. The architecture is really splendid. It is said that the temple name, "Eight chestnuts"[402] comes from a legend about the sprouting of eight roasted chestnuts that had been buried by Kōbō Daishi.

Going down was much easier than climbing up but the view seemed greatly inferior. However, I enjoyed the way my feet slipped and I slid to the foot of the mountain in an instant. From there, the so-called Table Mountain of Yashima was very close and seemed to be within hand's reach.

We threaded our way through human habitations, passed salt fields[403] and in the twinkling of an eye came to the mountain. En route there were places of historic interest: the tomb of Kikuōmaru, the tomb of Satō Tsugunobu,[404] and the temporary residence of Emperor Antoku.[405] Even while I was scrambling up the steep slope, the Genpei battle appeared entrancingly in my mind like a scroll painting, vanished and appeared again. The folding fan that was the target of Nasuno Yoichi,[406] and so on—how artistic the scenes were.

It was heartbreaking to think of the sad and beautiful lives

---

402 Yakuri means "eight chestnuts".
403 At this time Japanese harvested salt from the sea by first partially evaporating seawater in salt fields in areas near the sea. Before WWII seawater was the principal source of salt.
404 Kikuōmaru and Tsugunobu both died at Yashima during the Genpei war. Kikuōmaru was the servant of Noritsune of the Heike. He tried to cut off the head of Satō Tsugunobu of the Genji after Satō, when he was guarding Yoshitsune, pitched from his horse mortally wounded by an arrow. Seeing Kikuō attacking the body, Tsuginobu's brother, Tadanobu, sent an arrow into his back, which killed him. Kikuō was eighteen at the time. Tsuginobu and Tadanobu both died.
405 Emperor Antoku was the eight year old emperor, grandson of the leader of the Heiki, and drowned when his grandmother clasped him in her arms and leapt into the sea off the coast of Yashima.
406 Nasu no Yoichi fought for the Genji. At the Battle of Yashima in 1185, at the end of a day's fighting, a woman of the Taira tied a fan to the mast of a small boat and seemed to be challenging the Genji to shoot it down. Nasu no Yoichi, a young warrier, shot an arrow a great distance and succeeded with his first shot. Both sides applauded. This is one of the famous stories of the Genpei war.

of the many, many people who, like falling cherry blossom petals, had sunk and vanished in the sea, when it was reddened by the setting sun. Since then many days, months and eras have flowed from infinity to infinity; people are born and die.

Without my being aware of it, we had arrived at the temple.[407] It is a noteworthy temple, not inferior to Yakuri. We worshipped and prayed silently for several hours then went down. At a teahouse at the foot of the mountain, *genpei mochi*[408] were recommended and when we were resting for a little while, the rain completely stopped. I wonder how far we will go today. (Written at the tea house)

Article 84: A *KICHINYADO*

After Yashima, we went more than one *ri* and when we asked for Takamatsu,[409] a man walking on the road pointed west and said, "One *ri*".

Again we went on and asked. Again we were told "One *ri*". I was utterly exhausted. Today also it is very late. Where we came from and where we are going is an endless road—only mountains and rivers and the setting sun. Where are the mountains of my home? Like a wind-blown plant I am a forlorn traveller, suffering as I drift. Now the moon is overhead ....

A bell tolled—it seemed to die away—to vanish. The setting sun was already flowing like oil; stalks of grass and clods of earth were blood red on one side and, on the other, as bluish-black as a graveyard at night. All of a sudden there was a *kichinyado* beside the path.

Being invited, "Please stay here," we came back to life and entered a room in which a sooty lantern was waiting for us.

For a moment I didn't notice but when I looked carefully, there were narrow stairs going up to the attic from a dark corner where the light did not reach; I sensed signs of life up there. Feeling forlorn and tearful, I sat with my eyes cast down for a

---

407 Temple eighty-four, Nanmenzan Yashima-ji.
408 A sweet made of pounded rice.
409 Takamatsu is the largest city in Kagawa Prefecture and the capital of the prefecture.

while, then dinner came on two low flat tables and a dirty old *hibachi* made of wood.[410] There was a sloppy mixture of boiled food served on flat plates on the tables, and hot water was bubbling in a rather big earthen teapot set over the dying embers of a fire in the *hibachi*.

It was as melancholy and gloomy a scene as one would find in a Russian novel: the low ceiling, the lantern burning slowly, the densely rising steam and, in the midst of this, the silhouette of the pitiful old man eating something …. "If an overpowering, intense smell of vodka and the stench of smoked meat were added, and a pudgy old lady with a crooked pointed nose was waiting on us …."

While I was indulging in various fantasies like that, the aforementioned stairs made a creaking sound. I wondered who it was and when I looked furtively, a woman in her forties, was coming down, wearing a blackish *haori*[411] on top of her unlined, beige, flannel kimono. Her face was dark but her hair was freshly done up in the *marumage* style[412] with gaudy ribbons wound in it. She nodded briefly to us then went down to the earthen-floored entrance,[413] and after finding her *geta*,[414] went out.

Before long an employee of the inn brought our bedding[415] (surprisingly, this was clean) so I soon lay down, but I was wakeful and could not sleep. When it was late—maybe as much

---

410 A *hibachi* was a wooden table-like piece of furniture originally used to provide heat and boil water for tea. It had a copper ash receptacle where the tea kettle sat on a metal trivet over a charcoal fire.
411 A *haori* jacket is worn over a kimono and is held closed by a braided cord tied in a decorative knot.
412 The *marumage* style had a roll of waxed hair over the forehead and a big lump of waxed hair on top of the head. It was decorated with colorful pins and tassels. It was the most common style for married women. There is a strange contrast between the woman's dark clothes and unpainted face and her colorful hair style.
413 At the entrance to old Japanese houses was a dirt-floored room. People then took off their outside shoes and stepped up into the main part of the house where the floors were covered with tatami mats.
414 *Geta* are traditional Japanese wooden clog sandals with cloth thongs attached in the center. They were worn outdoors.
415 Japanese traditionally sleep on thin mattresses (*futon*) spread on the floor at night and stored in cupboards during the day.

as one or two hours had passed—I heard the sliding doors in the entrance rattle and open. I wondered what was happening and when I opened my eyes wide and looked, it was the woman of a while ago coming back with another person, a man of about fifty dressed in white. His appearance was strange. He had a white cloth headband wrapped around his forehead, and when I looked closely, he was wearing *hakama*.[416]

As he went up the stairs he glanced weakly in my direction with a tired looking, pallid face. While I was thinking that there are various ways to make a living in the world, I started thinking, as usual, about "death" and felt a morbid shuddering and, no matter how hard I tried, I couldn't sleep. Everyone has proceeded to death.

Leaving behind writings about various things, boys, young men, and beautiful women have all died. Time passes and people no longer exist; now, in the places of long ago where songs and dances were performed, we see only small birds and sparrows singing sorrowfully in the twilight.

The evening became late. I couldn't sleep, so I got up and was writing but I've decided to put down my pen because my eyes are a little tired.

Article 85: ALONE AT AN INN

October sixth. Today, we visited the seventy-first temple, Kengozan Iyadani-ji. That was probably at about three-thirty or four o'clock in the afternoon. After we had finished worshipping, the old man went to the temple office and I went again to the main hall. Then, enveloped in a lonely, sorrowful, sort of a reverent frame of mind, I worshipped the numerous Buddhist figures carved all over a cliff. Surprised to find that quite a bit of time had passed, I went to see the old man, but he had already left. Perhaps he thought that I had left just a bit ahead of him.

Hurrying, I went down to in front of the main gate where

---

416 The man's white clothes are strange. He is not a pilgrim as pilgrims do not wear *hakama*. In *Ohenro* p.176 Takamure says that the man was dressed like a Shintō priest and wearing an Eboshi hat, a tall black hat. She also states that he is the woman's husband.

there was one inn but the door was tightly shut and it seemed that no one was there. Then, right next to it, there was a small dark hut and because there were two or three pieces of washing hanging on a pole in front of the entrance, it seemed likely that people were there although I couldn't see what it was like inside.

For a while I hesitated, but then I mustered my courage and called out, "Is anybody there?" but there was no reply. When I timidly peeked in, I saw there was an old lady by herself, looking very decrepit, physically and mentally, working intently on some kind of cloth. Then I asked, "Perhaps an old man has passed by here? When was that?" but she seemed to be hard of hearing and didn't appear to understand. However, finally, she seemed to be able to discern me with her dim, lifeless eyes that looked as though they were glistening with tears, and after she had gazed at me, she listened as I repeated my question and, nodding toward my voice, she said, "Yes, the old man has passed on. I live alone. I am living with the Buddha this way." She barely spoke and when she did, her voice was extremely weak and quivered abnormally, so that she was very difficult to understand unless one paid close attention.

After that, she told me that she was eighty-six and that she had a son but he was a priest, and that in her old age she was spending a miserable time with no pleasure. I couldn't help feeling sad and deeply sorry for her. The old woman repeatedly tried to cut the cloth with scissors. However, watching, I saw that she couldn't cut it at all. When I looked closely, she was trying to cut the sleeves of an unlined kimono. It seemed that she was cutting off the end of the sleeves because they were too long,

I threaded the needle for her because she asked, "Excuse me but will you please thread the needle for me." Then, since I thought sewing was very difficult for her with her poor eyes, I told her to pass the work to me and borrowing her needle and scissors, I sewed it for her, crudely I must say.

Tearfully, the old woman fumblingly stroked the curved part of a sleeve and said over and over again, "Thank you so much, I am so grateful; it is very difficult for a person with bad eyes to do this part. Thank you very much." She repeated her thanks so many times that I blushed. In addition, I felt unbearably awkward because I had to speak in a loud voice when talking to this old lady.

While I was doing such things, it got still later. When I hurriedly tried to stand up, the old lady searched for something and taking my hand, she placed some objects in it. When I looked, they were coins. "No, I can't take them."

Becoming more and more uncomfortable, I tried to flee but she said, "Please listen to me; please accept these because they are the humble offerings of an old woman to Daishi *sama*. Please." Because she spoke so earnestly, I had to take them. One *rin*[417] coins together with five *rin* coins making all together, six or seven coins—how considerate the dear old lady was.

I went down the mountain, my heart buffeted by indescribable sorrow. Sighing and with tears spilling down, I walked despondently. I completely forgot about the old man and only felt deep sorrow in my heart concerning the loneliness of human beings.

Article 86: ALONE AT AN INN

For a little while, crying without realizing it, I walked pensively, thinking of the dear, tender hearted old lady, but all at once I thought of the old man and looked around the neighbourhood in amazement.

There was no one, just quiet rain continuing to fall. I suddenly became desperate and ran down to the foot of the mountain. When I called at a house just beside the road to make inquiries, I was told that he had passed by as much as forty or fifty minutes earlier. I thought, "Then, he's safe," and my mind was at last set at ease.

Then I inquired along the road again and again and received various replies such "an hour ago" and "just now". Not relying much on this information, I walked on for a long, long time in my torn, ragged *waraji* sandals, without changing them. Then, three people coming together from the other direction asked me "Pilgrim, haven't you become separated from your companion?" I said "Yes, I have."

---

417 One rin is one tenth of a sen.

They said, "Well, that companion asked us to please pass this on if you came along after him: he will be staying at an inn at the post station about five *chō* ahead." When I heard the message, I walked light heartedly in that direction.

When I arrived there after a short while, it was already dusk and in each house bright lamps had been lit, and people sitting at low tables appeared to be eating happily. In their midst, my despondent, soaking wet figure ….

There were two or three inns but when I asked at the first one, they said to me, "I guess it's that old man. He hurried ahead as fast as he could because he said that you were surely ahead of him. Yes, he asked for a room but I didn't give him one for certain reasons, although, if I'd known that you were with him, I'd have given him one. Anyway, because it is still one *ri* to the next post station, there's no use trying to go there. Take my advice—you'd better stay here tonight."

"Where has the old man got to in this rain—I'm worried. But, with my weak legs, I can't walk any longer. But shall I stay here? But the old man …." I considered what to do several times and sighed several times and finally made the decision to spend the night here.

When I washed my feet and went up into the house, everyone treated me with unlimited hospitality. "You poor thing, the rain has really drenched you. Please put this on." "You must be starving. Please eat something warm right away." I just sat there completely surprised and even forgot to say thank you.

When I had finished the meal, I was taken up to a large room on the second floor and they immediately put out my bedding for me. But when I took out my pen, they hung a lamp down low and brought out a desk for me. I was feeling somewhat at ease and at the same time unbearably tired, but I forced myself, and wrote the previous manuscript.[418] Then I went straight to bed and fell sound asleep, and I don't remember a thing until towards dawn.

When I woke up, the women at the inn were already working below and ladled water for me to wash my face and brought me tea.

---

418 Article 85

When I had eaten breakfast I immediately departed and again wondered about the old man. Then, as I was hurrying along the road, someone said from a house, "Pilgrim, the old man is waiting!" Before the words had ended, the old man came flying out surprised and delighted, and said "I'm sure you've probably been worried, I also was unable to sleep all night. Oh, I'm glad that you've come. You must have been cold. Oh, those straw sandals." He made a big fuss.

Me too–somehow or other tears streamed from my eyes and I couldn't say a thing.

Article 87: A DISGRACEFUL SCENE

October 14. This morning at daybreak we set out from the vicinity of Imabari, visited three pilgrimage temples and came to the highroad to Matsuyama. When I think that within four or five days I will have finally finished the eighty-eight pilgrimage temples, I can't help but be really, really glad.

We went through the seaside town called Kikuma[419] and continued walking for a long time along the shore beneath the cliffs. The old man[420] went from door to door and asked for free lodging at each house.

Covered with dust, I am walking along a road that is dyed blood red by the setting sun. What a traveller-like scene this is!

The sun set a little more. As for the old man's dealings, even though he'd walked and visited scores of houses, it seemed that all had refused. In despair, his face as white as a sheet, the old man said, "It's no use. We'll go to an inn," and went straight into the small post town ahead.

"It's no good! We can't stay." I wasn't surprised—I'd had a premonition it might be like that today. And so, after walking and begging at this village and that hamlet we finally came to stay at a house but there was just one room and the surprising thing was that there were no *tatami* mats or anything in it. We had to eat our meals and sleep on loosely woven straw

---

419 approximately 17 km from Imabari
420 She is now referring to the old man by the more respectful "sama", whereas before she used "san".

matting.

This I didn't mind, but how heartbroken I felt about everyone's loud voice and the snapping and shrieking between parents and children and between husband and wife and the old man's resulting short temper and anger, as he negotiated about various things and tried to cook dinner in the midst of the commotion. I sat pensively, worrying nervously, and concealed the surprise, sadness and anxiety that filled my heart. Beneath a lantern, the dirty-faced, pitiful children surrounded the old man, who was dishing out rice from a pot into a pail-like object, and they said, "Pilgrim, please give us some rice." When they did this, the woman of the house, pulled her hair and swore at them abusively. What was even worse was the wife's insolence towards her husband: her attitude was enshrouded in ignorance, lack of refinement, lack of restraint, and self-indulgence.

I shuddered because I felt that this time, this very time, the ugly side of women had been demonstrated to the full. I had formerly read several of the works of Strindberg and at times had harboured a certain animosity towards his intense hatred of women but the journey this time has shown me the ugly side of women; I couldn't help sighing deeply and being astonished.

Oh disgraceful one! Thy name is woman.[421]

Article 88: THE GRAFFITI HALL

We escaped from that disgraceful house and I walked to my heart's content along narrow paths through the fields, parting bush clover (*hagi*) flowers and asters and other various pretty autumn flowers as I walked. It was probably about five o'clock in the afternoon when we reached the town of Dōgo Onsen.

When we inquired at one traveler's inn, they said, "We don't allow pilgrims to stay." That was that, so we ended up being forced to stay in a dirty inn again.

The next morning, when I was changing my clothes, there were whispering voices behind me. When I casually turned

---

421 This echoes 'Frailty, thy name is woman!' which Hamlet says in the middle of his first soliloquy, as he is expressing his disgust at the speed with which his mother married again after the death of his father.

around, I was surprised. One person of about fourteen or fifteen with her receding hair arranged in the *momoware*[422] style had stuck faded artificial flowers in it in a ridiculous way. If that had been all, it would have been fine but she appeared to have gotten up just now and was wearing a single ripped *juban* that exposed her skin.[423] The other person was an old woman of about fifty, with scissored hair, who looked like the ghost of a nun. With complete absorption they stared boldly at my every action . Somehow I felt dazzled by them, so I organized my luggage with my back turned toward them. While I was doing that, the old woman went away somewhere but the young girl never left. Just then, the old man returned from washing his face and when he asked her, "Where do you come from?" She said, "Hiroshima Prefecture."

"Who did you come with?"
"I didn't come with anyone."
"Your father?"
"Everyone's dead."
"What kind of work are you doing now?"
"I'm not doing anything. I'm with that old lady."

When I turned around again and took a good look, she certainly seemed like a child of low intelligence but she didn't seem imbecilic. In addition, the thing that really surprised me was that although she had the face of a child, her body was extraordinarily developed. For example, it is blunt but the large size of her breasts somehow filled me with a feeling of pity and I did not dare to turn around and look at her any more.

Quickly we made our preparations and as we left this place, the dazed eyes of the child stared at us.

"Goodbye," I said weakly and parted from her. When we were out of the town, in an instant we arrived at the fifty-first temple Kumanozan Ishite-ji.[424]

---

422 A hair style in which the hair is rolled back from the face and has flowers in it. Traditionally it was the style worn by geisha after they had lost their virginity. *Momoware* means split peach.
423 The *juban* is like an undershirt and is worn under a kimono next to the skin.
424 Kumanozan Ishite-ji. The name of the temple, 'Stone-hand temple' comes from the legend of Emon Saburo, the legendary first pilgrim, (see Article 46)

I finished worshipping and when I happened to go around to the back of one building, I saw that graffiti had been written all over the wall. We often saw this at other temples and I didn't think it was particularly unusual, but suddenly my attention was caught and when I looked, I saw these lines just as I give them here.

"On a long spring day I took a stroll looking around at the Graffiti Hall."

"The evening cicada! At the Graffiti Hall the sun is setting with slanting beams."

I thought they were interesting and when I went on reading, this time in childish handwriting it said, "Dear newspaper reporter, Water Plant![425] It is really ridiculous that you quoted the graffiti of this temple in the precious space of your newspaper and titled the article, 'Graffiti Hall'."

With that I understood. It seemed as though something had been written in a newspaper in Matsuyama or somewhere else. Out of curiosity I continued to read and while doing so, I saw in many places handwriting that appeared to be that of young women and scrawled lines about various and sundry things.

"Having read Water Plant's article about the Graffiti Hall, I came here especially to see it. After a fall typhoon, the sound of water is refreshing."

"Dear Water Plant. Please be in good health. I sincerely hope that you will publish your Water Plant writings in the near future."

"The spring sun is shining warmly and the plum blossoms are falling soundlessly. Please think of this young person, relying only on her staff, going on a pilgrimage from one temple to another for the sake of her sick mother."

In addition to these, there were still many other graffiti but almost all the others were only extremely commonplace, full of so and so visited here on such and such a date.

---

who is said to have been reborn near this temple with a stone in his tightly curled fist which said "Emon Saburo reborn".

425 Water plant, (水草—mizukusa) also has a metaphorical meaning of floating, uprooted, or nomad. For example, Takamure uses it that way in Article 83.

Article 89: A NEW *ISOBUSHI*[426] SONG

Since first taking an interest in graffiti at Ishite-ji,[427] I have looked for other graffiti while walking to temples fifty and forty-nine,[428] one after the other. There were such lines as these:

"Before dawn in early autumn 1918, troubled with gloomy thoughts, I came here in the aftermath of the storm of the previous night when the wind had not yet completely died down."

"I had to set out on the pilgrimage alone. It is spring, but the fields are lonely. I pray that in the fall I'll be able to come with you as a couple."

There were a variety of other ones as well, but I will stop.

Today after visiting six temples, we are to cross the famed Misakatōge Pass of Iyo.[429] With these six, I will have finished eighty-four[430] pilgrimage temples. When I think that there are only two more to go, I feel rather pleased.

The rain was falling but not so very hard. However, the muddiness of the path up the hill greatly bothered us. Moreover, the hill was a long, long one rising to the left and rising to the right, so that when I finally reached the pass, I was drenched in sweat. We had heard that this place commanded a bird's eye view of the whole Matsuyama plain, a very fine view, but even though we'd heard that, there were thick clouds and fog surrounding us because it was raining and all I could see was my own body and the red earth of the mountain path and nothing else.

After we'd rested for a while at the teahouse at the pass, when we started down it was extremely pleasant; in addition,

---

426 *Isobushi* were originally sailors' boat songs from Ibaraki Prefecture sung to the accompaniment of a shamisen. These folk songs spread to other parts of Japan.
427 Temple 51.
428 Temple 49 is Sairinzan Jōdo-ji and Temple 50 is Higashiyama Hanta-ji.
429 A mountain pass near temple forty-six and Matsuyama, where three hills meet. There is a more famous Misakatōge Pass near Hiroshima.
430 It is not clear whether Takamure mistakenly wrote eighty-four when she should have written eighty-six, or whether she did not visit temples twenty nine and thirty (see also Articles 66 and 90).

before going even a few *chō,* we were surprised by a broad, gently sloped highroad running in front of us.

Because it had become late, we looked for a place to stay but could not find one. Even when there chanced to be one, they wouldn't let us stay. During this time it eventually became completely dark. Just then a person happened along and saved us saying, "That's too bad—please come to my house." Wondering if we looked like beggars and feeling forlorn, we were taken to the house of this man and looked after in various ways.

When I went outside, the moon was completely bright and clear. Without my being aware of it, the sky had cleared and there was not a wisp of cloud.

"Goodness, the fog is coming in." All of a sudden a pretty, young voice rose behind my back and the figure of a slender young girl was coming towards me.

"You're the pilgrim who is staying there, aren't you?" She was a cheerful person.

"Yes."

"Are you looking at the moon? Let's walk over there."

Before we realized it we had become good friends and we walked to the edge of the woods. Because she said, "What kinds of songs do you know? I know a lot. Shall I teach you some?" it came about that, against my will, I was taught a song called *"Shin-Isobushi"*.[431] She had an exceptionally good voice. Moreover, the song somehow had a lonely seriousness.

"I am a parentless child, and all I can do is sing and sing; I will sing myself to death."

So saying, she laughed, "Ho ho." For no real reason, I thought what a dear person she was and when I turned around fondly, her beautiful young face was smiling.

"Pilgrim, can you write songs?"

I don't know what she was thinking but she suddenly blurted this out. Then, she stared intently at my face. "Won't you please write a commemorative song for me."

She was a person of deep feeling, rare for a village girl.

"Well, goodbye."

In the light of the moon, I had scribbled one or two songs

---

431 Literally, "new isobushi".

that matched the melody of the *"Shin-Isobushi"* and after writing them for her, I left. I don't remember them well, but they were as follows:

"I am awake and bashful—the setting sun is red. I don't care if I cry, fall down, or sleep covered by the grass because I am nothing but a pilgrim girl."

"Worn out by traveling, I cross mountain slopes. I can't help feeling sorry for myself trudging along alone, not ringing my bell or wiping away my tears."

"Awakening from a dream of falling cherry blossoms, I wonder where I am or if I'm at the end of the transient world. At the small moon-lit window, leaning on my many layers of kimono sleeves, my heart is lost in a dream."

Article 90: REALIZING A LONG CHERISHED DESIRE

October 18. Now I am writing this sitting on a patch of soft grass deep in a deserted thicket of mixed trees. What a beautiful day it is! From the endless and completely clear lofty sky a fine light like mild, young *sake*[432] is pouring down, and everything is shining serenely and gloriously—the mountains above me, the stream faintly visible through the trees, and the weeds carpeting the ground all over. The silence is so immense that it seems that even if I were to shout "Waa!" in a loud voice, my spirit, which would at first be astonished, would then be sucked up by the immense silence while the sound was fading away or before it faded away. The shadow of a small bird has flitted by. The wind is blowing. The sound of something reverberates.

Yesterday we visited the pilgrimage temple called Iwaya-ji[433] and stayed overnight at the post town of Hatanokawa. At Iwaya-ji, there is a famous *oku-no-in* called Anazenjō,[434] but in the end we just came down the mountain without going there.

This morning we left the inn early, and with our visit to the forty-fourth temple, Sugōzan Taihō-ji, my long cherished

---

432 Japanese rice wine.
433 Temple 45: Kaiganzan Iwaya-ji
434 This is high on a rocky cliff and must be reached by a ladder.

desire has finally been realized. It's really like a dream. With this temple I have made the entire pilgrimage to all the eighty-eight temples. Because I left Kumamoto on June the fourth I've spent a lot of time but it still seems as though my leaving were only yesterday.

The humourous memory of sleeping outside for the first time on the pilgrimage suddenly arose in my mind. Wet with the evening dew and bathed in the light of the new moon, I wrote postcards. The next morning I put water in a saucepan and washed my face. That was a long time ago. Without my noticing it, the luxuriant groves of fresh leafed trees have thinned and it's become the time when autumn-coloured forests are often seen at the far end of fields and in mountain valleys. This is just the absolutely unrelenting way that time changes. There's no use crying over the transitions of nature. We can only open our eyes wide in amazement at them.

I shouted "Ah" and almost leapt up. That was because I thought that I could return home. I can return. I can return to my beloved Kumamoto. And now, I must try to think about what sort of situation will be waiting for me in Kumamoto.

The long dream-like trip is finally over. I expect the world that is soon to come to be more severe, more pressing, and more distressing. However, no matter what kind of scenes I encounter, no matter what kind of threats I receive, no matter what kind of scorn I meet with, once more I make a solemn vow to heaven to absolutely never lose this quiet, sincere, reverent, pure feeling or my integrity. Also, I will continue to embrace everything with warm affection.

I will go! I will go! I must go to my majestic battleground. Even if I am smeared and dyed in blood, I must walk the path of virtue, the serious, pure, pious path of virtue.

Article 91: MY REMAINING MONEY: ONE *SEN* AND FIVE *RIN*[435]

October twentieth. Today also is a refreshingly clear day

---

[435] In the Japanese currency system of 1918, a *rin* was one tenth of a *sen*; a *sen* was one hundredth of a *yen*.

of summery weather. Last night we were given free lodging near the town of Uchiko. Because chilly winds and fog constantly blew in through the torn *shōji*,[436] piercing our bodies, we spent the night freezing. This morning we left at dawn and are finally headed for Yawatahama.[437] When we get there, we will have made a complete circle of Shikoku.

Somehow I am delighted; for no particular reason, I am delighted. "I can't think of it as anything but a dream." As I walked along with my eyes shining, I repeated those kinds of words time and time again.

The weather was spring-like, peaceful and warm. Most of the houses standing along the road in ones and twos were completely surrounded by neat flowering plants such as cosmos, chrysanthemums and Chinese bellflowers.[438] Coming from the opposite direction was a pilgrim who looked like a beggar. It was a woman. She stood still and stared at me. She was still young and her features were pretty good, but her clothing was very dirty.

However, her eyes had the tender hearted gleam characteristic of young girls. Suddenly, her face went red and she said in a voice so small that it was almost inaudible, "Uh, will you be so kind as to lend me a little money?"

My face also went red. That was because, actually, there was no longer much money in my money bag. When I took it out furtively to see, my hand touched one ten *sen* silver coin. I was so glad. "Take this then …."

So saying, I parted from her and came away. When I looked in my money bag after we parted, there remained one *sen* and five *rin*. The money remaining is one *sen* five *rin*—those words have a good ring to them.

Somehow, my situation seems poetic. Even my straw sandals are already completely dilapidated, but I cannot buy new ones—that is a certainty. Tired out by the trip, out of money, going along dragging my broken down straw sandals—it seems like a novel or a play. I am now the heroine in a play. I don't

---

436 In summer rice paper was used for windows (In winter the paper was replaced by wooden shutters).
437 The harbour from which they would depart for Kyūshū.
438 *Platycodon grandiflorum*. They are blue in color.

know about the future. Anyway, this is a person's life, the limited lifetime of a person, a certain scene in a life.

The sun is shining. The mountain ranges on both sides are undulating, eternally, forlornly, and nobly. When we arrive at Yawatahama, things will be all right—I must not forget my pure soul!

My heart always cries out like this.

Article 92: PEOPLE WANDERING ABOUT THE WORLD.

This trip showed me various types of people—fortune tellers and priests and an *ukarebushi* singer,[439] a man who replaces stems on tobacco pipes,[440] a tinker, and so on—there are various and sundry people living in the world. In Tosa a man called Daikoku or something stayed at the same inn. He gobbled his *zōsui* rice gruel[441] and sometimes had a strange way of laughing; he was a somewhat creepy man. Another time, when I stayed in a place in front of the temple at Ichinomiya in Awa,[442] I met a man from Kyōto called Itō Yūzen.[443] He told me various stories about the world and gave me the Hannya Shingyō[444] and the Darani Sutra[445] of Jūichimen Kanzeon and so on. He was a

---

439 *Ukarebushi* was a gay samisen tune.
440 At that time a pipe consisted of a metal fire bowl for the powdered tobacco, a bamboo stem, and a mouthpiece. When the pipe became clogged, the pipe repairer (*raoya*) would replace the stem and clean both ends. The word *raoya* is derived from Laos, from where attractive bamboo with spots came.
441 A kind of rice porridge with bits of vegetable or meat in it.
442 Temple 15.
443 Or, Itō Tsukeyoshi; the reading of his name is not clear.
444 The Hannya Haramita Shingyō, also known as "The Great Heart of Wisdom Sutra" or "The Heart Sutra", is a concise scripture that contains the essence of Buddhist teachings. Kannon, the personification of compassion, tells the monk Shariputra that nothing –including human existence –has ultimate substantiality, which in turn means that nothing is permanent and nothing is totally independent of everything else; everything in this world is interconnected and constantly changing. Pilgrims chant the Hannya Shingyō at each temple.
445 Darani are often said to be half-way between mantras and sutras because they are longer than most mantras and shorter than most sutras. The mystic syllables of a darani are often regarded as the essence of a sutra and are found

person of about sixty and told me that he was interested in *haiku*.[446]

Moreover, while visiting the many temples I have met various young priests, and pretty complicated and poetic events have pursued me but, as though flowing with the current, I haven't looked back—that is the normal way of a vagabond traveler. I have bid a firm and final farewell to such people as a lovely young girl, a darling old nun, a dear woman, etc. In Sanuki, I visited the ruins of Emperor Sutoku's place of exile as well as his tomb[447] and visited the shrine of Kompira-*sama*[448] after going to Zentsū-ji.[449] On the steam train on my way back, I even became acquainted with a geisha. Truly, various kinds of people live in the world. Each of them lives, individually fashioning various worlds of ideas and worlds of morality. Even though they appear to be out of their senses, it is not so; one thinks they are imbeciles but they are actually ordinary people in those worlds. At any rate, this is an interesting world.

However, it seems that when you classify people broadly, they certainly divide into two, the material kind of people and the spiritual kind of people. However, on the whole, those whom I call spiritual people are very few. Among the people whom I have met on this trip I might say there are almost none. By comparison, material people are plentiful everywhere. Of course,

---

in the sutra with the sutra explaining the circumstances under which the darani was originally proclaimed. The recitation of a darani is believed to bring great spiritual merit and further the practitioner's progress towards enlightenment.

446 A three line poem of seventeen syllables in the form of 5, 7, 5. Takamure uses the older term, *hokku* which literally means "starting link" and was the beginning of a longer chain of verses called *haikai*. The independence of this poem was recognized in the 1890s when it came to be called a *haiku*.

447 These are found at the seventy-fifth temple, Gogakuzan. Emperor Sutoku was born in 1119 as a son of Emperor Toba. He came to the throne as the seventy-fifth Emperor in 1123. When he fought against Emperor Goshirakawa in the Hogen-War he lost and was exiled to Shikoku. He died there in exile in 1164 and was buried on Mt. Shiramine. After his death, there were severe famines and wars and it was commonly thought that these resulted from his unhappy spirit.

448 The Kotohira Shrine is the shrine of the guardian deity of seafarers, Kompira. There are 785 stairs to the main building and 1368 stairs to the innermost shrine.

449 This was the birthplace of Kōbō Daishi in 774.

there are various differences of degree, from pale to dark, and the more vulgar they are, the clearer their attitude is; almost all that they do is extremely egotistical and based on instinct. Although the structure of the higher plants and animals is complicated; by contrast, that of primitive things is extremely simple—it's the same as that.

Today is October 21. Yesterday we walked from over there straight through without stopping to here at Yawatahama and we are staying at a *kichinyado* called the Mitsuyama.

Although I was surprised because there are a lot of people staying here with us, I was also surprised by the variety of vocations they have. First, there is a blind, hard of hearing woman pilgrim and next, a darkly tanned *ukarebushi* singer with parted hair. In a comical tone of voice, the *ukarebushi* singer was reading aloud Kōdan stories,[450] which pleased everyone there, including a young pilgrim boy of fifteen or sixteen, who listened engrossed.

Here this *ukarebushi* singer seems to be the central character. He is actively involved in everything; his energy extending as far as the hard of hearing female pilgrim whom everyone ignores. They seemed to have agreed to something, judging from his shouting, "Have you decided? Do so! I'll catch up with you and we'll go together." The gullible looking female pilgrim was pleased and, giggling, pretended to slap him from time to time.

Other than these, there is an old man pilgrim and a fortune teller leading his family and a bad tempered old lady who always sits in a corner. Each and every one of them is talkative. They do only what they want and don't hesitate to meddle with others. Actually, even just observing them as a bystander, at first I was

---

450 These were stories of heroes of various kinds, warriors, faithful wives, dutiful children, outlaws, gamblers, millionaires, etc. At first they were recited, but later, in the Meiji era, they became available in book form. The recitation of the stories lost popularity with the advent of movies but since 1985 there have been female kōdan reciters and more topical themes, and interest in the art has revived. The kōdan reciter sits behind a low table rhythmically reciting tales, punctuating the rhythm of his words and emphasizing important phrases by rapping his fan and striking wooden clappers.

almost frightened by the lack of reserve, lack of humility, and lack of moderation in the language and conduct of such people.

Article 93: THE FIGURE OF A MAD WOMAN

October 22. Today we are still staying here. So are the *ukarebushi* singer, the blind woman pilgrim, the old man pilgrim, the fortune teller and his family. Everyone talks only about making money. In everything they do, their only criterion is money.

"Training in the samisen is best for a girl; what good will it do her to go to school? Being a geisha is best; being a geisha is best; or else, being a prostitute is good. First of all, she lazes about, she is dressed in a good kimono and she can have any delicious food she wants. Is there any job better than this?" The fortune teller talked this way to his wife and daughter. Both the wife and the daughter seemed convinced that this was certainly reasonable.[451]

The *ukarebushi* singer said his birthplace was Ōsaka. "Even if I go back home it's unpleasant because my stepmother's there. Anyway, I'm a lazy fellow you know." So saying, he laughed loudly, but there were also times when he was apt to sigh.

The state of mind of the old man pilgrim seemed a little strange. He often talked to himself.

The attic, where our room was, had been divided in two and, even in the daytime, the rooms were dark. In the midst of the faint light the wriggling shadows of people seemed like apparitions from another world. Feeling gloomy and exhausted, I thought of Poe's last moments,[452] Oscar Wilde's last

---

451 In this period it was not uncommon for poor families to sell daughters into prostitution in order for the family to survive financially.
452 The circumstances of Poe's death are still a mystery. He was found on a street in Baltimore (where he did not live) and taken to a hospital where he died alone five days later. There is speculation as to whether he was mugged, died as the result of an alcoholic binge, had a disease (rabies, TB, diabetes have been suggested), or was shanghaied by a political gang and forced to vote over and over again (It was election day in Baltimore) and beaten and given alcohol to achieve his compliance.

moments,[453] etc., one after the other.

This morning I got up really early and took a stroll by the light of the moon. It was as quiet as if the people were sleeping silkworms, their heads in a row.[454] All of a sudden, I recalled the time we stayed at a house standing alone in the vicinity of the eighty-second temple, Negoro-ji. There were probably five or six people at the same inn. Among them was a couple traveling together; the wife was in her early forties and it was said she was mentally unstable. Glancing at her, there was nothing particularly unusual, but she never stopped talking about something or other.

In the evening at bedtime her husband warned us, "Everybody, I'm sorry but towards morning she'll probably become a little strange."

As we'd been told, around one or two in the morning—there was moonlight at that time also—she suddenly got up and rushed outside. The others were all sound asleep and didn't seem to know, but because I happened to be awake I was scared, wondering what would happen.

Being concerned, I quietly opened the door and when I looked, she was holding her hands together and fervently praying for something. When she finished that she walked here and there in a clump of trees in the moonlight, her face as pale as a ghost's. That figure will never ever leave my heart. When I walk around in the light of the moon this way, I am even inclined to feel that I myself have become like that woman.

Article 94: THE *HOTETEN GEKYŌ*[455]

There was a temple in the neighborhood of the inn where

---

453 Oscar Wilde died of acute meningitis following an ear infection in a hotel room in Paris. It is said that his last words were "This wallpaper is terrible—one of us will have to go."
454 As Japanese families often raised silkworms in attics, it was natural for Takamure to think of silkworms.
455 The Hoke Kyō or Lotus Sutra was and is a major influence in Japanese Buddhism. In the Kamakura era, Nichiren advocated chanting its title, Namu Myōhō Renge Kyō, (I take refuge in the Lotus Sutra) as the ultimate act of devotion. Nichiren believed that if all Japanese chanted the title, the country would be transformed into a Buddha land.

all day long believers were chanting the title of the *Hoke Kyō* as they beat fan drums.[456] When the *ukarebushi* singer said, "You know they're chanting, '*Namu Myō Hoteten Gekyō*'—listen carefully,"[457] everyone burst out laughing.

The fortune teller interrupted, "I don't approve of Hoteten Buddhism at all. And the Ikkō religion of the outcastes[458] is even more detestable. If a religion gives money, I won't say two words; I'll become a believer right away."

"Well, then become a Christian. Mention illness, there's medicine; mention education, there's money for school fees. It's great." This was the *ukarebushi* singer speaking.

The fortune teller said, "You know, Christianity preaches the present but with other religions it's the future."

When I thought the talk had become more and more interesting, the old pilgrim began chanting,

"Thanks be to Kōbō Daishi! Thanks be to Kōbō Daishi!

"Ga shaku sho zō sho aku gō. Kai yū mu shi don shin chi. Jū shin go ishi sho jō. Is-sai ga kon kai san-ge.[459]

"All the evil karma, ever created by me since of old; on account of my beginning-less greed, hatred and ignorance; born of my conduct, speech and thought; I now confess openly and fully.

"Nōmaku sanmanda bazaradan senda. Makaro shada. Sowa taya un tarata kan man.[460]

"Homage to all the deities of Vajra rank! O Violent One of great wrath! Destroy any evil enemies totally! Exterminate any

---

456 Fan drums look like fans and are held in the hand and hit with a stick.
457 The ukarebushi singer changes the sounds of the syllables Myō hō Ren ge Kyō, to the nonsense sounds of Myō Ho Te Ten Gekkyō. Perhaps he is mimicking the sound of the drums beaten by Nichiren believers in the word "hoteten".
458 The word the fortune teller uses is *eta*, which means the outcaste class in Japan of that period. He is speaking of the Jōdō Shinshu School of Japanese Buddhism, which is also known as the Ikkō School. At present it has the largest number of adherents.
459 This is the Sangemon, the verse of penitence.
460 This is the mantra of Fudō Myōō, a fierce guardian deity in Buddhism. It is well known as it is chanted at funerals to help the deceased become a Buddha. Four of the 88 Shikoku temples have Fudō Myōō as the chief deity.

defilements! Kanman!"

When the old pilgrim began to recite a sutra fervently, someone joked, "Homage to the farts of Kōbō Daishi the stink, the stink, homage to the farts...." There was an unbearable racket.

By and by the fortune teller, who had been lying sprawled out idly looking at an elementary school reader, stood up. "The policy of the government towards education is very mistaken. Look at this, made up stories such as *Hanasaka Jiji*[461] have been dragged out and printed here. These kinds of things never happen—it's the same as instilling superstitions in little heads and it's dangerous." He said it as though he thought it was a great discovery. Without a second thought, all present agreed with him.

This is not the just the fortune teller. There are probably still many people in the world who think this kind of thing. Facts, facts; they are people who cannot accept things unless they have factual evidence before their eyes.

There is war; the cabinet collapses, is reorganized, and collapses again; the price of rice rises; the world is in fear and trembling. People go on more and more enslaved to material things. Nerves are on edge; senses are dulled. People are totally under pressure. Life is intolerable without occasional indulgence in hedonistic pleasures. What will be the result of this situation? From the flesh to the spirit, from the spirit to the flesh—the world spins round and round, but as it turns, perhaps it is necessary to give a thought to the many costs that are paid. I am being presumptuous but at one time I felt indignant about various things.

These were chiefly concerned with women's education, which is truly too makeshift and too irresolute. It is the same everywhere in Japan. I want education to be a little more lively and practical. Isn't every woman who is a product of this education like an eyeless, numb, pale potato worm?

Women's education is too narrow-minded, too

---

461 *Hanasaki Jiji* (The Man who made Trees Bloom) is the story of an honest old man whose dog finds buried treasure. The neighbour, a cruel man, kills the dog. In the end, the kind old man sprinkles the ashes of the dog on trees and makes them bloom just as the lord of the area is passing. For this, he receives much gold.

condescending. I want women to be people who understand poetry rather than being women taught Moral Philosophy one letter at a time.

Article 95: HUNTING FOR LICE AND HUNTING FOR PILGRIMS

October 23. I cannot tell you how happy I am thinking that tomorrow I will finally return. Before daybreak I was lying awake in my futon, joyful as a happy child, thinking "Let tomorrow come quickly! Let tomorrow come quickly!" when, suddenly, the old man leapt up from the next futon shouting "I've caught something! Very suspicious—it appears to be a louse!"

When he took it under the electric light in order to examine it carefully, it was as he thought. It was a whitish, indistinct color. What a flat bug it was!

"It's terrible!" The room was in a great uproar. "Oh, there's one here too!" "Take a look!"

Day came and we ate breakfast and finished our preparations, and this was the only topic of conversation until each of us went out to do whatever we were going to do. Over and over again the old man said the futon was suspicious. The futon was certainly suspect but actually, from two to three days before, the old man had been saying, "My whole body has become so itchy. This is certainly because Kōbō Daishi is helping me by making the fever throughout my body go away. It's a blessing." Although he had been saying this, I had thought to myself that perhaps it was lice.

During the time that we were making a racket, the voice of a policeman was heard below. "An old man and a young woman? Is that so? Tell them to come here."[462]

In the end, when we were called down, there were two policemen. They were in the entrance of the house, one sitting on

---

462 The expression used here "Chotto koi" is well-known as the phrase used by police during the militaristic period prior to the end of WWII. Those to whom it was said were then taken to the police station for interrogation and even beating, sometimes to death. The phrase had a very ominous sound as innocent citizens could be jailed without warrant, injunction, or even evidence.

the raised floor, the other standing on the earthen floor.[463]

"What? This young woman? Is she your granddaughter? State your name and permanent residence." We were treated like criminals.

They also said, "Actually, since they say pilgrims are in a pitiful state because the price of rice has become high like this, the authorities decided to give a small handout of money to each pilgrim And you, have you been doing some begging? If you have, I'd like you to speak up without hesitation. Do you need the money?"

"No—we're already on our way home so there's no necessity but it's a nice offer."

"Well, do you accept it or not?"

"No, I don't need it. I'm expecting a money order by telegraph."

"For sure? Is that really so?"

"Yes, absolutely."

"Well then, I guess it's not necessary to give it you. It's been decided to give quite an amount per head. If you don't need it, it's not necessary to give it …."

Watching nearby, I was amused and thought they were people who stated the obvious.

"Young woman, what was the reason that you left home and came here?"

The thundering voice now turned in my direction.

"It was a vow."

"Your name? Say it once more."

"My name is Itsue."

When the two of them had stared at me intently for a while, they said, "Hey, pilgrim. What are you two? You're certainly dressed like pilgrims, aren't you." This time they thrust in the direction of the old man.

"Yes, because we're on Daishi *sama*'s pilgrimage, we have to dress as pilgrims."

"You fool! I called you pilgrims—what's wrong with

---

463 Traditionally Japanese houses had an earthen floored entrance where people removed their shoes before going up onto the raised floor inside the house.

that? Are you angry? No matter how much social status you have, you're pilgrims."

"Hey! I'm tired of this. Let's go."

The two left promptly. I also went back upstairs.

Somehow it seemed comical. As I was smiling, wondering if that was the policemen's duty, the old man came upstairs fuming with rage.

"They considered us criminals—what an arrogant attitude."

Some people tend to be high-handed and threatening and some people flare up in response—there are various types in the world. I happened to recall the policeman in *Les Miserables*. He was a machine through and through ....[464]

The *ukarebushi* singer returned and informed us all, "Today they're hunting pilgrims. They say that a lot of people have been taken to the police station." That accounted for the blind pilgrim woman having finally been caught and taken to the police jail that night. Everyone said that once pilgrims are caught they are escorted to the border of the prefecture and expelled.

Article 96: TO ŌITA

October twenty-fourth. Since morning the sky has been looking extremely threatening. Everyone says that judging from the way it looks, it will probably be stormy. When we were resting for a while at a teahouse in the harbour, a steam whistle sounded offshore.

At last the time has come. Finally I have to part from Shikoku and leave behind my dream-like wandering journey. My destiny that is bound to come—what will it be? The world that is bound to come—what will it be? Somehow or other I feel a vague uneasiness. For a moment I thought of the English ship in Ibsen's *The Lady from the Sea*.[465]

---

[464] Javert, the petty, regulation-bound bureaucrat who relentlessly and unreasonably pursued a good man, Jean Valjean, for stealing a loaf of bread.
[465] Written by Henrik Ibsen in 1888, the play, *Fruen fra Havet* is about a seaman who comes back from a long voyage, after a ten year absence, and tries to reclaim the girl to whom he was unofficially engaged. She, however, is now married to a doctor.

Fantasizing has long been a habit of mine, but recently, I have begun to have a particular interest in poeticizing, fictionalizing, and dramatizing myself and my surroundings. While I was rapturously lost in honey-like, pleasant thoughts, the ship approached in front of me before I realized it.

People were noisily excited. I remained lost in a trance until, at a little after eleven in the morning, upon entering the third class cabin of the Misōmaru, a small steamship, I looked around at my surroundings. The old man and I sat against the portside hull of the ship as though fastened to it, but against the starboard hull across from us, four brazen, ungainly, fat women were reclining, eating uninhibitedly and laughing in loud voices. In spite of that it was really an enviably beautiful scene; to all appearances they were enjoying themselves as they held hands and talked together familiarly.

Ah, how happy are people who have friends to talk and laugh with, simply and sincerely like that! If I lose everything else it will not matter; I just want to live with an unreserved and open-minded, peaceful and sacred, beautiful feeling that does not make the slightest distinction toward anyone. Without intending to, I could not help giving a deep sigh when I looked back at my narrow heart that has been annoyingly entangled in empty forms and empty display.

The wind is gradually becoming strong. The waves are making a terrifying noise. The people who were on the deck have fled back in, saying, "We felt as though we were going to be blown away."

Right up at the "nose" of the boat, we were unbearably pitched about. Pillows on the shelves fell down and pails rolled about and so on. Had that been all, it would have been fine, but I was very surprised by the commotion caused by a rice ball that was being eaten across from me landing on my knee, with the pickled plum still sticking out, and then, suddenly, saltwater spray flying in through a porthole.

People vomiting, people who had collapsed and were lying on the floor, voices calling for the steward, the wind howling; it was an appalling scene. Wondering what I should do, I nervously watched a young woman right beside me who had been suffering for some time. Her hair was in disarray, her limbs were sagging, her face so pale it was unlike that of a person of this world.

I was barely able to say just, "Hey, why don't you vomit into this," and give her a cup out of the old man's bag into which she vomited without saying a word. Oh, how distressing and pitiful it was. Unaccountably, the old man and I didn't get sick but almost everyone else had collapsed and was lying down. When I realized the waves had become somewhat calmer, the boat had already arrived in Saganoseki port.

Swept along by a piercingly cold wind we landed, and probably about eight o'clock in the evening arrived at an inn, feeling relieved and safe. This is Kyūshū; this is Saganoseki; this is the land of Higo. Ah, I have finally come back.

Article 97: HELPED THREE TIMES

"Am I back already? It's like a dream." Repeating such words over and over again I walk along the coastal road to Ōita. October twenty-fifth and the sky is completely clear, with no sign of the previous bad weather, and the Kunisaki Peninsula is clearly bounded by the silvery sea.

Rapturously intoxicated by various memories of the past, I don't know how many times I check myself from saying to the old man, "Remember…."

"Kōbō Daishi be praised, Kōbō Daishi be praised; no matter how I think about it, I am grateful." The old man harps on the same string every day. But this time his gratitude has a somewhat profound meaning like this:

Not long before my remaining money became one *sen* five *rin*,[466] we were in such difficulty that we barely managed to pay for our lodging. Then we unexpectedly received some money as a gift from a man from Ishikawa Prefecture who stayed at the same inn as we did in Dōgo. He also was begging on the trip and although, of course, we did not reveal the true state of our affairs to him, he gave us money saying, "Please don't take offence but let me give you this as a parting gift." We had not expected this.

---

466 See Article 91

Tears streaming down, the delighted old man merely said that this was Daishi *sama*'s help.

By and by we didn't have enough money again. And then, this time, right in the middle of the highway, I caught sight of several silver coins clumped together that someone had dropped. Being sure that a person we had just jostled had dropped them, I hurriedly ran after him but couldn't find him. Then the old man said, "This is also certainly Daishi's help. Daishi be praised! Daishi be praised!" and picked up the coins.

After that, arriving in Yawatahama we spent two or three days waiting for a reply telegram from Ōita. Actually, the money had arrived earlier but, because the post office was irresponsible and said that nothing had come in spite of our repeated questions, we had to borrow money and send a telegram. From Ōita came a reply by telegram, "Sent already investigate further." Finally, the money for the steamship fare was in our hands but, having bought our tickets, only fifty *sen* remained and we would not be able to manage on that because even after going by ship to Saganoseki, it is still seven *ri* from there to Ōita.

"Alright! Even though it will be the middle of the night, it doesn't matter; we'll walk all the way!" Although, of course, not one of the passengers knew about our situation, while we were consulting together, we received a completely unexpected gift of money from one of them who said it was for Daishi *sama*.

Thanks to that, we could pay for our lodging and were saved. It seems I have written pretty much only about money, but, in fact, it was a terribly cold night and if we had walked all the way, indeed, we would probably have felt frozen, so again we were saved. Because this kind of occurrence happened not just once, but twice, three times, it was not unreasonable that the old man in his single-minded heart considered it to be the assistance of Kōbō Daishi.

His tears were already rolling down as he said, "Besides, there's no doubt you are a child born in answer to your parents' prayers to Kannon. Because of you at my present age I have been able to make the Shikoku pilgrimage—it is more than I deserve."

If you will grant there are miracles in the world, my life is truly turning out interestingly. I'll write a little about the connection between Kannon *sama* and myself.

Article 98: KANNON *SAMA* AND I

Perhaps I have written a bit about this before but in my home we particularly believed in Kannon *sama*, especially my mother. On Kannon *sama*'s festival day,[467] the eighteenth of each month, she always, without fail, cooked something and made an offering. Thus, it had been our habit from childhood never to neglect worshipping each morning and evening. When the younger of my two brothers and I were living on our own in Kumamoto while he was going to school there, we unfailingly bought something for an offering on the eighteenth. Of course, we had ulterior motives; using the festival day as a pretext, we bought many delicious things, offered them for only a minute on the desk, then happily ate them. At any rate, I knew the origin of our faith and our practices had an extremely deep connection with me because my mother constantly told me so. The connection is this.

My mother told me that many male children were born before me, one after the other, but they all soon died. The boy who lived longest, a child called Yoshito, lived until he was two and died. Because the grief of my mother, who was still young at that time, was extreme, she said that she composed poems such as "Don't think of dying alone, Yoshito, lead your mother on the same path." Then when she had prayed and made a vow to the Kannon at the Yabekawa River in Chikugo[468] as someone one day had recommended, I was born, precisely on January eighteenth, Kannon's festival day.

I don't know for certain if her prayers were the cause but

---

467 This is actually "ennichi" or Day of Connection which means a day on which a Buddha or divinity is believed to have been born, manifested himself, attained enlightenment, died, etc. According to popular belief, religious services held on such a day have particular merit.

468 This area is in southern Fukuoka Prefecture in Kyūshū. The Yabe River Kannon is perhaps the Senju Kannon image in Setaka Town on the Yabe River, that is said to have been carved by Saichō in 805 on his return from China. Prayers to this ancient Kannon are even now considered effective for good fortune, marriage, pregnancy and safe delivery.

I was the picture of health, just like a boy, full of vitality and thriving, and the children after me all grew up. This gave rise to my mother's great faith. Moreover, she said, "I don't know how many times you have received divine protection since you were small," and she often talked to me about various things. I well remember that I was made to wear a beautiful amulet next to my skin when I was young.

Then, when I grew a little older, my mind became strangely pessimistic. Also, I learned the pleasure of fantasizing by myself. When I was still very young, for several nights in a row I was in anguish thinking, "I will die" and even in my childish heart I was in agony, in the depths of despair.

Then, when I began to go to school, I brashly organized family discussion sessions and a little later, produced with my younger brothers a magazine-like thing called *Yuai no Tomo*, (Friendly Companion),[469] and wrote fairy tales and and a collection of poems and so on. While I was doing those things I started to forget to worship Kannon *sama*. The memory of being taken by my mother and going to worship at the Yabekawa River was a warm one which never left my heart but ….. My mother always said things such as "You will surely be struck by divine punishment." When I heard that, I was certainly frightened.

At one time the following thing happened. We were living in a village called Moritomi. At that time there were young people who came to our house to hear my father's lectures on the Chinese classics. Among them was a man called Washiyama Torayoshi from Tajiri village who often attended enthusiastically. I think I was twelve. He was doing *Jūhachi shiryaku*, the Eighteen Outlines of Chinese History, and I, who was precocious, took my father's place in teaching him, but teaching him only the oral reading of the text.[470] However, it was unbearably

---

469 A magazine circulating among her siblings.
470 This is oral reading and recitation of a Chinese text without the meaning being comprehended. Students imitated the teacher's reading and memorized the Chinese characters. This enabled them to read other texts in Chinese. This method is called "*sodoku*"—reading aloud without being concerned with meaning. The *Jūhachi shiryaku* (十八史略) was used from the Muromachi period until after the Meiji period to introduce this type of reading. The textbook presents the history of China in a simplified form.

unpleasant. This is what happened one day.

That day Mr. Washiyama made his appearance. When I saw him, I was disgusted by him for no reason and took off. Later I was severely scolded by my mother. "Think about your duty. Do you not understand what kindness is? Mr. Washiyama ended up going home early."

That was what happened. When I thought of why I had run out, I was repentant—how repentant I was—and going to the path between the rice fields in front of our house I cried for a long time. After that, I wrote a strange thing I called a vow and secretly put it behind the doors of Kannon *sama*'s shrine in our house and prayed earnestly, joining my hands together and saying, "Please forgive me."

I grew up doing those sorts of things but, even concerning the trip this time, there were things such as the rebuilding of the Kannon Hall by the family of the old man and Kannon's appearing to the old man that night. At any rate, even if it is by chance, it seems as though Kannon *sama* and I have a deep connection.

Article 99: INFLUENZA

I have been afflicted with influenza and suffering for a long time but now, finally, I am on the verge of recovery.[471]

Today is November twelfth, and I am presently staying at the old man's house in Ōno County, Ōita Prefecture. Various things have happened since I last wrote. While I was taking it easy for a while in Ōita City (Actually, I spent most of those days in bed.) I received visits from two or three prominent people and listened to edifying talk. I was invited to a certain gentleman's

---

471 It is estimated that, worldwide, more than forty million people died in the Great Flu Epidemic which began in September 1918. No area of the world was spared. More people died from the flu than from World War I. Unlike the usual flu which particularly affects children and old people, this virus particularly attacked those between 20 and 40. Most people affected by the second wave of the disease, which began in the fall, developed only a 3-5 day illness, initially a cough and stuffy nose, but later a dreadful ache in every joint and muscle and a temperature as high as 40 degrees. However, the illness was usually over within a week.

home and chatted with his wife and was able fortuitously to learn something about activities in the women's sphere in Ōita. When I returned here still sick, I immediately saw several people who presented me with some interesting cases. However, having somehow become insensitive to things along those lines, for me now, writing in detail, item by item, would be agonizing.

Through the good offices of a certain person, I can now read the Kyūshū Nichi Nichi newspaper[472] every day and I was surprised by the paper's report that influenza was raging there too. Here in Ōno County also the flu was severe for a while, but it now seems to be subsiding somewhat. Because I felt extremely listless and every joint ached terribly, I thought at first this was surely the result of walking around Shikoku. However, after being examined by a doctor, I realized that I had been stricken with influenza, the disease of the hour.

I am feeling much better now. If the good weather continues, I am thinking that I would really like to leave here within two or three days. I am grateful for the old man's kindness in insisting that he will come to the Aso Miyaji station to see me off, but I have firmly refused him and am resolved to go to Kumamoto as a solitary figure once more with just my sedge hat and staff and the flying wind and flowing clouds.

It's like a dream. It's been six months since I left Kumamoto. That explains why it has become cold without my knowing when it happened. And I'm still in my summer clothes. A wintry wind and summer clothes—they seem incongruous but aren't. I live my pathetic life within that incongruity. Every day I thought about such things as I coughed.

I was told by the doctor several times "You know, if you are not careful, you will develop pneumonia," but, in spite of his warnings, I always dared to go outside twice a day, in the early evening and at night. The setting sun and the moonlight invariably make me feel not only crazy and tense, but also serene.

I gave a wry smile as I remembered the night I upset the old man on a road in Shikoku by suddenly saying that I would enter into the state of the Gatsuai Zammai, the moon-loving

---

472 This is the newspaper for which she has been writing throughout her pilgrimage.

samadhi.[473]

It is like a dream—no matter how many times I think of it, it is like a dream—Tosa Bay—Awaji Island—Kompira Shrine. It is like a magic lantern show.

> Ringing a bell I visited
> A dream-like village
> In the province of Bungo
> One day on a trip and
> Chanced to meet you.

Yesterday, I presented such a frivolous poem to someone and, without a doubt, this also will become a remembrance of my dream.[474]

I will leave soon; I don't want to wait until I am completely recovered.

Article 100: THE GOD OF COLDS

Past noon on November fifteenth, just as I was changing the cord of my hat and organizing my luggage thinking that I would leave tomorrow for sure, an old lady of about fifty came, falling on her knees before me. I was surprised by her strange behaviour but after she had worshipped me for a while, she finally broached the matter of her visit. Speaking very politely, she said, "I am from the outskirts of Mie, Ōno County, a little way from here and I deal in used clothing and since your reputation is famous I really wanted to meet you at least once. The people of the neighbourhood constantly talk about wanting to see you and hearing the news that you were staying here at this very moment—it's very rude of me but I have come to see you

---

473 Gatsuai-zammai. *Sammai* (zammai/ samadhi) denotes a state in which the mind is free from distraction and is absorbed in intense concentration. The Buddha once entered this samadhi in order to cure a king. Spiritual diseases can be cured by this samadhi in the same way as moonlight releases a person from uneasiness and brings calmness of mind. Moonlight is compared to the boundless compassion of the Buddha.
474 Horiba thinks she presented the poem to the young man who studied hard and who lived at the house with the bath. (Article 25)

about a small favour."

Wondering what the favour was, I could only listen in amazement.

"Earlier we heard that you had kindly saved one old woman when you passed through the outskirts of Taketa."

The more she talked, the stranger it was.

Finally I blushed and said, "I beg your pardon? I don't understand at all."

"No, everyone knows. As that old lady said, 'When I was weak from a long term illness, she honoured me by staying at my house, and just by receiving her staff, my illness was completely cured and the next morning because of her I had recovered enough that I could cook rice for her.' Everybody's talking about this."

Good heavens! Judging from "She honoured me by staying at my house", it was surely the old lady in that house in the suburb of Taketa (I have momentarily forgotten her name; I wrote it in my diary but I've already sent it home in a parcel.) I wonder what I did with my staff then; I've completely forgotten. At any rate, the situation was odd.

"Well then, there are people sick with colds in the home of the head of Mie village and many other places as well. Much as I hate to bother you, I would be very grateful if you would grant my request for help and come. Please grant us your mercy."

She was an old lady who spoke exceedingly politely. In spite of myself, I was charmed by the melody of her words but then I had to reply something to her.

"Please forgive me. I can't …."

The old lady just would not give up. For an eternity she kept bowing again and again without stopping.

What should I do? I was completely at a loss.

However, after a long time I finally escaped the difficult situation and felt relieved. For a while I stared in blank amazement at her as she left saying over and over, "I am grateful just to have met you."

It's a strange world. I had been thinking that since rather a lot of people had come lately in order to receive the touch of my staff that they were acting strangely. Now, it seems that I was about to be ordered out on official business as the God of Colds.

I will go back soon. I no longer care whether my influenza is better or not.

I was asked by the old man and the doctor to stay but I must return, no matter what. Oh, Kumamoto, I miss you so much.

I can see Mount Aso from the mountain behind. Soon, soon—soon I'll go back.

Article 101: SCRAWLED HASTILY

November fifteenth. No sooner had I sent the strange old lady back and was feeling greatly relieved, than right after her a peddler of patent medicines made his appearance. He was from a village called Funaki several *chō* northeast of here and he said his surname was Hirosue.

He said that hearing that I was leaving tomorrow he'd come in great haste and hurriedly thrust a sheet of paper at me. I was nervous, certain that something was going to happen again. Then he said, "I'm sorry to trouble you, but, please, will you leave me a line or two? Anything at all is fine. Actually, I have been thinking of asking you for this for a long time, but I thought it would be rude to ask out of the blue …."

"I shall write." I have to admit that for a moment I thought my behaviour was high handed and really ridiculous.

Then, when I took up the paper I was stumped for a while as to what to write but then I wrote, "All of a sudden Mr. Hirosue has pressed me to write something. I am very much at my wit's end but, following his orders, I have taken my brush in hand and playfully written something light:

> Cry or laugh,
> The transitory world is
> The transitory world,
> A dream world like
> The falling of
> Cherry blossoms.

Insufferable pretentiousness….

When I had written it, I immediately felt uncomfortable, so I excused myself and went outside alone.

It was just twilight and the sorrowful red light of the setting sun flowed, piercing through the sparse woods in front of me. Crossing an earthen bridge to a grassy hill—even when I saunter leisurely like this, time is moving steadily on. This year also, I don't know when, it has become the time of falling leaves. My heart is filled with intense grief, a feeling of wanting to cry but being unable to do so.

Time is flowing along, and my life.

What a superficial person I am! When I think about that, my head begins to ache. At any rate, I must return soon.

****

When I woke up it was finally the sixteenth. I was delighted when I thought that I was leaving today. Since last night the old man has repeatedly said that it is finally time to part and that he is certainly going to miss me.

When I had finished my preparations and left the house, it was after two in the afternoon. There were various difficulties as well, but I will skip them. Today at the town called Tanaka about two *ri* ahead, I expect to be taken care of because I have repeatedly received invitations from Miyazaki Kotoji there but have not been able to take him up on them.

Because I had not walked for a while, I began to feel strangely tired after I had gone not even one *ri*. The old man is seventy-three but very strong. Talk about good health! Thinking that the old man has treated me lovingly for a long time, better than a blood relative would, and that tonight is all that remains for us to be together, when I saw him walking along ahead of me my tears spontaneously welled up.

Article 102: "ODON"

November eighteenth. Now I am at Aso. How my heart leapt hearing Kumamoto expressions such as "Odon ni kashinahari" [475] or "Odon ga oshiyurutai" [476] after a long time. Ah, I also want to call myself "*odon*".[477] I also am a Higo person, a person of Kumamoto Prefecture. I am one of them.

When I was listening to such expressions with shining eyes, inexplicably delighted and inexplicably joyful, before I knew it, everyone was looking at me. Behind my back housewives kept saying, "Her father and mother must surely be worrying. Letting a young girl like this go off alone."

"She's probably the person who was in the newspaper."

"Is that so? I thought she didn't look like an ordinary person."

Again, even here, it's started. Both at Tanaka and at Taketa, a lot of the same things were said.

My departure from Tanaka was yesterday, the seventeenth, and people accompanied me as far as on to the bridge on the outskirts of the town and, parting from the dear old man, I was finally plodding along alone. As one might expect, I was sorry to leave and turned around again and again looking up at the mountains that had been familiar for a long time. Also, my heart was further filled with tearful sadness thinking of the people who had come to see me off who were still there in the town at the foot of those mountains.

Goodbye you people of Bungo! My dear old man!

All of a sudden, the things I did in the town of Tanaka, returned to my heart one by one and I couldn't help feeling a painful feeling, rather like regret, in my heart.

Because one and all brought various papers and folding fans and insisted that I write something on them, I was completely disconcerted. First of all, the phrases to write didn't come easily to me. I could do nothing but dash off such extremely commonplace phrases as "Chūai", [478] "Kanshū",[479]

---

475 Please lend it to me.
476 I'll tell you.
477 This is a combination of "ore" (I) and "tono" (lord) and means "I". It is an unusual combination of a humble form and a respectful form.
478 loyal and loving subjects
479 finish what you start

"Shūsui", [480] "Shinkō ichizu", [481] "Unsui ruten". [482] What was ridiculous was that I wrote the same words, "Kikyorai" [483] on several pieces of paper. Although I was really self-indulgent, even this was just fine because people were happy. Furthermore, they made me write on a number of wide sheets of paper they said would be made into hanging scrolls, but that was pleasant. Making charcoal ink soak into a big brush, fixing my eyes on the paper, gathering force into my lower abdomen, courage filling my whole body—dashing these off on the scrolls was an unparalleled pleasure. It was really a delight. Nothing existed, not people, not myself, not any other thing; there was only the sky and the void.

In Taketa I was put up in the home of Mr. Furuya Yoshijiro, where I had stayed previously. The grandmother was as glad as if I were her grandchild returning. I also was deeply happy. Then I proudly told her my tales of Shikoku.

"My dear, after you left for Ōita, I don't know how many people came to this house in order to inquire about you. You created a big sensation."

She also told me various absurd and exaggerated rumours about me. This morning they kept telling me to stay longer but I left. The old lady was reluctant to have me leave and saw me off with tears streaming down her face.

Article 103: BACK IN KUMAMOTO

November twentieth. Now I'm back and am writing this. I am in Kumamoto. Am I already back? How dreamlike it seems. I

---

480 a burnished sword; another translation of this might be a clear stream in autumn.
481 believe wholeheartedly
482 clouds and water flow eternally
483 Let's go home. This is from an ancient Chinese poem by the Jin dynasty poet Tao Yuanming, who is known in Japanese as Tōenmei. The poem, "Let us go home" [帰去来の辞], was composed in 405 when Tao Yuanming resigned his official post and returned to his native rural village. The ode praises the merits of simple life in the countryside, away from the temptations of the material world. In Japan, the poem was a popular theme for both painters and calligraphers and was felt to sum up the ideals of the recluse.

haven't the slightest idea what I should write about or where to begin. I came by steam train, I came by rickshaw; everything seems faint and indistinct, as if in a scroll painting.

The flower-like light of the Tateno Station[484]—me in a kimono of grayish blue *shibori*[485] with *Genroku* sleeves[486] and a vest, and, over that, a mantle—everything seems to be floating gently away in a land of fantasy far, far from reality. I do not know my future in the least, not in the least. Sometimes I am excited and sing a song or leaf through a collection of poems. My cheeks burn, my eyes shine, my tears flow, ah, my tears flow. I don't know whether I am sad or glad.

When I think that I am already here, my heart is full. I have returned to Kumamoto, to my solemn battlefield, to my heartbreaking battlefield, to my gruesome battlefield. What shall I do? I will battle on, taking the most righteous, the most honourable, the mightiest path.

Two letters from my hometown were waiting for me at the inn. My parents warmly wrote, "We cannot wait, we are worrying, hurry back,"… . How could I help crying?

Please wait, I am coming back, I am coming back, I am flying back. For the sake of my parents, for the sake of my younger brothers and younger sister, I must contend with and overcome each and every difficulty. The road runs straight.

That's right, the road is straight. It is my steadfast intention to create a self that is sincere and uncompromising by struggling with all might and main against vanity, falsehood, and all other vices and conquering them.

Because I was tired writing up to this point, I went to bed. November twenty-first. With some difficulty, I have become a little calmer. I can see the weather station. I can see Shinsaka. At one time, it was this highway and the trees lining it and Mount Tatsuta that I looked at enveloped in sorrowful thoughts and with

---

484 Takamure mentions a song about Tateno station in Article 5, "There is a light burning at the station at Tateno on the border of Aso and Kikuchi counties."

485 This is a traditional form of dyeing in which the fabric to be dyed is tied into intricate patterns before being put into the dye.

486 The Edo Genroku period was from 1604 to 1866. Genroku sleeves on a kimono were short, rounded sleeves.

tears in my eyes. Reality is always sad and lonely; I must struggle on. I clenched my teeth and thought; a courageous, glittering, and determined smile rose to my lips. The sun is shining brightly. I will work hard—what a pleasant feeling this is.

****

It was the next day that I returned to my hometown. It was twilight. I stood lingering in the gate in my newly bought, air-cushion *zōri*[487] that were already falling apart. My appearance—my feelings—at that time.

> Coming back
> With feelings of delight and sadness
> At first I hesitated to enter
> This place, my home.

That night was completely ecstatic. Seeing my mother I cried; seeing my sister and brothers, I cried. From my flood-like happy tears arose various feelings, tangled, entwined, melting, flowing, so passionate and strong as to make both my head and heart ache.

Happiness that was like fragrant *kunshu sake*,[488] filled my entire body to overflowing, but made my unending sadness all the more darkly melancholic.

I don't know how to describe it. I, who more than others, am a person of passion verging on insanity, at such a time I did not know what to do other than cast down my eyes in front of my parents, brothers and sister, who are unrivalled in the world, whom I have tearfully missed and been longing to see.

Article 104: MY LIFE HENCEFORTH

The indistinct, hazy dream of the pilgrimage has already ended. When I think about it, it seems to be an invention.

"Why is she doing such a drastic thing?"

---

[487] Takamure's term is "air zōri".
[488] Kunshu is a fragrant type of sake.

"No, that's a rumour. I hear she's in Kumamoto."

Even amongst people in my hometown I heard that various rumours had been circulated. It seems that there were some people who were surprised because they'd thought I had become a real nun. Become a nun? Indeed. I have a pretty strong aspiration to be a nun. I probably would already have become one if I had not thought of my parents' sorrow. There's no maybe about it. Actually, I even had the experience of secretly sneaking away from home in the spring of my twelfth year with the intention of entering a temple.

My fear is "death". It is always "death". Permanent nothingness—the eternal void. How empty, fathomless, large, inextricable, and terrifying a pit it is!

I'm a person with a death sentence! I always think that. Life is threatened by impending death! I always think that. My parents' death—when I inadvertently think about a matter of such intense grief, I am racked with fear. I become so frightened that I'd rather die before them. "Death" is terrifying. It is unbearably frightening.

My laughter, my sorrow, my confusion, and my uneasiness always arise from this. Consequently, in the midst of great despair I pass each day of my life only by sculpting small dreams. The usual sorrow and joy, grief and pleasure of human beings are small dreams for me. I continually think of the vast sky. I think of death. Ah ….

Yes, I am much more emotional than others. In my heart are surging blood and excitable tears. Uncontrollable passions, intoxicated, crazy, singing, burning, torrential passions suddenly arise. Yes, they are uncontrollable passions. This is what I thought: Maybe I would be happy if I died suddenly enveloped by these strange feelings, my whole body bathed in suffocating blood and tears.

I was unable to move my pen further. All at once ardent emotions swarmed together and overcame me and I was utterly bewildered.

Well, I will skip that and think about the problem of "my life henceforth". To tell the truth, I had intended to be in

Kumamoto. I had intended to look for sweat-smeared pearls.[489] However, my parents do not agree. That is natural. So I have immediately changed my mind. I don't think this is inconsistent or weak willed. I want nothing more than to live an honest life. I want nothing more than to live a serious life.

    I will be glad if, overcoming all temptations, I can become a warm and gentle, kind and good natured, noble, modest, godly, and devout woman. Making my parents happy is my greatest and only pleasure. I will do the laundry, I will cook, I will read and I will write poems.

    Above my head clouds are flowing leisurely, before my eyes water is flowing slowly; time is flowing, carving out the inner reaches of my heart.[490]

    Flowing! Flowing! Everything is flowing!

Article 105: (UNTITLED)

Today, also, it has become evening. The sky above the forest is pinkish. It is sunset. I am thinking of going down to the water's edge later, as I usually do, and walking about, crossing over hills and threading through fields. Yesterday my sister and I, like two little birds, went on an enjoyable, beautiful walk in the mountains.

    At one time, with hot blood overflowing in my heart, I used to think of and long to be like that young girl, Joan of Arc. Even now, thinking of that makes my blood stir. I also am a human being; I want to bless my happy youthfulness, to glorify it, to cry about it, to laugh about it.

    While I was smiling for no particular reason, an old lady of the village came by. When I am alone, I pretentiously sink into deep thought and when dealing with people of the real world such as old men and old women, I blunder greatly in my words and actions—I think this is not good. In Shikoku, also, I had that kind of experience. That was when I was walking through Tosa

---

489 What does she mean by this—diamonds in the rough?
490 Perhaps here she intends to echo the opening sentences of 'An account of my hut" (Hōjōki) by Kamo no Chomei: 行く川のながれは絶えずして、しかも本の水にあらず. The flowing river never stops and yet the water never stays the same.

and was, as usual, intently absorbed in thought— thinking about the power of freedom.

"I must love; I must love. Everything is my beloved." When I had become wound up, at that point there was a teahouse where an old lady was sitting.

"Won't you sit down? You're a sweet thing. How old are you?"

When she asked me various things, I had neither freedom nor love. I just stiffened up, blushed bright red, and fidgeted. When I think about what happened that time, I cannot help but laugh.

But I am determined; I am determined.

While I was foolishly getting worked up it became dark. I have an unbearably heavy feeling in my chest as though there is something important that I have to write.

But, I will put an end to my tale right here. I don't need to say anything, to write anything. Farewell to the dreams, large and small, of my pilgrimage journal! Flying things, fly away! Departing things, be gone! If you want to drift, drift! If you want to vanish, vanish! Just let everything be as it is ….

- "origin Mandala" photo project
- Suzuka Yasu, born in 1947
- pilgrimage for his mother's death
- starts on 8/8/01 on 54th bday
- ends on his 55th bday
- buddhist priest: live like you're excited for each day
- "one"-ness of the many, the "many"-ness of just one
- Someone standing in front of the temple holding a pic of (cycle)
- infinite regress

MAP OF THE SHIKOKU PILGRIMAGE

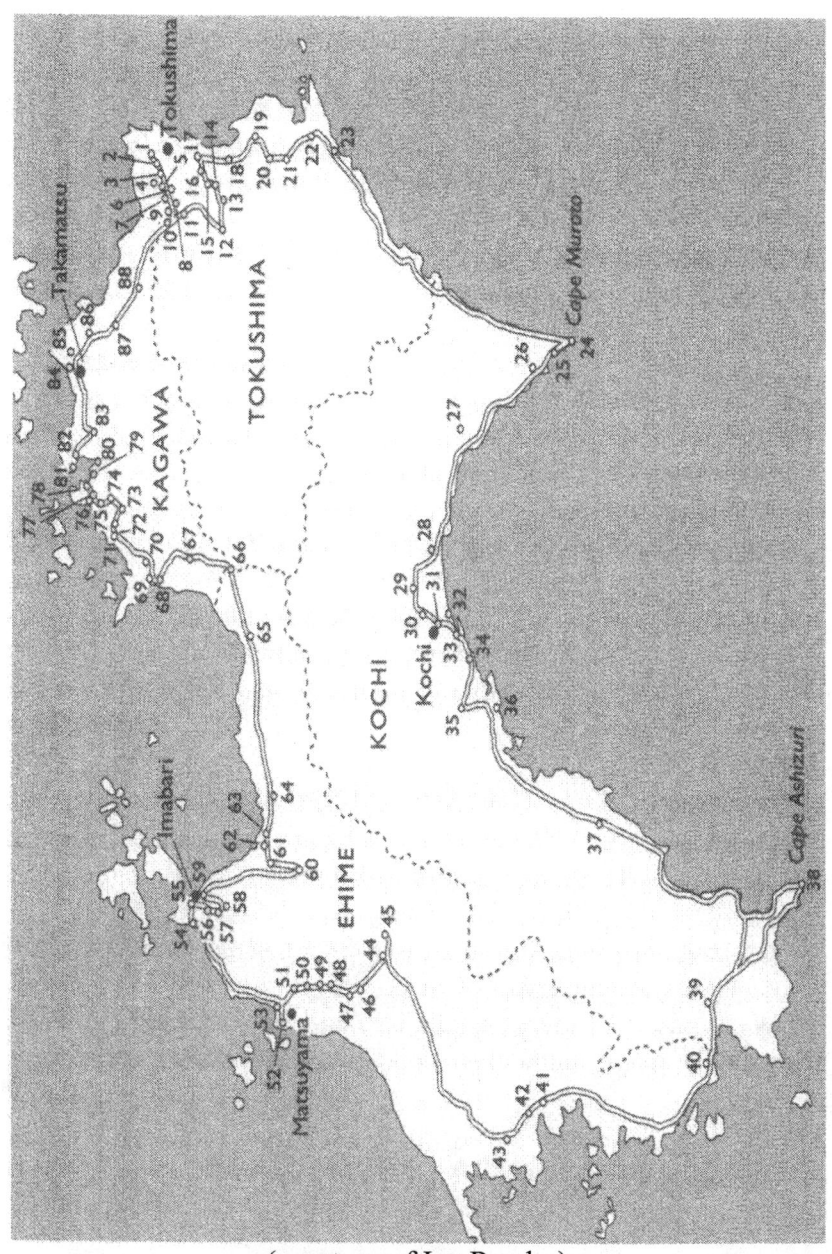

(courtesy of Ian Reader)

WHAT IS THE SHIKOKU PILGRIMAGE?

Every year more than one hundred thousand pilgrims of every Buddhist denomination visit the island of Shikoku, the smallest of the four main islands of Japan, in order to follow in the footsteps of a great Buddhist saint, Kōbō Daishi (also known as Kūkai; 774-835).

Kōbō Daishi was born in Shikoku to a powerful family and sent at an early age to Nara to study to be a court official. He was told by a monk he met there that if he chanted the mantra of Kokuzō Bosatsu one million times, his memory would so improve that he would be able to memorize all the Buddhist sutras. Hoping to achieve this, he returned to Shikoku and engaged in ascetic practice in the mountains and by the sea, in places where practitioners of Shugendō, Japanese mountain religion, also practiced. When he was nineteen, he attained enlightenment at Muroto Cape in southern Shikoku.

In 804 he traveled to China to study Esoteric Buddhism and, while there, he was appointed the eighth patriarch of Esoteric Buddhism. Upon his return to Japan, he founded Shingon Buddhism, and became an important religious leader. He also became an influential figure in the Japanese court and was one of the great Japanese calligraphers. He was a multi-talented genius, an artist, engineer, educator, philosopher, poet, and writer, and, for that reason, is sometimes referred to as the Leonardo da Vinci of Japan.

In 818 Kōbō Daishi asked the Emperor to grant him the land of Mount Kōya in Wakayama Prefecture so that he could build a temple complex. This request was granted and a large religious community grew up on the mountain. In 835, after predicting the date of his own death, Kūkai entered into a state of deep meditation on Mount Kōya. Even now his followers believe that he did not die and that he will, in future, return from this state of eternal meditation. Pilgrims to Shikoku believe that he is traveling with them and for that reason, written on each sedge hat, staff, and bag are the words *dōgyō ni nin* meaning, "Two people traveling together." Pilgrims also believe that any pilgrim they meet may be the saint himself.

The Shikoku pilgrimage is a circular one. Along the route there are eighty-eight temples which pilgrims visit. All of the temples have some connection with Kōbō Daishi but the place of his birth is not at the first temple but, rather, near the seventy-fifth temple, and the twenty-fourth temple, not the eighty-eighth temple, commemorates the place of his enlightenment. Many pilgrims also visit *bangai*,[491] unofficial temples which have a deep connection with Kōbō Daishi, as well as inner sanctuaries of pilgrimage temples. These are called *oku-no-in*. The *oku-no-in* is often in the same compound as the main temple but it can be located at a considerable distance from it.

Pilgrims may begin the pilgrimage at any point but in the past it was traditional for pilgrims to begin at either the first or the forty-third temple as these are the temples closest to the ferry ports for ships from Honshū or Kyūshū. Although most pilgrims today travel by car or chartered bus, or even by helicopter, in the past pilgrims walked the 1400 kilometre pilgrimage route, which roughly traces the circumference of the island. Most walking pilgrims take approximately two months to complete the route.

Although the ideograms for the name of the island, Shikoku, denote "four countries" and refer to the four prefectures on the island, the sound of the first syllable, "shi", is the same as the pronunciation of the word "death". Indeed, the pilgrimage to Shikoku has always been connected with the idea of death; the long pilgrimage journey was dangerous and many pilgrims died en route. Furthermore, in Japan the color of death is white and the pilgrims' white robes signify death to the everyday world and preparation for death. Pilgrims are often dressed in their pilgrimage robes when they die.

Pilgrims make the journey for various religious and secular reasons. Some are praying for health for themselves or loved ones; others are praying that they will be spared senility in old age and have a quick and painless death. Some are hoping for success in some aspect of life, perhaps entry to a prestigious

---

491 The number of *bangai* and *oku-no-in* are not clear. Hoshino (1997) says that Henro Michi Hozon Kyoryokukai (1991) lists 248 sites at which pilgrims should worship: the 88 temples, 148 *bangai* temples (these would include the *oku-no-in*), and numerous wayside statues and shrines.

university, economic prosperity, or finding a good marriage partner. Those who are sorrowing hope to find relief; those who have been bereaved often carry the memorial tablet of the person who has died. Nowadays some may travel more as tourists on a sightseeing trip and some who walk may see the pilgrimage mainly as a physical challenge.

Shikoku pilgrims are known as *"o-henro-san"*, a name with both an honorific prefix and an honorific suffix, both of which denote respect for the person engaged in the spiritual practice of the pilgrimage. Shikoku residents are known for their generosity in giving food, money, small necessities, and even shelter to o-henro-san. This custom of *osettai* is based on the Buddhist belief that those who give alms to monks who support themselves by begging gain merit. In the earliest days of the pilgrimage, those who were travelling were priests and monks and even now, the pilgrims' clothing sets them apart as sacred. In addition, since it is believed that any pilgrim may be Kōbō Daishi himself, giving *osettai* to the Daishi himself would be an act of great merit. Pilgrims receiving *osettai* give a small slip of paper (*osame fuda*) to the donor on which the name of the pilgrim is written. Formerly, this paper was believed to have miraculous power and was kept by the Shikoku family as a talisman to ward off evil.

Although the custom of *osettai* remains, the custom of providing free lodging (*zenkonyado*) is now seldom practiced, probably because most pilgrims now travel as part of large tours. Although there are still pilgrims walking alone, estimated at one thousand a year, they are not usually poor and can afford to pay for accommodation; in addition, they can book lodging before arrival by using a telephone. A number of the Shikoku temples provide accommodation for pilgrims.

In the past there were pilgrims known to Shikoku residents as *"hendo"*. These were people whom society considered undesirable, lovers involved in illicit relations, people accused of or found guilty of crimes, people with mental afflictions, those with leprosy (Hansen's disease), cancer, tuberculosis, or venereal diseases. In the past, "going to Shikoku" was a euphemism for having an incurable disease.

People with Hansen's disease, which was considered a form of divine punishment, were often driven away from their homes in other parts of Japan and sent to Shikoku. There they might experience a miraculous cure but, if not, at least they would not bring shame on their family at home.

In addition, there were also pilgrims who swindled the gullible, especially women, by selling medicines and offering exorcisms. There were even vaudeville groups who entertained the travelling pilgrims. Many of these "professional pilgrims" would walk the Shikoku pilgrimage path until they died, begging for their food, lodging, and other necessities. In the Meiji and Taisho eras, it is said that there were almost one thousand professional pilgrims, who can be considered to be similar to the homeless people of today, wintering in Kōchi.

WHO WAS TAKAMURE ITSUE?

Takamure Itsue (1894-1964) is known in Japan as a pioneering feminist scholar who wrote extensively on the history of Japanese women. After studying the institution of marriage in Japan for thirty years by reading ancient documents and records, she concluded that the Japanese marriage system until the Heian period had been a matrilineal one with the man being summoned to the woman's home for marriage. This idea challenged the then-accepted belief that the original Japanese family system had been a patrilineal one in which the family line was passed on through male children and a woman married into the husband's family. She wrote voluminously about her research findings, publishing many scholarly books. She also authored a four-volume *History of Women.* Takamure's ideas remain controversial in Japan today and her contributions to the history of Japanese women are not included in Japanese high school textbooks.

Scholars outside Japan have shown interest not only in her writings on women's history but also in Takamure's autobiographical writing,[492] which she began in the 1930s but was unable to complete before her death in 1964. In particular, attention has been paid to Takamure's remarkable relationship with Kenzō Hashimoto which began with infatuation on her part,

---

492 For example, Ryang, Sonia, (1998) "Love and Colonialism in Takamure Itsue's Feminism: A Postcolonial Critique", Feminist Review No. 60, Autumn, pp. 1-32; Reynolds, Katsue and Christine Andrews, (1994) "Conflict and Resolution: Takamure Itsue as a Woman Scholar", Women in Hawai'i, Asia and the Pacific, The Office for Women's Research Working Papers Series, Volume 3, (K.Heyer ed.), pp. 37-44; Ronald P. Loftus, (1996), "Female Self-Writing: Takamure Itsue's Hi no Kuni no Onna no Nikki", Monumentica Nipponica: Studies in Japanese culture, Vol. 51, No. 2, pp. 153-170; Monnet, Livia, (1989)," 'In the beginning woman was the sun': Autobiographies of modern Japanese women writers--1", Japan Forum, Vol. 1, No. 1, April, pp. 197-233; Chabot, Jeanette Taudin, (1985), "Takamure Itsue: The first historian of Japanese women", Women's Studies International Forum, Vol. 8, No.4, pp. 287-290; Tsurumi, E. Patricia, (1985) "Feminism and Anarchism in Japan: Takamure Itsue, 1894-1964", Bulletin of Concerned Asian Scholars, Vol. 17 (2) pp. 2-19; Germer, Andrea (2003) "Feminist History in Japan: National and International Perspectives", Intersections, Issue 9, August 2003.

continued with her submission to his physical and emotional abuse during the early years of their marriage, and ended with Hashimoto's willing subordination of his life and career to her research. It was Hashimoto who completed her autobiography, *Diary of a Woman from the Land of Fire,* in 1965 after her death and published it as the tenth volume of her collected works, *Takamure Itsue Zenshū,*. Unfortunately, these ten volumes do not include Takamure's original account *Musume Junreiki* (The Pilgrimage Journal of a Young Woman), of her pilgrimage journey to Shikoku in 1918 when she was twenty-four. This was first published in 1979 following the discovery of her original newspaper articles in Kumamoto. *Musume Junreiki* is the book translated in this volume.

WHY DID TAKAMURE MAKE THE PILGRIMAGE?

It is not clear why Takamure decided to make her pilgrimage. In the first sentence of *Musume Junreiki*, she says, "Even I myself don't know why I resolved to make the pilgrimage ...." Clearly, she was not deeply motivated by faith in Kōbō Daishi as her first plan was to visit the thirty-three Kannon temples in western Japan which comprise the Saigoku pilgrimage, but she impulsively changed her mind when she heard some religious songs of Kōbō Daishi from a man from whom she was seeking advice about making the Saigoku pilgrimage. Perhaps the idea of a pilgrimage occurred to her because her mother had promised before Takamure's birth that if she had a daughter who grew up healthy, she would send her on a pilgrimage.

Takamure was entranced by the idea of a wandering pilgrimage and spoke of wanting to drift with no fixed destination. Japan has a long tradition of travellers who kept diaries and composed poems as they roamed;[493] perhaps thoughts of such writers were at the back of her mind although she does not mention them.

The adventure of a pilgrimage appealed to her romantic

---

[493] For example Bashō 1644-94), poet, essayist, writer of travel sketches in the early Edo period.

and spiritual nature. As she says in Article 1, "Going on a pilgrimage—that's particularly easy for me. There is nothing in the world more painful than stagnating. I even think that venturing recklessly into an unknown world has perhaps more significance than that." When she made her pilgrimage in 1918 it was a dangerous journey and she speaks often of death, of which she was greatly afraid, but she also says, "Life and death are of no concern. I want to acquire faith and a sense of wonder; I want to acquire joy or frenzied passion. Somehow or other, while I am suffering in agony and wailing loudly, I may arrive at an incomparably majestic and lofty faith." (Article 9)

However, she was probably motivated most of all by her personal problems at that time. She had no job or money and the man she loved was unhappy with her insistence upon chastity while another man was pestering her with his avowals of love. It seems likely the pilgrimage was a means of escape from the chaos of her life. Throughout Takamure's life she tended to flee when circumstances became difficult.

TAKAMURE'S LIFE BEFORE THE PILGRIMAGE

Takamure Itsue was born in 1894 on the island of Kyūshū, the southernmost of the four main Japanese islands, in the village of Toyokawa, Kumamoto Prefecture. She was the first child to survive in her family, her mother having previously lost three sons, one being stillborn and the other two dying soon after birth. Hoping for a healthy daughter because of the Japanese saying, "First a daughter, then a son",[494] her mother, Tōyoko, decided to travel to Fukuoka Prefecture to worship a famous Kiyomizu Kannon there[495] but, because she became pregnant before setting out, she traveled only as far as Aso where, in a small temple, she prayed fervently to the Kiyomizu Kannon. At that time, Takamure's mother promised Kannon that if she had a healthy daughter who grew up, she would send her on a pilgrimage.

Because Itsue was born on the eighteenth day of the month, a day sacred to Kannon Bosatsu, her parents considered

---

494 いちひめにたろう； 一姫二太郎

495 in the Chikugo Sanmon district

her to be the "child of Kannon". She was taught to celebrate the feast days of Kannon on the eighteenth of each month by kneeling before the Kannon image on the family altar and making food offerings; according to popular belief, religious services on such a day have particular merit. In her childhood Takamure truly believed herself to be the child of Kannon, and her parents and two younger brothers and sister, believing the same, treated her with unusual respect.

Takamure's father, Katsutaro, an elementary school teacher and headmaster of village schools, taught his wife Chinese history and literature, Japanese poetry and literature,[496] and read newspapers and magazines aloud to her. This was unusual behaviour. Takamure described them as a devoted couple who did everything together from mountain hiking to performing in village plays. However, at times her father became an abusive drinker and when he had been drinking, he pursued his wife and forced her to have sex with him. When his wife resisted demands made in front of the children, he kicked and hit her and at those times, Takamure used to take her brothers and sister outside. Takamure commented that her mother, who had once been so beautiful, became thin and haggard because of this treatment by her husband. His excessive drinking may have been the cause of his moving from one village to another.

At that time girls studied only subjects which would make them "good wives and wise mothers" with emphasis placed on sewing, cooking, childcare, and reading *Onna Daigaku* (Greater Learning for Women), the eighteenth-century Confucian treatise on female subservience.[497] Itsue always received high marks and was usually the top student in her class. She learned classical

---

[496] Statler, p. 276
[497] 762. Thought to be by Kaibara Ekken or by his wife, Kaibara Tokken, Onna Daigaku stated, for example, that "More precious in a woman is a virtuous heart than a face of beauty. The vicious woman's heart is ever excited; she glares wildly around her, she vents her anger on others, her words are harsh and her accent vulgar. When she speaks it is to set herself above others, to upbraid others, to envy others, to be puffed up with individual pride, to jeer at others, to outdo others, all things at variance with the "way" in which a woman should walk. The only qualities that befit a woman are gentle obedience, chastity, mercy, and quietness.."

Chinese from her father and is said to have taught her younger brothers and other young people in the village how to read a Chinese classic when she was twelve. In later years her skill in reading classical Chinese enabled her to read and understand the ancient records which she used in her research into the history of Japanese women. Her familiarity with the Chinese classics can be seen in her pilgrimage account.

Takamure was a person of extreme emotional sensitivity. Even as an adult, she was described as meek, shy, and able to speak only with great difficulty. At six, she was so deeply troubled by being present at her Grandmother Takamure's death that she was unable to eat. When she was twelve, she ran away from home in order to become a nun, but abandoned the idea and returned home when she thought of her parents' feelings. This was the first of her home-leaving experiences.

Because her father wanted her to become a teacher, she entered the women's section of the Kumamoto Prefecture Normal School at the age of fifteen. She found life at the school stressful. She was humiliated when she was unfairly accused of and publicly reprimanded for seeking attention by sending money to a needy orphanage; she had sent the money anonymously and the newspaper which published an article praising her generosity had been able to identify her only through the postmarks on her envelopes.[498] While at the school she developed beriberi and was absent for a long period of time. The following year her parents received a notice asking for her withdrawal from school. This was a terrible blow as she had been her parents' pride and joy. It is not clear why she was asked to leave, but the school was very strict, allowing no make up or fancy hair styles and her classmates remember Takamure as using much make up, her face very white, lips very red, and her hair in the butterfly (*chochomage*) style. She also dressed very fashionably. The school's philosophy did not allow such freedom of personal expression.

After leaving the normal school, she studied on her own and was accepted as a fourth year student at Kumamoto Girls School. After the year of study she expected to become a teaching

---

498 Statler, p.277

assistant, but through some sort of bureaucratic error her name was not on the list of candidates for the exam to qualify her as a teacher. She was secretly pleased as it was her father's desire that she become a teacher, not hers. She then decided to help her family financially by becoming a factory girl in a cotton-spinning mill. It is estimated that at this time her father's drinking consumed half of his monthly salary.[499]

At that time many female workers entered spinning mills in order to help their families and the Japanese government encouraged women to be hard working and productive. The living conditions were appalling, with insufficient and poor quality food, unsanitary dormitories, and inadequate bathing facilities. Within the mills, lighting, heating, and ventilation were poor, and the air was full of cotton dust. In exchange for their low pay, the women worked at least twelve hours a day, and chronically fatigued workers who developed tuberculosis or beriberi were sent home to die in their villages.

Recruiters from factories attracted girls from country villages by promising that they would learn to read and write, but most girls were too tired after twelve hours of work to study anything, even if there were a teacher available which was unusual. However, Takamure steadfastly continued her studies during the four months she spent working in the factory. Her work ended when her father discovered that his daughter was working in a cotton spinning mill, and wrote to the manager. The manager sent her home saying that the mill was no place for a teacher's daughter.

One year after leaving Kumamoto Girls School, Itsue began working as a substitute teacher. She first worked in a school about four kilometres from her home, walking a mountain road to and from school each day. Because she looked so young, students there often thought she was a high school student. Her father soon arranged for her to transfer to his school in Haraigawa, the town where the family was living. She worked there for three and a half years and in later life continued to have an interest in education, writing many essays on the subject. This interest can also be seen in her account of her pilgrimage journey.

---

[499] *Waga Takamure Itsue* (p.76)

TAKAMURE'S ROMANCE WITH HASHIMOTO

When she was twenty-three, because of a short piece which she had written for an educational journal in Kumamoto Prefecture, she received a postcard from Kenzō Hashimoto, a man three years her junior, who was also an assistant teacher in a village school in Kumamoto Prefecture. He invited her to write for a round robin magazine that he was going to circulate.[500] They began an exchange of letters and eight months later, they met in Yatsushiro, a town midway between his hometown and Matsubase, the town where, for the purpose of meeting him, she had arranged to attend a summer training course. Although she had previously sent him ardent letters, Takamure was shy and uncommunicative when they actually met. She wore a white kimono, which was a strange choice as white is the color of death in Japanese culture.

After meeting at the station they walked by the river and then went back to the room he had reserved in a Japanese inn. They ate their dinner in the room in silence. After the maid had prepared their bedding on the floor, they got under the mosquito netting together but Takamure sat, fully clothed, in a corner. Hashimoto tried to force himself upon her but, in the end, abandoned the attempt.

In the morning Takamure took the first train back, without eating breakfast. Hashimoto walked her to the station but could not go on to the platform with her. When the old lady with whom she was staying told her that she had mismanaged things, Takamure telegraphed Hashimoto to say that she would come the next day to the town next to his hometown. This time she dressed more stylishly, wearing a silk kimono with violet sleeves, but they had only thirty minutes together before she had to catch her return train. During that short time, she did not speak but Hashimoto kissed her.

Upon returning, she wrote to him saying, "I vow eternal love to you. If I am false to you, I'll accept whatever you do. I'm

---
500 One copy was made and circulated among a group of teachers

keeping your letters carefully. My beloved." She was upset and hurt when, after some time, he replied saying, "There is nothing in this life that is eternal. There is only the moment so shall we go as far as we can?"

Hashimoto's ideas concerning love had been influenced by the ideas expressed in *Sanin*, a notorious Russian novel by Mixail Artsybashev (1907) in which Sanin, a selfish and cynical hedonist, has sexual relations with various women without becoming emotionally involved. Hashimoto, although attracted by the idea of this kind of love, did not, in fact, have such experience despite the fact that at that time in Japan it was not uncommon for men to have sex with many women and with prostitutes. Furthermore, Hashimoto was in no position to pledge eternal love as his family was poor and he had graduated only from upper primary school, had lost the sight of one eye because of a childhood accident, and was physically weak. In addition, Hashimoto was interested in the Japanese naturalist movement, which viewed the possession of a fully developed sense of identity as most important and sought to look objectively at family ties, the position of women in society, and the life of people in the provinces. Hashimoto's new ideas were in startling contrast to the traditional Confucian virtues Takamure had absorbed at home.

Takamure was a firm believer in chastity and at the age of sixteen had written in a poem, *A Girl's Chastity*, "I want to be pure. I detest wantonness. Unchaste women are animals." Her position may have been the result of her father's drunken lust for her mother and may also have been influenced by the old custom of yobai, night crawling, which continued to exist in the mountain villages of Kumamoto Prefecture where she was raised although it had been forbidden by the Meiji government. *Yobai* often involved young men and women pairing off during village festivals and retreating to the bushes for sexual encounters. In some places, groups of bachelors would visit the homes of young women, do *janken*[501] outside the house to choose one young man to enter the house and the girl's room, the door of which would

---

501 Choosing someone through the game of paper, scissors, stone done with the hand.

have been left open. The other young men proceeded on to another house with an eligible young woman in it.

In October 1917, a little over a month after meeting Hashimoto, Takamure quit her teaching job at her father's school in mid term and moved to Kumamoto to attempt to become a newspaper reporter with the Kumamoto Nichi Nichi newspaper and also to increase her opportunities to meet Hashimoto. She and her youngest brother lived in Sennen-ji temple where she had lived before when going to school in Kumamoto. She became a member of a female poetry group and both with the group and independently contributed a number of articles and poems to the Kumamoto Nichi Nichi newspaper but was not able to become a reporter. This may have been because at that time the newspaper was an organ of a political party and it was impossible to get a job without political connections .

Life in Kumamoto City was difficult for Takamure. After her brother had graduated and returned home, there was no longer any money from her parents. That year the price of rice rose rapidly in Japan and she had no regular job. She did piece work in her room, making both hemp rope and thongs for geta;[502] she also helped the cooper who lived in the back room at the temple sell his products on the street. She was so troubled, poor, hungry, and desperate that at one point she even took a small amount of money from the donation box at the temple and bought some food with it; however, she found she could not eat the food for fear of divine punishment.

In the next eight months she saw Hashimoto only twice. The first time was in December. He surprised her by an unannounced visit to the temple. They climbed a hill near the temple and spent two hours talking. The second visit was late in January. Itsue told Kenzō that they would meet at the Someya, ("dyed inn") and Kenzō asked her "What is it dyed with?" Itsue felt that his reply had a sexual connotation so she immediately changed the arrangements. On the day of the visit, she did not take him to the inn and within an hour she had sent him to the Upper Kumamoto station where he boarded the train and returned home. After this second meeting, he wrote to her and said, "Don't

---

502 Japanese wooden sandals

make a fool of me." She wrote back assuring him that she loved him dearly but said that although sexual love was natural, she had no desire for it. She also said, "Although I say I don't want it, really I am afraid of it."

Hashimoto came to Kumamoto a third time and booked a room in a Japanese inn near the temple but they did not meet. She later wrote him a letter of apology in which she said that her mother had come to visit at the same time and that when she and her mother walked the street in front of the inn on their way to the public bath, she had thought longingly of him.

Another man was courting her at the same time; a young man who three times in one day sent her letters written in his own blood. This man, called "H" by Takamure and Hashimoto and now thought to be Furukawa Setsuo, was active in poetry circles in Kumamoto City. He was an emotional man who cried easily and had even threatened to commit suicide by jumping off a cliff. Because of her tenderhearted, sympathetic nature, Takamure was unable to reject H outright but her inability to do so complicated her relationship with Kenzō, who treated her coldly. Takamure loved Hashimoto but wanted to remain chaste. At the same time she did not reject suicidal, tearful Furukawa, which angered Hashimoto.

When, on the spur of the moment, she decided to make the Shikoku pilgrimage, she had been living in Kumamoto like this for about seven months and had told neither her parents nor Hashimoto about her financial difficulties. She visited the City Editor of the Kumamoto Nichi Nichi newspaper, Miyazaki Daitarō and was given ten yen for travel expenses, in exchange for which she promised to send dispatches to the newspaper describing her experiences. Other than that preliminary payment, she set off with nothing, trusting everything to fate. Later, she received an additional thirty yen from the newspaper, but the total amount of money she received was not enough for a five and a half month trip. From June 6 to December 16, 1918, she contributed one hundred and five articles to the newspaper describing her physical and emotional journey, the people she met, and her unusual experiences. These articles, unchanged, were published together as *Musume Junreiki*.

The day before leaving on the pilgrimage she wrote a letter to Hashimoto saying, "Please do not tell people that I am going on a journey crossing fields, crossing mountains." He replied, "Wear a sturdy pair of drawers."

TAKAMURE BECOMES A CELEBRITY

Takamure began the pilgrimage on June 4, 1918, setting off on foot from Kumamoto City to walk across the island of Kyūshū to Saganoseki, Ōita Prefecture, where she would board a ferry to Shikoku. Although not yet on Shikoku, she dressed in pilgrim robes and thus received help from people whom she met en route because of her status as a pilgrim. Although she makes no mention of this in her newspaper articles, it is known that Furukawa, the Kumamoto suitor, accompanied her for the first day.

Hashimoto did not know of this until he read Furukawa's novel, serialized in five installments, which was published from October 26-30, 1918 in the rival newspaper, the Kyūshū Shinbun. The story, *The Tale of Tamiko and Me*, told of a man seeing a woman off as she left on a pilgrimage and walking with her for the first day. Although the story implied that the two were lovers, it was a fictional work and one cannot assume that there was a sexual relationship between Furukawa and Takamure; however, the readers of the newspaper probably made that assumption.

The day after Furukawa's story ended, October 31, the first installment of Hashimoto's story, *Mountain Woman*, was published in the same newspaper, in the same column. Four other installments were later published in January 1919 at the request of readers, which probably indicates that people in Kumamoto were keenly interested in Takamure. Hashimoto's story told of a man who trifles with a young, beautiful, independent woman who has left her home and gone to live in the city and states that their relationship has progressed to a deep level.

The newspaper stories written by the two men led to exaggerated rumours about Takamure. In addition, there were also rumours about another man, a friend of Hashimoto named Koyama Katsukiyo. He was the son of a doctor near Kumamoto and later became a writer of children's books. It is possible Koyama was also in love with Takamure. Hashimoto reported that Koyama had called Takamure "a vampire sucking men's blood", "a walking monster eating men" and a "she-devil".

It was against this background that Takamure's own articles about her pilgrimage were published in the Kumamoto Nichi Nichi Newspaper. The newspaper was surprised and pleased by their popularity. Their sensational success can be attributed to a number of factors: first, at that time it was unusual for a young woman to travel alone; second, because there was not the same access to information as there is now, Takamure's descriptions of pilgrim life were fascinating; and third, because Takamure's emotional writing style was compelling. However, the chief reason for the astonishing success of her articles was perhaps people's interest in Takamure herself, the interest having been fueled by Hashimoto's and Furukawa's published stories. One young man living near Kobe who had followed the course of her pilgrimage in the newspaper became so enamoured of her that he tried to drown himself when her engagement to Hashimoto was announced after her return to Kumamoto.

The newspaper articles reveal her intelligence, emotional intensity, spirituality, wit and charm. The reader can sense Takamure's personal confusion and can also gain insight into her ideas and philosophy of life at that time. Although Takamure later criticized her writing saying, "At that time I didn't yet know the technique of filling … a page, I just wrote my feelings and thoughts as they were," it is this breathless spontaneity that is so appealing to the reader. Because the writer of the accounts seems very young, it is hard to remember that at the time of the pilgrimage Takamure was already twenty-four years old and had been working as a teacher for three years.

Although Hashimoto treated her coldly before the pilgrimage and during it, he clipped her articles at night at the school where he worked. However, these clippings were later lost when they moved and she had no access to her newspaper articles during her lifetime.

TAKAMURE'S PILGRIMAGE JOURNEY

When Takamure set out on her journey, she was not very concerned about having only ten yen because of the pilgrimage traditions of *osettai* and *zenkonyado* on Shikoku. It seems that *zenkonyado* was a custom not only on Shikoku but also in Kyūshū, because Takamure was given accommodation by local people as she traveled towards Saganoseki.

Takamure's travel plans changed dramatically when she met old man Itō . Now she had a protector, a man of deep faith but an ignorant and superstitious man. Takamure arrived at Itō's house on June 10 and by June 13, articles she had written were being published in the Ōita newspaper (in addition to the ones being published in Kumamoto). Altogether nine articles appeared in the Ōita newspaper, the last one on June 27. These articles created much interest and she became a celebrity with people travelling long distances to catch a glimpse of her. Many people also wrote letters and postcards to her. Although she speaks of this attention being upsetting to her, in fact she appears to have sought it. When she was in Ōita City en route to Shikoku, she went uninvited to the newspaper company and had an interview, which was also published in the newspaper.

After spending a month at the old man's house while he prepared for the journey, they finally reached Shikoku on July 14. The old man insisted upon walking the route counter-clockwise because travelling in that direction is more difficult and one's spiritual merit increases. In fact, it is said that one trip counter clockwise is equivalent to three trips clockwise. There is also thought to be a greater chance of meeting Kōbō Daishi when travelling this way. This decision meant that they reached Kōchi Prefecture in the southern part of the island in the typhoon season, when there is great heat and humidity, heavy rain and floods. As a result, instead of taking the customary two months to circle Shikoku, they required over three months, not leaving Shikoku until October 24.

The pilgrimage involved considerable physical discomfort. Because Shikoku is very mountainous, going up and down the mountain trails in the heat and humidity of the Japanese summer was exhausting for Takamure, despite the fact that the old man insisted on carrying all the luggage. The pilgrimage was also a dangerous journey, as was attested to by the pilgrim graves she saw beside the path and the news of pilgrims dying. "Since we are human beings, since we are living creatures, we don't know where we will die. It is possible that even I who am writing this will pass away on the pilgrimage. I hear that the other day forty pilgrims died while crossing the Shimanto River .... On the road that I must travel from now on, I will go there." (Article 45)

Takamure and the old man were sometimes forced to sleep outdoors because there was no accommodation nearby when night fell. At other times they were refused accommodation because they were pilgrims and therefore undesirable. After camping out she awoke one morning to find bugs crawling over her and another time to find the sea lapping at her. Even when they did find a home or inn in which to stay, the accommodation was not always clean: there might be dirty bath water or bedding with lice; once they slept in a room attached to a stable with a strong stench. The life that she endured while on the pilgrimage was very different from her life at home.

Their pilgrimage occurred during a period of economic hardship in Japan; the skyrocketing price of rice in the country ultimately lead to the Rice Riots which occurred all over the country during the months that she was traveling, although she does not mention them. Takamure and Itō relied upon gifts from local people and on the proceeds of begging which he insisted on doing by himself; he would not allow Takamure to beg because of her connection with Kannon Bosatsu. This meant that there were days when they went hungry and days when they had plenty to eat. Their relationship was like that of lady and servant; he did all the cooking, ate after her, insisted on carrying all the bags, and when they arrived at an inn, he immediately massaged her feet with salt.

Itōs ignorance annoyed Takamure greatly; "Really, I don't pay the slightest attention to the old man. Sometimes when I think that he is probably very bored, I turn around and look at him. At that time, I suddenly feel sorry for him and try to engage in a few words of conversation, but I soon become disgusted and give up." (Article 50) She took refuge in reading as she walked in order to avoid speaking to him. Her choice of reading material, such as works by Tagore and Björnson, both Nobel prize winners, is indicative of her intelligence and interest in the world beyond rural Japan.

Those three months tested Takamure physically and emotionally. Her loneliness and sense of isolation were intense; again and again she writes of longing for her parents and Kumamoto and of weeping with loneliness. She seems to have been happiest when she met young girls along the way with whom she could exchange girlish chatter. She waxed lyrical about such encounters. "She was a lovely young girl with beautiful hair, a young girl who seemed the embodiment of pure beauty. I like females best when they are girls. Pure, childlike and innocent—I want females to be like that forever." (Article 51)

Takamure's fellow pilgrims were, for the most part, uneducated, ignorant, diseased, handicapped, materialistic, and sometimes even frightening, not the sort of people with whom a young woman from a good home was familiar. Takamure was a keen observer and describes these people so that they come alive. The reader not only sees them as individuals but also understands the condition of outcasts in Taishō Japan.

Because begging was forbidden by the authorities, for these moneyless Shikoku pilgrims there was always the danger of arrest and expulsion from a prefecture. When she was in Yawatahama at the end of her journey, the police visited the *kichinyado* where she was staying and offered money for rice but this was a ruse; they were hoping to arrest pilgrims who had been begging.[503] That same day a woman staying at their pilgrim inn was taken to jail because she had been begging.

Takamure's pilgrimage account became less detailed after she reached Sanuki (now Kagawa) and when she was traveling in the remaining part of Iyo (now Ehime). (She had started her pilgrimage in Iyo.) From Sanuki until the time she reached home she wrote only about one fifth of the whole series although the distance was probably closer to two fifths of the total distance. However, it was in Sanuki that the anguish that she had been suffering for months lifted.

---

503 *Waga Takamure Itsue*, p. 188

That the pilgrimage was a period of personal transformation for Takamure can be seen if one compares her feelings about her fellow passengers on her way to Shikoku with her feelings on her return voyage. Going to Shikoku she wrote, "In the cabin, really, it is unbearably ghastly. .... If even this cabin is like this, how much worse it must be in third class. It is almost no different from a group of wild animals living together. Forlornly sitting upright on a tatami mat in a corner, I shudder to think of the scene when all the people sleeping uncouthly like this stand up at the same time." (Article 33)

Returning to Kyūshū she wrote, "The old man and I sat against the portside hull of the ship as though fastened to it, but against the starboard hull across from us, four brazen, ungainly, fat women were reclining, eating uninhibitedly and laughing in loud voices. In spite of that it was really an enviably beautiful scene; to all appearances they were enjoying themselves as they held hands and talked together familiarly.

Ah, how happy are people who have friends to talk and laugh with, simply and sincerely like that! If I lose everything else it will not matter; I just want to live with an unreserved and open-minded, peaceful and sacred, beautiful feeling that does not make the slightest distinction toward anyone. Without intending to, I could not help giving a deep sigh when I looked back at my narrow heart that has been annoyingly entangled in empty forms and empty display." (Article 96)

Perhaps the last words of her pilgrimage articles sum up what she learned on the pilgrimage: "Just let everything be as it is." (Article 105)

TAKAMURE'S LIFE AFTER THE PILGRIMAGE

Takamure arrived back in Kyūshū on October 25 and reached her family's home in Haraigawa, Kumamoto Prefecture on November 22. There, readily acceding to her parents' request that she remain near them, she appeared to accept cheerfully the common expectations of Japanese society. "To tell the truth, I had intended to be in Kumamoto City .... However, my parents do not agree. That is natural. So I immediately changed my mind. I don't think this is inconsistent or weak willed. I want nothing more than to live an honest life. I want nothing more than to live a serious life. I will be glad if, overcoming all temptations, I can become a warm and gentle, kind and good natured, noble, modest, godly, and devout woman. Making my parents happy is my greatest and only pleasure. I will do the laundry, I will cook, I will read and I will write poems." (Article 104)

However, this domestic life in the village did not occur. After being away almost six months she felt a longing for spiritual union with Hashimoto, "...for a perfect love and communion between our two souls... Feeling light and with my body and mind purified by my recent pilgrimage, I resumed writing passionate letters to him, letters full of naïve romantic fantasies he usually dismissed as 'mad ravings'. It was as if all the suffering and doubts of the past year had vanished. I felt I absolutely had to attain the most exalted goal in life—the union of my soul with my lover's, the fusion of our minds and bodies into one, just as the goddess Kannon had directed me to. I felt pretty sure I wanted to become one only with Kenzo, that I would never love anyone else, and that I wanted him—that nihilistic, tyrannical and brutish egoist who pretended not to give a damn about the rest of the world—to be mine forever."[504]

At the end of January 1919 she published *The Dawn of Love* in five installments in the Kyūshū newspaper. Hashimoto was moved by these articles in which she explained her philosophy of loving all. He wrote her a letter that pleased her and they became engaged in April 1919 and began living together. She was now able to support herself by writing prose and poetry which she submitted to newspapers.

During this period the old man Itō with whom she had made the pilgrimage came to visit her. He had not known where she was living so had first gone to her parents' house then turned back and come to her home near Hitoyoshi. This was the last time that she saw him although they had some further correspondence. She was later informed of his death in accordance with a request in his will.[505]

---

504 Quoted in Monnet, p.71
505 *Ohenro*, p.62

Hashimoto and Takamure lived together for three months, but she found her life with him unsatisfactory: "I didn't necessarily feel that I was a budding scholar or poet, but there was something there and it made me a somewhat contemplative woman. This did not bode well for my life as a 'service wife'. Anyway, needless to say, this absurd, illusory love state that I was in did not fit at all with [Hashimoto's] demand for a wife who would take care of him. His hot temper would flare up and he would beat me violently."[506] She returned home to her parents, where she wrote and published poetry and made plans to go to Tōkyō. When she reached Tōkyō she published two volumes of poetry, *Nichigetsu no ue ni* (Above the Sun and Moon) and *Hōrōsha no shi* (A Wanderer's Poems), making a brilliant debut and being praised by one famous literary critic as a "genius". These are usually considered her maiden works but, in fact, her newspaper articles that later became *Musume Junrei* had been published three years earlier.

In June 1921 Hashimoto came to Tokyo and persuaded her to return with him to live in seclusion at Yatsugi on the coast of Kumamoto Prefecture. They returned to Tokyo in the early spring of 1922. Itsue, who became pregnant while living in Yatsugi, had a stillborn baby boy on April 10, 1922. She was heartbroken and said later that this sad event made her aware of society's neglect of mothers and children.

In 1923 Hashimoto got a job with the Heibonsha publishing company, and their house began to resemble a clubhouse, full of his friends and co-workers coming by to eat, drink, gamble, or to stay; Takamure was forced to look after them while trying at the same time to do her own writing. It was a frustrating and difficult time for her and on September 19, 1925 she fled the household with Fujii Hisaichi, a man working for Heibonsha who had been living in the house. Although both of them said they were simply planning to visit the thirty-three Kannon temples of western Japan, the route known as the Saigoku pilgrimage, Japanese society was scandalized by the behaviour of Takamure, who was now a well-known writer. Eventually Hashimoto came and escorted her back to Tokyo

---

506 Quoted in Loftus, p. 162

while Fujii continued his pilgrimage alone.

Takamure subsequently wrote a long poem *Ie de no shi* (Leaving Home Poem) in which she defended her flight from home and attacked the marriage system of Japan. Her leaving home in 1925 marked a turning point in her relationship with Hashimoto. He acknowledged the importance of her work, and began to help her. In July 1931, they moved to a house in Setagaya, outside Tokyo, which they called *Mori no ie* (the house in the woods). There she remained until she died, never leaving the house, never meeting people unless necessary, never spending less than ten hours a day on her research. Hashimoto did the housework, searched for materials and brought them home, and devoted himself to helping her with her research and writing, except for four years when he worked for Heibonsha again.

Takamure said that during the pilgrimage she had learned to leave things to fate, that, although her later life had ups and downs, she remained unworried.[507] The pilgrimage was such a powerful experience that she tried twice more to go on a pilgrimage. The first time was the "leaving home" incident of 1925 when she planned to make the Saigoku pilgrimage saying that she felt called by the spirit of her dead child, and the second time was in 1953. At that time she was fifty nine years old and exhausted from her heavy schedule of research and writing; it is even said that she spent so much time at her desk that the side of her clothing which faced the sun became faded. She had become sick with numbness in her limbs, and was confined to bed. Hashimoto suggested another pilgrimage to Shikoku, but she never actually went because her health improved.

Not only did Takamure attempt to make other pilgrimages, she also wrote two books and a number of shorter articles about her pilgrimage. In 1938 she published *Ohenro* (Pilgrim; 282 pages) and in 1939, *Ohenro to Jinsei* (Pilgrims and Life; 265 pages). Her later writing was based upon her notebooks and memory because she did not have access to her original articles despite the fact that Hashimoto had clipped and saved them in 1918. They were unfortunately lost in a move he made in 1925. The Kumamoto newspapers themselves were unavailable,

---

507 Hoshino, p. 84

having been stored away in company warehouses. Her later accounts are much less emotional than her original account and lack its charm.

Takamure died June 7, 1964, of peritonitis resulting from cancer.

THE IMPORTANCE OF TAKAMURE'S PILGRIMAGE ACCOUNT

Other strong and independent women have travelled and written of their adventures. Isabella Bird, an English woman, published fascinating and opinionated accounts of her journeys to distant lands such as Tibet, Persia, America, Hawaii, Japan, China, Malaya, and Korea.[508] Alexandra David Neel, a French Buddhist, made a forbidden pilgrimage to Tibet and described it graphically.[509] Takamure's account of her pilgrimage to Shikoku belongs to this body of literature. She was an adventuresome traveller, an intelligent and observant narrator.

Not only does Takamure tell an excellent story, she also, like Bird and Neel, tells her readers much about the people of the area where she travelled. Hers is a first hand account of a Japan that has now vanished, and readers can experience vicariously rural life in the Taisho period (1912-1926), when large numbers of people living in the rural areas of Japan moved to big cities in order to seek work. Many of the people whom she met on her travels through Kyūshū and Shikoku, were members of a substrata of society: the poor, the sick, the handicapped, the blind, the insane, and the illiterate. When people had jobs, they were sometimes in occupations that no longer exist or are no longer common: such as fortune teller, pipe stem mender, *ukarebushi* singer.

Many of these people were staunch believers in divine acts which could be achieved through the intervention of Kōbō

---

508 For example, *On Horseback in Hawaii: A Canter Across the Sandwich Isles in 1873; A Lady's Ride in the Rockies: Travels on Horseback in 1873; Unbeaten Tracks in Japan: Travels on Horseback in 1878; Journeys in Persia and Kurdistan: Travels on Horseback in 1870; Among the Tibetans: A Legendary 1893 Journey.*
509 *My Journey to Lhasa*, 1927.

Daishi, Kannon Bosatsu, *tengu*, or even Takamure herself. For people with health problems: scabrous boils, Hansen's disease (leprosy), mental afflictions, venereal disease, their only hope was divine intervention and some such sick people, considering Takamure to be a manifestation of Kannon Bosatsu, came to her to be cured.

Takamure was unusually well educated for a young woman at that time; there were many who considered education to be useless for women. The fortune teller extols the life of a geisha for his daughter saying that she will wear fine clothes and eat plentifully. Men in rural communities were also often prevented from getting a higher education because of financial difficulties and family responsibilities. Takamure devotes one article to stories of young men eager to seek educational opportunities and leave their rural communities. At the same time, uneducated people were ready to trust those whom they considered educated, even when such trust, as in the case of a charlatan doctor, was undeserved.

This was a society which was poor. Children were hungry; straw was used as toilet paper; neighbours took turns providing bath water for their community in order to save money and time. Pilgrims were begging for both food and accommodation and knew that if they were caught by the police, they would be expelled from the prefecture in which they were travelling.

Readers will not find discussion of world or national events in Takamure's pilgrimage account. It is interesting to note that during her travels, the First World War ended (November 11, 1918), an event about which Takamure says nothing. Beyond calling it "the disease of the hour", she says little about the world-wide flu pandemic, which began in March 1918 and ultimately afflicted 23 million people in Japan, including herself, and killed 390,000 Japanese. The Rice Riots, unparalleled in modern Japanese history in terms of size and violence, began in July 1918. By September, more than 2 million participants had caused disturbances all over the country causing the prime minister and his cabinet to resign. About this she says only: "There is war; the cabinet collapses, is reorganized, and collapses again; the price of rice rises; the world is in fear and trembling." (Article 94)

A further reason that the pilgrimage articles written by Takamure are important is that these are the only writings of Takamure that can be said with certainty not to have been heavily influenced by her husband Kenzō. Even the two books of poetry which established her reputation as a poet, although written while she was living with her parents after leaving Kenzō, may possibly have been influenced by him. After they returned to Yatsugi from Tokyo, Hashimoto became her first reader and copy editor, and continued to act in that capacity until her death. Because he helped with any work published after that time, it is difficult to separate Takamure's ideas and writing from Hashimoto's. These newspaper articles are the only prose writings that we can say with certainty are in her own voice.

Hashimoto once described Takamure as a combination of dream and will,[510] which seems an apt characterization. The newspaper articles reveal a painfully shy but determined young woman who, at times, went out of her way to attract attention. Her intelligence and wit are palpable; at the same time, she was also a person critical of ignorance in others who could be both arrogant and condescending. She had extensive knowledge of literature, both Asian and Western, intense interest in Buddhism, and delighted in words and in expressing her ideas. In addition, she had a good eye and ear for human foibles. She was curious, observant, amusing, and knew how to win people's hearts, as is clear in her tale of the two young men who were attracted to her en route. She was extremely emotional: "I am much more emotional than others. In my heart are surging blood and excitable tears. Uncontrollable passions, intoxicated, crazy, singing, burning, torrential passions suddenly arise. Yes, they are uncontrollable passions. " (Episode 104)

Although Takamure herself thought her writing in these articles immature and did not want them republished, her passion and naivety are appealing and her voice is as captivating now as it was in 1918. Her style of writing is demanding, with long, complicated sentences but at the same time, Takamure's intense,

---

510 *Waga Takamure Itsue*, p.7

passionate prose has a youthful transparency that allows the reader to see into the sensitive nature of Takamure herself and her pilgrimage account is compelling. The woman who later went on to become a well-known feminist, anarchist, historian and magazine editor, began here, as a woman of flesh and blood, as a young woman who both delights and exasperates her readers.

TANKA POEMS AND *GOEIKA* HYMNS

In the articles Takamure includes poems composed en route. In this she was undoubtedly influenced by traditional Japanese travel diary literature *(kikō bungaku)* in which poems are mixed with prose accounts of places visited, philosophical reflections, and anecdotes. The poems composed by Takamure and the temple hymns (*goeika*) which she quotes are in the form of *tanka*, a poem of 31 syllables with a configuration of 5/7/5/7/7.

Goeika are Buddhist hymns which are sung to the accompaniment of hand bells and small metal gongs. Each of the 88 pilgrimage temples in Shikoku has its own *goeika*. There are various themes for the temple hymns; Buddhist teachings, legends of the temple, the possibility of a future life in Paradise, or the benefits arising from praying to the principal deity of the temple,. For example, the *goeika* of the second temple, Gokuraku-ji, states, "If you wish to go after death to Gokuraku, the Land of Perfect Bliss over which Amida Nyorai presides, always chant 'Namu Amidabutsu'!" Formerly, pilgrims rid their minds of distracting thoughts and attachments by singing the temple hymn as they approached each temple.

The *goeika* are intended to convey Buddhist teachings to lay people; there are often two layers of meaning, a surface layer and a deeper, religious meaning. Often the name of the temple is used as a *kakekotoba*, or pivot word, in the hymn. *Kakekotoba* are rhetorical devices, word plays similar to English puns, that are used in Japanese poetry to suggest several interpretations. Words with the same pronunciation but different meanings are used; for example, the word "matsu" can mean either pine tree or "to wait", depending upon the character used to write it. Often the *kakekotoba* of the hymn is based on the temple name.

Thus, the mountain name of the forty-third temple is Akeishi. The similar-sounding word "ageishi" means to lift a big rock. The *goeika* for that temple is "We hear that Thousand Armed Kannon made a mystic vow and was able to lift a great huge rock". The name of the eleventh temple, Fujiidera, means Wisteria Well Temple and the *goeika* is "Even the colour or scent of wisteria never fails to accord with the Middle Way, always reflecting the ultimate truth."[511]

Tanka and *goeika* have the rhythmic pattern of 5, 7, 5, 7, 7 but are almost always written by the Japanese as one line. The *goeika* in Takamure's pilgrimage account have been translated as one line but her *tanka* have been transformed into four line poems to meet the expectations of English readers regarding poetry. Readers must not judge the worth of these *tanka* and *goeika* by the translations presented here. Not only is a deep knowledge of Buddhism necessary to translate the *goeika* well, but also, in both the *goeika* and the *tanka*, the ambiguity of the words used, the different poetry traditions in English and Japanese, the grammatical inversions and other stylistic devices, references to things inside and outside the poem that would be clear to Japanese readers, and the great differences between the two languages make it difficult, if not impossible, to translate the poems well. Arthur Waley once compared a Japanese poem to a watch saying that a translated poem no longer ticks—it is like a disassembled watch which only a watchmaker would recognize as a possible watch.[512] Thus, unfortunately, it will be impossible for readers of this book to judge Takamure's poetic ability accurately, although she was famous as a poet.

---

511 *Awa Henro: A Bilingual Guidebook for Pilgrims in Tokushima*, 1993, p.121.
512 *As I Crossed a Bridge of Dreams*, 1971, p.18. Quoted in the introduction by Ivan Morris.

GLOSSARY OF TERMS

Amida Nyorai	principal deity of the Pure Land Buddhists (Jōdo). He promised in his eighteenth vow to bring all sentient beings who called upon him to his Pure Land. Thus, believers who invoke the name of Amida (see *nembutsu*) with a sincere heart can achieve rebirth in his Pure Land.
ascetic practice	there are various forms of ascetic practice including standing under waterfalls, meditating in caves or on mountain tops but the Shikoku pilgrims generally used the term to mean begging.
Awa	present day Tokushima Prefecture
bangai	an unofficial temple of the pilgrimage circuit. "*Bangai*" means "without a number"
Bon festival	(or obon) A Buddhist festival honouring the spirits of the dead which are said to return to their homes in mid summer. Families visit their ancestors' graves, welcome the spirits home with food offerings, then see the spirits off.
Bosatsu	a future Buddha who seeks enlightenment not for only for himself but for others. Instead of becoming a Buddha immediately, a Bosatsu vows to save all beings and compassionately helps suffering beings.
bu	one tenth of a *sun*; 3.03 millimeters
Bungo	now Ōita Prefecture
chō	measurement of length equal to 109 meters.
Dainichi Nyorai	principal deity of Shingon Buddhism who is an idealization of the truth of the universe. All things in the universe

	constitute the body of this deity.
Daishi	great teacher
dango	dumpling, cake or other round food made from rice flour and water. It can be sweet or savoury.
dō	a temple building or hall
earthen bridge	the simplest type of earthen bridge is made of bundles of small logs laid on top of longer logs, and then covered with several inches of gravel and soil
fuda	pieces of paper that pilgrims put into a special box at each temple. On them are the pilgrim's name, address, prayers for happiness, peace and prosperity, and a drawing of Kōbō Daishi.
fudabasami	the box in which the pilgrim's fuda are carried
Fudō Myōō	a form of Dainichi Nyorai. A frightening looking deity with a rope in his left hand, a sword in his right, and a halo of flames behind him. He destroys evil.
futon	Japanese bedding. Japanese traditionally sleep on a thin mattress on the floor that is folded and put away each day.
gassho	putting one's palms together in worship, veneration, thanks, or other forms of respect
goeika	Buddhist hymn. Each of the 88 pilgrimage temples has a goeika.
Gyōki Bosatsu	(668-749) a great priest of the Nara period who traveled to various districts with his disciples doing social welfare work and who is said to have founded 49 temples.
hakama	pleated, skirt-like garment worn over a kimono; it was originally worn by men on formal occasions and was part of the school uniform for girls in the Meiji era.

hara-kiri	suicide by disembowelment
henro	a Shikoku pilgrim. They are respectfully called "ohenrosan".
henroyado	inn specifically for pilgrims where pilgrims supplied their own rice but pickles, etc., were provided by the inn
higanbana	red spider lily which blooms in autumn at the time of the autumn equinox when people visit their ancestors' guests
Higo	present day Kumamoto Prefecture
Horiba	Horiba Kiyoko, editor of *Musume Junreiki* and Takamure researcher
Iyo	present day Ehime Prefecture
Izu	present day Shizuoka Prefecture
ji	suffix meaning temple
Jizō Bosatsu	Jizō Bosatsu is one of the most beloved deities in Japan. He is the guardian of children, especially those who have died. He is regarded as the saviour of those who are suffering in the underworld. In Japan he is almost always depicted as a shaven-headed monk.
jō	measurement of length. One jō equals 3.03 meters.
Jūichimen Kannon	the eleven-headed Kannon. The eleven faces symbolize the all seeing power of Kannon
Kanjizai	another form of Kannon Bosatsu. Kanjizai means the Boddhisatva that sees and acts freely at will.
Kannon Bosatsu	the bodhisattva of great compassion, mercy and love. Kannon was originally a male but is now often regarded as a female deity. The name means "He who perceives the sounds of the world" Kannon Bosatsu made a vow to listen to the suffering and the afflicted, and dispel the evil and calamities that surround

	sentient beings. Kannon can manifest in any of thirty-three forms, the most common being Jūichimen Kannon—the Eleven Faced Kannon, Senju Kannon—the Thousand-armed (and thousand-eyed) Kannon, Nyoirin Kannon—the wish fulfilling Kannon, and Bato Kannon—the horse headed Kannon.
Kanzeon Bosatsu	another name for Kannon Bosatsu
ken	a measurement of length equal to 1.82 metres
kichinyado	lodge with a fee for wood. Travelers either carried their food or purchased raw ingredients and cooked their own meals. Later, *kichinyado* became cheap lodging houses where street minstrels and travelers with little money stayed.
Kii	present day Wakayama Prefecture.
Kōbō Daishi	(774-835) founder of Shingon Buddhism in Japan, poet, artist, educator, engineer, scholar, calligrapher, and political statesman. He is considered by many Japanese to be a saint, a semi-divine entity who did not die in 835, but entered into a state of eternal meditation on Mount Kōya in Wakayama Prefecture.
Kokubun-ji	In the Nara era, Emperor Shōmu ordered the building of two temples in each province of Japan: a temple for priests and a temple for nuns.
Kōmyō Shingon	the light mantra. According to Shingon teaching, the light mantra contains in its syllables the entire power of the Buddha.
Kumamoto City	the capital of Kumamoto Prefecture
Kumamoto Prefecture	a prefecture on the island of Kyūshū; it was formerly known as Higo Province.
Kompira Shrine	(Kotohiragu) Large Shintō shrine in Kanagawa Prefecture.

Mikkyō	Esoteric Buddhism
Mount Kōya	sacred mountain in Wakayama Prefecture where Kōbō Daishi is interred. Pilgrims should visit it before and after their pilgrimage.
Nembutsu	invocation of the name of the Buddha. In the majority of cases the word refers to invoking the name of Amida by the formula "Namu Amida Butsu" in order to be reborn in his Pure Land.
nokyō chō	a book carried by pilgrims which is stamped and inscribed at each temple visited
Obon	(see Bon Festival above)
oku-no-in	the inner sanctuary and most sacred part of a temple. It is usually a separate building containing the most sacred object of worship.
post town	From the Nara (710-794) through the Edo period (1600-1868), a network of officially regulated post towns was established throughout Japan to facilitate and control travel. They provided food, lodging and stabling and ranged in size from tiny stations along mountain passes to large castle towns. They were like links in a chain that crisscrossed Japan.
ri	measurement of length equal to 3.93 km.
rin	a coin worth one tenth of a sen
sama	an honorific term applied to a person
Sanuki	present day Kagawa Prefecture
seiza	a kneeling posture, a traditional sitting position of the Japanese
sen	coin, 100 sen equaled one yen
shaku	measurement of length. One shaku equals 30.3 cm.
Shingon	the school of Buddhism founded by Kōbō Daishi on his return to Japan from

	China, a kind of Esoteric Buddhism
Shōmu	45th Japanese emperor, 724-749.
sun	one tenth of a shaku; 3.03 centimeters.
tabi	a type of sock in which the big toe is separated from the other toes
Tanabata	the Festival of the Weaver celebrates the meeting once a year, on the seventh day of the seventh lunar month, of two lovers, a cowherd and a weaving girl, who are separated by the Milky Way the rest of the year.
tanka	a poem of 31 syllables in the form of 5,7,5,7,7 syllables
tatami	a tatami mat has a thick straw base and a soft rush covering. Traditionally, Japanese people kneel on mats rather than sit on chairs.
tengu	long nosed, red-faced creatures that dwell in forests and in cryptomeria (a type of cypress) trees near temples. They are said to kidnap human beings or play tricks on them.
tera	the suffix tera (or dera) means temple. See also 'ji'.
Tosa	present day Kōchi Prefecture
vajra	a weapon used in India that is used in Esoteric Buddhism as a symbol for the Buddha mind because it is hard and can destroy any defilement
waraji	rough straw sandal with a thong between the big toe and second toe and tied on to the foot with straw straps. They were worn when taking a long journey on foot.
wasan	A Buddhist hymn of praise. It may praise a Buddha, *bodhisattva*, founder of a sect, a doctrine or a sutra.
Yakushi Nyorai	the Buddha of medicine
yukata	unlined summer kimono

zengonyado	literally, "good deed inn", a home where pilgrims were given free lodging
zori	a kind of sandal with a thong between the big toe and the second toe but with no straps. They are the type of sandal women wear with a kimono.

SELECTED BIBLIOGRAPHY

In English:

AWA 88. 1993. *Awa Henro: A Bilingual Guide for Pilgrims in Tokushima*. Tokushima: Tokushima-ken Kyoiku Insatsu, Inc.

Chabot, Jeanette Taudin, 1985, "*Takamure Itsue: The first historian of Japanese women*", Women's Studies International Forum, Vol. 8, No.4, pp. 287-290.

Hoshino, Eiki. 1997, "Pilgrimage and Peregrination: Contextualizing the Saikoku *Junrei* and the Shikoku *Henro*" Japanese Journal of Religious Studies 24/3–4, pp.271-299.

Loftus, Ronald P. 1996, "Female Self-Writing: Takamure Itsue's Hi no Kuni no Onna no Nikki", Monumentica Nipponica: Studies in Japanese culture, Vol. 51, No. 2, pp. 153-170.

Miyata, Taisen. 1984. *A Henro Pilgrimage Guide to the 88 Temples of Shikoku Island Japan*. Northern California Koyasan Temple, Sacramento, California.

Monnet, Livia, (1989), "'In the beginning woman was the sun' : Autobiographies of modern Japanese women writers—1", Japan Forum, Vol. 1, No. 1, April, pp. 197-233.

Morris, Ivan.1993. *As I Crossed a Bridge of Dreams: Recollections of a Woman in Eleventh-Century Japan*. Translated with an introduction by Ivan Morris. Penguin Books. London, England.

Reynolds, Katsue and Christine Andrews, 1994, "*Conflict and Resolution: Takamure Itsue as a Woman Scholar*", Women in Hawai'i, Asia and the Pacific, The Office for Women's Research Working Papers Series, Volume 3, (K.Heyer ed.), pp. 37-44.

Ryang, Sonia, 1998, *"Love and Colonialism in Takamure Itsue's Feminism: A Postcolonial Critique"*, Feminist Review No. 60, Autumn, pp. 1-32.

Statler, Oliver. 1983. *Japanese Pilgrimage.* Tokyo: Charles E. Tuttle Co., Inc.

Tsurumi, E. Patricia, 1985, *"Feminism and Anarchism in Japan: Takamure Itsue, 1894-1964"*, Bulletin of Concerned Asian Scholars, Vol. 17 (2) pp. 2-19.

In Japanese:

Hashimoto, Kenzō Horiba Kiyoko. 1981. わが高群逸枝 (Waga Takamure Itsue: My Takamure Itsue) Volume I and Volume II. Tokyo: Asahi Shinbunsha

Horiba, Kiyoko. 解説 (Commentary) inTakamure, Itsue. 1979. *Musume Junreiki* (The pilgrimage journal of a young woman). Tokyo: Asahi Press pp. 245-270.

Takamure Itsue. 1938. お遍路 (Ohenro: Pilgrim). Tokyo: Kōseikaku.

Takamure, Itsue. 1979. 娘巡礼記 (Musume Junreiki: The pilgrimage journal of a young woman). Tokyo: Asahi Press.

Made in the USA
San Bernardino, CA
14 August 2019